Published by Posttime Press
4905 Drew Avenue South
Minneapolis, Minnesota 55410

Library of Congress Catalog Card Number:
86-90437

Printed in the United States of America.

FIRST EDITION

Illustrations & design by Jennifer Ellis

Cover photography by Reed Palmer

If Your Father Didn't Leave You A Fortune ... Maybe A Horse Will!

Tom Pritchard

Posttime Press
Minneapolis, Minnesota

Dedicated to Liz Pritchard

A devoted racing fan and wonderful mother.

ACKNOWLEDGMENT

I could not have written this book without borrowing liberally from the thoughts of other authors in the field. I want to acknowledge these unwitting contributors and advise them that, regretfully, their rewards lie in heaven and not on this earth. (Any temporal compensation to these distinguished turf scribes would most likely be consumed by the mutuel machines anyhow).

The reality is that a single acknowledgment will serve justice because every author on the subject was weaned on the writings of my friend, Tom Ainslie, and have subsequently woven his wisdom into their works.

We all thank you, Mr. Ainslie.

A Word From the Author

I've always said ... "Aside from attorneys, the last thing this planet needs one more of is a book on playing the ponies!" I must recant. The new breed of racing enthusiasts, spawned by the opening of Canterbury Downs, prompted me to consult my library for books to recommend.

Although there are quite a few books on thoroughbred handicapping, they tend to fall into one of two categories. The first group assumes that the reader understands the *Daily Racing Form* and is fully grounded in the fundamentals of handicapping. These books focus on very specific nuances and complicated approaches to the game (many of which are beyond my grasp). Further, these books tend to be bogged down with the author's euphoric recall of betting coups scored in the past — flagged by long chapters which usually begin with ... "It was a hot, and somewhat humid, August morning in Saratoga when I awoke to the sensual aroma of sizzling bacon ..." Give me a break! I want info — not memoirs of your summer vacation!

The second type of book takes the "global" approach. They include everything ever written or murmured on the subject — rambling from topic to topic. This variety tends to be "more than anyone cares to read" on the subject, especially when the reader is relatively new to the game.

As a consequence of this review, I was convinced that there was a need for a small, concise and well organized guide for new fans who want to learn the fundamentals of the game. I wanted the book to follow a logical and sequential path — with a minimum of examples and extraneous commentary. With these modest objectives in mind, I sat down to write this blockbuster.

My goal was to condense and organize the handicapping "process," rather than to expose new and previously unpublished "winning formulas." I've minimized or omitted some of the more esoteric theories on the game. I've also eliminated long, drawn out examples to support the principles being discussed.

There are a number of references to Canterbury Downs herein, and I don't mind admitting to having parochially slanted my examples. However, this book's utility is not limited to playing the ponies at Canterbury Downs. The fundamentals discussed are basic to the game and will work at any thoroughbred track. In fact, if you read this book carefully, you will be able to handicap a dash between two fat ladies racing from the front door of Macy's to Ladies' Sportswear during a Labor Day Sale.

Thoroughbred handicapping is a lot of fun and provides the player with a constant challenge. To play the game, you have to understand the fundamentals. Once these principles are understood, I urge the reader to continue his or her education. To that end, I've included a recommended reading list in the Appendix.

One last comment ... For years, authors and self-proclaimed "experts" have developed and espoused "systems" designed to make you a winner at the "pony palace." And many of these prophets have enjoyed tremendous financial rewards through these systems — not at the pari-mutuel windows, but through publishing royalties! If you bought this book with the idea you are going to get rich at the track, please call me, collect. I have some land in Wyoming you might be interested in ...

CONTENTS

STEP ONE

DOING YOUR HOMEWORK

I. Doing Your Homework

Before we begin, let me suggest a couple of ideas to help you survive this book. First, the subject is a little more involved than you may think. In order to get the "big picture" across, I have compressed the discussion of certain topics, and these areas may require re-reading or separate study. Secondly, there is logical sequence to the material, so if you have a question about something, please read on — the answer probably lies on the following page or in the next section. In this vein, I may touch lightly on an item in the beginning, then more fully explain that item later in a more appropriate context. Thirdly, I sometimes suggest rather extensive analysis or tracking (e.g. the maintenance of "privates files") which is probably more work than the recreational racegoer cares to do. That's okay. You don't have to do it all to have fun and improve your handicapping skills. Lastly, I have developed a rather bizarre vocabulary after 20+ years of hanging around the racetrack — understood only by fellow degenerate horseplayers. So if you encounter a bewildering word or expression, please consult the Glossary. All set? Let's go ...

Homework

Don't groan! If you want to avoid being prematurely separated from your paycheck at the racetrack, you're going to have to do your homework — and I do mean homework. The textbook we all study is the *Daily Racing Form* (DRF) — a daily newspaper published in five regional editions by Triangle Publications. It is unquestionably the single most important tool for the handicapper — providing a detailed history (Past Performances) of every horse racing that day.

Each regional edition contains from three to five tracks, depending on the edition and time of year. All but the Eastern Edition are tabloid size and present the information in a standardized format. The Eastern Edition is larger and provides more data than the other editions. The following chapter deals with how to read the Past Performances and explains their various abbreviations and symbols.

Study at Home

It's important to get your homework done at home, before going to the track. I've tried, without success, to do my analysis at the track, before and between races. It just doesn't work! There are too many distractions and not enough time. Moreover, you have other things to do between races such as checking out the horses in the paddock and monitoring the odds and the tote board. Further, you should arrive at the racetrack with a budget for the day and a rough game plan as to which races offer the best wagering opportunities.

So pick up a *Daily Racing Form* the night before, check the weather forecast for race day, sequester yourself from spouse and "rug rats" — then dive into your analysis. The following is a general approach I use in this exercise and suggest it as a starting point. All horseplayers develop their own "study habits" — but the following might be helpful to those who are initially intimidated by the abundance of data the *Daily Racing Form* thrusts at you ...

Reading the *Daily Racing Form*

I start by reading the news pages, particularly the articles and columns which discuss the local track (in my case, Canterbury Downs). Frequently, answers to questions you might have regarding certain horses are answered in these articles. Then I turn to the "Latest Workouts" section and note any outstanding "works" posted for that day. Works or workouts are timed exercises (brisk gallops) that horses perform during the morning training regime.

LATEST Workouts

Key b Breezing d Driving e Easily g Worked from gate h Handily o All out u Eased up bo Bore out ro Ran out Names of horses making fastest time at each distance appear in black face type Track record after distance

Wednesday, August 14

CANTERBURY DOWNS - Track Fast

Three Furlongs		
All Decked Out	:39	b
Bet My Cannon	:38	b
CherokeePrince	:35⅘	bg
Dakota Albie	:38	b
Ferdy	:36⅘	b
Girl Named T. J.	:36	b
GraniteMountin	:36	b
Harem Pants	:37	bg
Hesa Winner	:37	b
High Due	:35⅘	b
Intrusion	**:35⅗**	**hg**
Jancandance	:37	b
Jessica'a Jewel	:38	b
Jody Sweet Bell	:40	b
Line of Sevens	:36⅗	b
March of Ides	:37	bg
Never Now	:41	b
Noble Camel	:37⅖	b
Prize Victory	:39	b
Quote Me Later	:37	b
Song Singer	:37	bg
Sonoita Mley	:38	b
Spunkyville	:38	b
Whin to Win	:36	bg
Whistling Burg	:37⅗	b
Winged Star	:37	b
Winooski	:38⅖	b
Four Furlongs		
Big Band	:49	b
Black Wench	:50	b
CpturedHerHert	:49⅗	b
Cerise Bouquet	:48	h
CleverArrngmnt	:51⅕	b
CleverDestroyer	:52	b
Climit Control	:50⅖	b
Coryza	**:47⅗**	**bg**
Cream Um	:49⅖	b
Crystal Dawn	:52	b
Czarlotta	:52⅖	b
Excalibur	:52	b
Faneuil K.	:49⅖	b
Fire Native	:49⅗	bg
Flemingsburg	:52⅕	b
Flickering's Uno	**:47⅗**	**h**
Four Turns	:49	b
Grand andLucky	:48	hg
HvMySuspicons	:52⅖	b
Hot Circuit	:48⅖	b
Katzenjammer	:48	h
Keep the Faith	:48	h
Late to Name	:49	b
Light Fling	:49⅖	b
Lt. Kid Heilman	:48	h
Molly's Seven	:49⅖	b
MyFriendPhillis	:52	b
Naskra's Note	:52⅖	b
Piper's Pride	:48⅖	b
Rapid Gray	:47⅘	h
RunforButtrmlk	:51⅗	b
Shecky'sPrincss	:48	h
Sly Perfections	:49⅗	b
Steady Naskra	:49	b
Steven'sSuprem	:51⅖	b
Super Quack	:50	b
Swingtown	:48	hg
SyndicteMoney	:51⅕	b
T.'s Turn	:52⅖	b
TheRoyalFreeze	:49⅖	b
Travel Dancer	:48⅘	h
Tribe Dancer	:51⅖	b
Tuly ASerenade	:50⅖	b
Venturette Miss	:49⅘	b
What Fun	:52	b
Five Furlongs— :59		
A Firm Kiss	1:02	bg
Amabeauty'sJoy	1:02⅖	bg
Becky's Alibhai	1:04	bg
BrodwyMistress	1:03⅕	b
Bud Is Back	1:02⅖	b
Clever Wake	1:02	b
Come Summer	1:03⅘	b
Dynamo Doc	1:02	b
Far Gallant	1:01⅕	hg
Flaming Irish	1:01⅖	bg
FortyEightFcets	1:02	b
Freddie theFirst	1:04	b
Genuine Glory	1:03⅖	b
Gustosette	1:02	bg
Halo Ice	1:00⅗	h
J. R.'s Pleasure	1:03⅖	b
Jolie Femme	1:01⅗	hg
Keahi	1:00⅕	h
Laughing Lester	1:05⅗	b
Lord Petersham	1:01⅘	b
LuckyStriksAgn	1:02⅖	b
Lyphard'sLassie	1:01	h
MumelleMickey	1:06⅗	b
Mean WhatISay	1:01⅖	h
No Mas X.	1:04	b
Plexus	1:06⅗	b
Prole	1:01⅗	hg
Queens Palace	1:01⅘	h
Refocus	1:01⅘	b
Rudloff	1:00⅘	h
Russian Flush	1:03⅕	b
Sheets N Pillow	1:01⅗	h
Silver Wraith	1:00⅘	h
Sir Session	1:01	h
Sovereign's Ace	1:00⅗	h
Spiritualistic	**:59⅗**	**h**
Stomp 'n'Smash	1:01⅘	bg
Vestor	1:02	b
Your My Star	1:00⅖	h
Six Furlongs—1:09⅗		
Mr. Alligator	**1:15⅕**	**b**
Petite Reviere	1:16	b
Seven Furlongs		
Tartesh	1:32⅗	b
1 Mile—1:36⅕		
Sultan's Gold	1:41⅖	b

INTRUSION(3f) came from the gate in handy fashion. CORYZA(4f) with Dickey Winnant up looked very impressive coming from the gate. RAPID GRAY(4f) was asked for a good effort in this fine prep. SPIRITUALISTIC(5f) is being kept at his best form. SILVER WRAITH(5f) looked very sharp in this fine move. MR. ALLIGATOR(6f) went evenly. SULTAN'S GOLD(1m) turned in a fine mile work here.

Be sure to read the Clocker's Comments at the end of the workout section. Horses who put in outstanding "works" are generally mentioned and should be noted.

[A word about "notes". Even those of you who are blessed with incredible memories will benefit greatly from having files, notebooks and other reference aids. I keep a number of different files — one for workout logs, another for Results Charts — plus a notebook on individual horses. This may seem like a lot of work — but it really isn't once you start. And the rewards for keeping good notes or "private files" will be evident as the season progresses.]

After the editorial and workouts, I then turn to the "Experts' Selections" page *(sample on facing page)* to get an overview of the day's races. Examine Sweep's Graded Handicap Ⓐ and the Selections Box Ⓑ prepared by the *DRF's* handicappers. I look at this information to determine:

1) **Quality of the Card** — the types of races being run — maiden races, claiming and allowance races (definitions coming, gang).

2) **Size of the Fields** — the number of entrants per race.

3) **Competitive Level** — Are the fields well-balanced or are there a number of races with prohibitive favorites or "stick-outs"

4) **Equipment changes** — indicating those horses running with or without blinkers.

5) **Medication List** — listing horses racing with medication, e.g. Lasix or phenylbutazone (bute).

Once you have this overview, turn to the Past Performances (PPs). Handicapping is a lot of fun. Each race is a puzzle waiting to be solved — and every race is a little different. Your first run through the Past Performances should be viewed as a whittling down or "elimination" process. The objective is to reduce each race to a manageable number of possible contenders — not to

AMERICA'S TURF AUTHORITY Daily Racing Form

Experts' Selections

Consensus Points: 5 for 1st (today's best 7), 2 for 2nd, 1 for 3rd. Today's Best in Bold Type.

Canterbury Downs
Sweep's Graded Handicap

FRIDAY, AUGUST 23, 1985

Post Times in Local P.M. Time, Unless Otherwise Noted.

FIRST RACE–6 Furlongs. 4:00
2-Year-Olds. Maidens Claiming ($16,000). Purse $4,000.

P.P.	Horse	Jockey	Wgt	Odds
6	Clever Destroyer	Woods C R Jr	117	3-1
10	Major George	Orona W	117	4-1
8	Coffee's Swinger	Hansen R D	117	6-1
1	Secret Cal	Melancon G	117	6-1
4	Mc Fella	LaGrange D L	117	8-1
7	Chief's Award	Bianchini J	117	8-1
2	Payforthefence	Bass S H	5112	10-1
3	I. C. Bull	Martinez N C	117	20-1
5	Cash Draw	Rashall R D	117	15-1
9	Norwest	Finnegan P M	117	15-1
11	Doc Ranck	Melancon G	117	20-1
12	Minndak Prince	Warhol V L	117	15-1

COUPLED–Norwest and Minndak Prince.

SECOND RACE–6½ Furlongs. 4:30
3-Year-Olds, Fillies. Claiming ($20,000 to $18,000). Purse $9,750.

P.P.	Horse	Jockey	Wgt	Odds
4	Chaotic Eruption	Montoya D	119	2-1
6	Bryce's Idea	Martinez N C	112	5-2
3	Sharp And Pretty	Solomone M	119	4-1
1	Dinner Show	Bass S H	5109	4-1
5	Unbroken Circle	Smith L S	114	8-1
2	Charmin Bug	Martino M	114	15-1

THIRD RACE–6 Furlongs. 5:00
3 & 4-Year-Olds. Maidens Claiming ($10,000). Purse $3,500.

P.P.	Horse	Jockey	Wgt	Odds
9	Roaring Bear	Melancon G	115	5-2
8	Security Anthem	Fernandez A L	115	3-1
2	Dine With Dev	Hansen R D	115	4-1
7	Riki Niki Waldman	Smith M E	115	5-1
5	Virtual Lady	Rubbicco P	120	10-1
1	Tahari	Moyers L	115	20-1
3	Harem Pants	Warhol V L	115	20-1
4	Regalo Gratis	Woods C J Jr	115	20-1
6	Sam's Sunny Cat	Robley J J	115	20-1
10	Rosy Outlook	Kaenel J L	115	20-1

FOURTH RACE–1 Mile. 5:30
3 & 4-Year-Olds. Maiden Special weights. Purse $10,400.

P.P.	Horse	Jockey	Wgt	Odds
8	Bet My Cannon	Hansen R D	115	2-1
1	Strohsburg	Montoya D	115	5-2
7	Ken Smoke	Solomone M	110	4-1
6	Lavish Feast	Kaenel J L	115	5-1
3	Intriging Times	Smith M E	115	10-1
2	Gypsy Jovan	Smith L S	110	15-1
4	Notthrutheironduke	Craig K	5110	20-1
5	Real Tare	Rashall R D	116	20-1

Trackman, Jim Dunleavy

CANTERBURY DOWNS

Selections Made for Fast Track

	TRACKMAN	HANDICAP	ANALYST	HERMIS	SWEEP	CONSENSUS	
1	PAYFORTHEFENCE CLEVER DESTROYER CHIEF'S AWARD	SECRET CAL MC FELLA CHIEF'S AWARD	MAJOR GEORGE CLEVER DESTROYER MC FELLA	MAJOR GEORGE CLEVER DESTROYER COFFEE'S SWINGER	CLEVER DESTROYER MAJOR GEORGE COFFEE'S SWINGER	MAJOR GEORGE CLEVER DESTROYER SECRET CAL	12 11 5
2	CHARMIN BUG CHAOTIC ERUPTION BRYCE'S IDEA	BRYCE'S IDEA SHARP AND PRETTY CHARMIN BUG	BRYCE'S IDEA CHAOTIC ERUPTION DINNER SHOW	SHARP AND PRETTY BRYCE'S IDEA CHAOTIC ERUPTION	CHAOTIC ERUPTION BRYCE'S IDEA SHARP AND PRETTY	BRYCE'S IDEA CHAOTIC ERUPTION SHARP AND PRETTY	15 10 8
3	SECURITY ANTHEM RIKI NIKI WALDMAN VIRTUAL LADY	REGALO GRATIS HAREM PANTS RIKI NIKI WALDMAN	SECURITY ANTHEM ROARING BEAR RIKI NIKI WALDMAN	ROARING BEAR SECURITY ANTHEM DINE WITH DEV	ROARING BEAR SECURITY ANTHEM DINE WITH DEV	SECURITY ANTHEM ROARING BEAR REGALO GRATIS	14 12 5
4	BET MY CANNON KEN SMOKE INTRIGING TIMES	KEN SMOKE REAL TARE GYPSY JOVAN	STROHSBURG BET MY CANNON LAVISH FEAST	LAVISH FEAST BET MY CANNON STROHSBURG	BET MY CANNON STROHSBURG KEN SMOKE	BET MY CANNON KEN SMOKE STROHSBURG	14 8 8
5	MT. TABOR RD. NINETEEN DREAMS VALENTINE LEW	**THE RIGHT EXIT** CENTRAL SET PORSCHE II	GRANITE MOUNTAIN MT. TABOR RD. NINETEEN DREAMS	MT. TABOR RD. THE RIGHT EXIT GRANITE MOUNTAIN	MT. TABOR RD. GRANITE MOUNTAIN PORSCHE II	MT. TABOR RD. THE RIGHT EXIT GRANITE MOUNTAIN	17 9 8
6	MACON COUNTY KEY'D UP BRILLIANT PASS	KEY'D UP GAYLE'S TIME GALAROB	MACON COUNTY KEY'D UP BRILLIANT PASS	KEY'D UP BRILLIANT PASS MACON COUNTY	KEY'D UP MACON COUNTY IT'S COALIE	KEY'D UP MACON COUNTY BRILLIANT PASS	19 13 4
7	ARCTIC ANGEL CLASS COUNTS GOODNIGHT MY LOVE	CLASS COUNTS IRISH LORA ARCTIC ANGEL	ARCTIC ANGEL IRISH LORA GOODNIGHT MY LOVE	ARCTIC ANGEL SMOOTH N' GOOD GOODNIGHT MY LOVE	ARCTIC ANGEL GOODNIGHT MY LOVE SMOOTH N' GOOD	ARCTIC ANGEL CLASS COUNTS GOODNIGHT MY LOVE	21 7 5
8	**JOVIAL WITNESS** KENNEDY EXPRESS INDIAN HEATHER	JOVIAL WITNESS INDIAN HEATHER QUALIA	**JOVIAL WITNESS** KENNEDY EXPRESS INDIAN HEATHER	**JOVIAL WITNESS** KENNEDY EXPRESS MISTY PROSPECT	**JOVIAL WITNESS** KENNEDY EXPRESS QUALIA	**JOVIAL WITNESS** KENNEDY EXPRESS INDIAN HEATHER	33 8 4
9	JEKYLL J. B. ON THE ROCKS HOME INA BREEZE	SNEAK SPY SULTAN'S GOLD J. B. ON THE ROCKS	J. B. ON THE ROCKS JEKYLL FRIENDLY FELLER	JEKYLL SULTAN'S GOLD STAR SONG BIRD	J. B. ON THE ROCKS FRIENDLY FELLER JEKYLL	JEKYLL J. B. ON THE ROCKS SNEAK SPY	13 13 5

FIFTH RACE–6 Furlongs. 6:00
4-Year-Olds and Up. Claiming ($6,250). Purse $4,500.

P.P.	Horse	Jockey	Wgt	Odds
6	Mt. Tabor Rd.	Montoya D	115	5-2
2	Granite Mountain	Hoverson C	119	3-1
1	Porsche II	Orona W	115	4-1
4	The Right Exit	Melancon G	115	4-1
5	Nineteen Dreams	Martinez N C	119	5-1
3	Central Set	LaGrange D L	115	15-1
7	Valentine Lew	Hamilton M	115	20-1

SIXTH RACE–6 Furlongs. 6:30
3-Year-Olds, Fillies. Claiming ($5,000). Purse $3,500.

P.P.	Horse	Jockey	Wgt	Odds
3	Key'd Up	Kaenel J L	116	2-1
4	Macon County	Bass S H	5111	3-1
1	It's Coalie	Smith M E	114	4-1
7	Brilliant Pass	Fernandez A L	114	5-1
2	Gayle's Time	Martinez N C	114	30-1
5	Hot Socks	Melancon G	114	12-1
6	Fran Chris	Hoverson C	114	30-1
8	Vying	LaGrange D L	114	15-1
9	Fleet Harbor	Woods C R Jr	116	20-1
10	Galarob	Oldham J	116	30-1

SEVENTH RACE–6 Furlongs. 7:00
3-Year-Olds and Up, Fillies and Mares. Claiming ($10,000 to $9,000). Purse $6,500.

P.P.	Horse	Jockey	Wgt	Odds
4	Arctic Angel	Bass S H	5115	1-1
2	Goodnight My Love	Kaenel J L	115	3-1
1	Smooth N' Good	Craig K	5107	5-1
5	Irish Lora	Smith M E	109	3-1
7	Class Counts	Hamilton M	118	6-1
3	Sonoita Mley	Warhol V L	114	8-1
6	Partner's Express	LaGrange D L	114	30-1

COUPLED–Goodnight My Love and Irish Lora.

EIGHTH RACE–1$\frac{1}{16}$ Miles. 7:30
3-Year-Olds and Up, Fillies and Mares. Allowance. Purse $14,000.

P.P.	Horse	Jockey	Wgt	Odds
2	Jovial Witness	Melancon G	114	2-1
3	Kennedy Express	Bass S H	5109	4-1
6	Qualia	Melancon L J	111	5-1
5	Indian Heather	Smith M E	108	6-1
1	Flo Control	Baze D	114	15-1
4	Misty Prospect	Moyers L	114	20-1

NINTH RACE–1$\frac{1}{16}$ Miles. 8:00
4-Year-Olds and Up. Claiming ($8,000). Purse $6,000.

P.P.	Horse	Jockey	Wgt	Odds
7	J. B. On the Rocks	Smith M E	119	7-1
8	Friendly Feller	Melancon L J	115	4-1
9	Jekyll	Bass S H	5110	6-1
4	Roman Hills	Woods C R Jr	115	7-1
10	Intermediary	Adkins R M	115	8-1
1	Sneak Spy	Moyers L	115	20-1
2	Star Song Bird	Hamilton M	115	20-1
3	Sultan's Gold	LaGrange D L	115	8-1
5	Home Ina Breeze	Hansen R D	115	10-1
6	Bat An Eye	Martinez N C	115	15-1

COUPLED–Roman Hills and J. B. On the Rocks.

Equipment changes

2—Little Irish Magic, blinkers on.
6—Important Business, blinkers on.
10—Outrageous Too, Vintry, Game Bidder, blinkers on.

Medication List

BLEEDER MEDICATION

1—Washington Leader, Grey Ruler, Neat Patty(X), Felix Hill, Doing Great, Portuguese Picnic.
2—What a Smash.
3—Point Guard, Diana's Delight, Prize Pretender, Damon Runyon, Full Flame, Chiefo, Wild Exuberance, Sunderly, Dou-

select a single horse. That comes later. After your first pass through the data, you should be able to eliminate a number of horses from each race and you will be left with three to four "possibles" circled. This initial analysis will also separate the "playable" from the "unplayable" races.

But to do all of this, we must first learn how to decipher the Past Performances ...

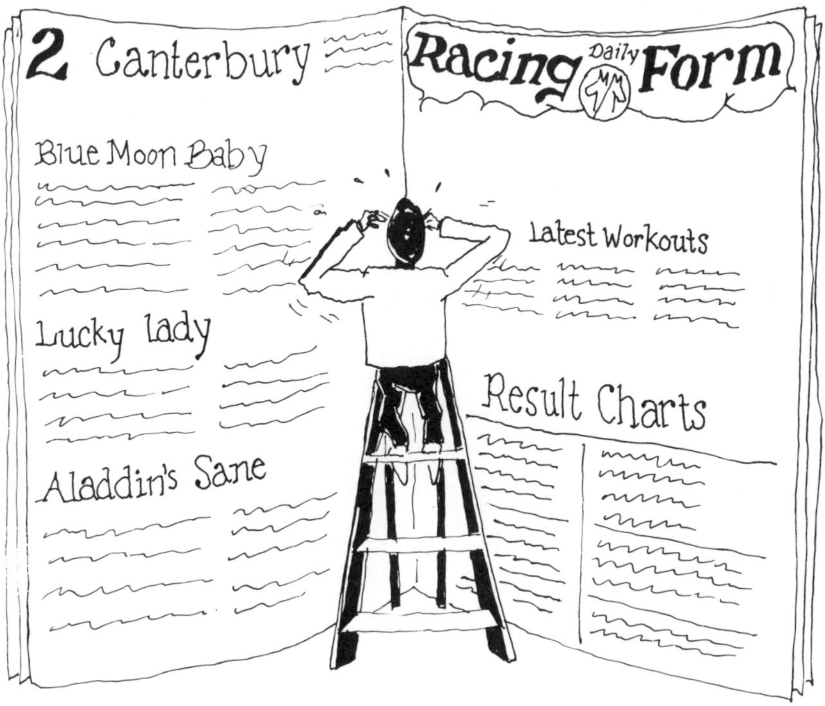

II. How to Read the Past Performances

Most newcomers to the game take one look at Past Performances in the *Daily Racing Form* and groan "Uffda!". Believe me, it's not nearly as confusing as it might appear at first glance. And you must be able to read and understand the PPs in order to learn the game. So stay with me ...

On the following page is the set of Past Performances we are going to examine element-by-element. In a later chapter, we'll look at ways of marking these data and some short cuts for absorbing this wealth of information.

7th Canterbury

6 FURLONGS. (1.09$\frac{3}{5}$) CLAIMING. Purse $6,500. Fillies and mares. 3-year-olds and upward. Weight, 3-year-olds, 115 lbs.; older, 120 lbs. Non-winners of a race since July 15 allowed 2 lbs.; since June 15, 4 lbs. May 15, 6 lbs. Claiming price $10,000; if for $9,000 allowed 2 lbs. (Races when entered for $8,000 or less not considered.)

Coupled—Goodnight My Love and Irish Lora.

Smooth N' Good

CRAIG K **107^{5}**
Own.—Huntington K

Dk. b. or br. f. 4, by Smooth Dancer—Alien Flower, by Good Turn
Br.—Cox & Jarvis (La) — **1985 11 2 3 2 $12,216**
Tr.—Huntington Dougie **$9,000** — **1984 18 4 1 3 $19,448**
Lifetime 30 6 5 5 $32,564 — **Turf 1 0 0 1 $770**

18Aug85-10Cby	1	:48^{2}	1:13^{2}	1:39^{1}ft	6$\frac34$	116	3^{2}	4$^{3\frac12}$	5$^{5\frac12}$	7$^{9\frac14}$	Melancon G^{6}	c6250	76-11	Adobe Chief, SpeedSpy,TonicMajor	9
3Aug85-10Cby	1$\frac{1}{16}$	:48^{3}	1:13^{4}	1:47^{4}ft	*2$\frac34$	114	2$^{1\frac12}$	2$^{\frac12}$	1^{hd}	1^{3}	LaGrange D L^{8}	Ⓕ 6250	77-10	SmoothN'Gd,EnglshWzrd,Dwnsflng	8
26Jly85-1Cby	1$\frac{1}{16}$	:47^{4}	1:12^{4}	1:46 ft	*1	109^{5}	4^{2}	3^{1}	2^{hd}	1$^{1\frac12}$	Bass S H^{7}	Ⓕ c5000	— —	SmoothN'Gd,MystclSng,SlvrStrshn	7
12Jly85-9Cby	1	:48^{4}	1:13	1:39 ft	7$\frac34$	107^{5}	3^{nk}	3^{nk}	3^{nk}	3$^{\frac34}$	Bass S H^{1}	Ⓕ 7500	— —	Snderell,SheWillTll,SmoothN'Good	8
11Jun85-3CD	1	:46^{3}	1:11^{3}	1:38^{2}ft	2$\frac12$e	116	6^{6}	4$^{5\frac12}$	4$^{6\frac12}$	4^{8}	Montoya D^{5}	Ⓕ 7500	69-18	TwinHerts,JestersJoy,TrojnGoddss	9
15May85-5CD	6f	:21^{2}	:45^{1}	1:11^{4}ft	3$\frac34$e	116	7^{15}	7$^{9\frac14}$	7$^{8\frac34}$	6$^{6\frac14}$	Melancon G^{4}	Ⓕ 10000	80-14	Countess Suzie, PorchCat,IronGold	7
3May85-1CD	1	:47^{3}	1:14^{4}	1:41 ft	*8-5	116	7$^{2\frac34}$	4$^{\frac34}$	3^{3}	3^{3}	Fox W I Jr^{6}	Ⓕ c7500	61-14	She Will Tell, Joby, SmoothN'Good	8
29Mar85-11FG	1$\frac{1}{16}$	:47^{1}	1:13	1:47^{4}ft	*2	112	8^{10}	8^{11}	3^{4}	2^{hd}	Fox W I Jr^{4}	Ⓕ 8500	73-20	JestersJoy,SmoothN'Good,TiffyK.	10
8Mar85-7FG	6f	:22^{1}	:46^{2}	1:12^{2}ft	*7-5	116	10^{13}	8^{14}	6$^{6\frac14}$	4$^{6\frac14}$	RomeroRP^{4}	Ⓕ[S] 12500	77-19	ClrCrkCt,Mg'sBlossm,HnrAndGlry	10
15Feb85-8FG	6f	:22^{3}	:47^{1}	1:13^{1}ft	16	114	7^{9}	8^{13}	5^{6}	2^{hd}	Faul J H^{1}	Ⓕ[S] 15000	79-21	Dr.PrttyFst,SmothN'Gd,LdyL.AndL.	9

15Feb85—Steadied to avoid tiring horse

Aug 21 Cby 3f ft :36^{3} b

Goodnight My Love

KAENEL J L **115**
Own.—Shamie E

Ch. f. 3, by China Silk—Upcuma, by Crozier
Br.—Shamie E (Cal) — **1985 10 1 0 2 $8,250**
Tr.—Pappalardo John W **$10,000** — **1984 0 M 0 0**
Lifetime 10 1 0 2 $8,250

8Aug85-6Cby	1^{70}	:48^{1}	1:12^{3}	1:45^{2}ft	7	109^{5}	7^{13}	7^{12}	5^{7}	5^{5}	Bass S H^{3}	Ⓕ 20000	76-16	QutThVocs,JstBrlyAbl,StrdstMlody	7
1Aug85-5Cby	1	:47^{3}	1:14^{3}	1:41 ft	*9-5	109^{5}	8^{10}	4^{3}	1$^{2\frac12}$	1^{5}	Bass S H^{7}	ⒻM16000	76-12	GoodnghtMyLv,ChthmHgh,KnSmk	8
18Jly85-4Cby	1^{70}	:47^{4}	1:12^{4}	1:44^{2}ft	11	113	9^{11}	6^{11}	4$^{9\frac12}$	4^{10}	Hamilton M^{5}	ⒻMdn	— —	Opulence,VenturetteMiss,Bbu'sKey	9
30Jun85-7Cby	6f	:24	:47^{2}	1:13^{1}ft	8$\frac14$	115	6^{12}	6^{11}	6$^{7\frac34}$	4$^{6\frac12}$	Hamilton M^{3}	ⒻMdn	— —	FeelsLikeLove,MeCry,DineWithDev	6
7Jun85-3Hol	1$\frac18$	:48^{1}	1:12^{4}	1:50^{2}ft	19	109	7^{11}	7^{10}	7^{11}	7$^{13\frac14}$	Hawley S^{4}	Ⓕ 12500	84-06	Cecile,DuchessPetrone,MerryHdlinr	8
16May85-2Hol	1	:46	1:11	1:36^{4}ft	28	113	12^{17}	10^{19}	10^{19}	7$^{18\frac34}$	PedrozaMA^{1}	ⒻM28000	70-08	Don A Top, Grenalda, LuckySilver	12
11Apr85-3SA	1$\frac{1}{16}$	:46^{1}	1:11^{1}	1:45^{2}ft	7	114	10^{11}	8^{14}	8^{12}	3^{6}	Hawley S^{9}	ⒻM28000	68-18	TAtTn,RoylCurvs,GoodnghtMyLov	12
5Apr85-2SA	1	:46^{2}	1:11^{3}	1:38 ft	20	110^{5}	9$^{6\frac12}$	8^{12}	8^{8}	6^{6}	DomngzRE^{7}	ⒻM45000	72-14	‡PussyCat,SenstionlDrm,KeepDting	9
22Mar85-3SA	1$\frac{1}{16}$	:46	1:11^{2}	1:45 ft	6	109^{5}	9^{17}	10^{12}	4$^{7\frac12}$	3^{6}	DomngzRE^{2}	ⒻM28000	70-17	RcklssMss,DonATop,GdnghtMyLv	12

22Mar85—Very wide into stretch, bumped at 1/8

22Feb85-3SA	6$\frac12$f	:21^{3}	:44^{3}	1:18 ft	20	110^{5}	10^{19}	10^{24}	9^{16}	7$^{5\frac12}$	DmngzRL^{5}	Ⓕ[S]M35000	74-18	Sntequos,SusnnRose,KpStorming	10

Jly 14 Cby 6f ft 1:15 b **Jly 8 Cby 5f ft 1:03 b**

Sonoita Mley

WARHOL V L **114**
Own.—Williamson R M

Ch. m. 6, by Yorkville—Tattling, by Commanding II
Br.—Short D (Cal) — **1985 8 0 1 0 $1,454**
Tr.—Crowe Marcel J **$10,000** — **1984 16 6 2 3 $24,137**
Lifetime 56 14 7 6 $52,996 — **Turf 5 1 0 0 $3,985**

16Aug85-9Cby	5$\frac12$f	:22^{3}	:46^{1}	1:05^{4}ft	6$\frac34$	114	1$^{\frac12}$	2^{hd}	4^{3}	6$^{6\frac34}$	Warhol V L^{3}	Ⓕ 12500	84-09	Sotetta, La Liz, Porch Cat	8
13Jly85-8NP	6f	:22^{2}	:46^{1}	1:12^{1}gd	12	108^{5}	1^{3}	1^{2}	2^{nk}	6$^{5\frac14}$	Jumpsen N^{7}	Ⓕ 20000	83-22	LittlePrincess,EstrLit,Nlee'sFshion	7
30Jun85-7NP	6$\frac12$f	:23	:46^{4}	1:18^{4}ft	4$\frac12$	115	4$^{3\frac14}$	4$^{3\frac12}$	6^{7}	6^{21}	Turcotte Y A^{7}	Ⓕ 16000	67-14	TirelssLdy,OwlwoodLn,FigonroLssi	6

30Jun85—Reared st.

14Jun85-7NP	6f	:22^{4}	:46^{4}	1:12^{4}m	3$\frac14$	115	1^{2}	1^{4}	1^{nk}	5$^{9\frac12}$	Levine C^{3}	Ⓕ 20000	75-25	Drwin'sDrlin,Nl'sFshon,OwlwoodLn	6
24May85-9NP	6f	:22^{4}	:46^{3}	1:13^{4}sy	5$\frac14$	115	3^{1}	3^{3}	5^{10}	6$^{25\frac14}$	Levine C^{6}	ⒻAw6800	55-26	BrightBouquet,Snowder,RinbowSkr	6
11May85-9StP	6f	:22^{1}	:45^{2}	1:10^{4}ft	11	114	1^{3}	1^{3}	1^{nk}	6$^{4\frac14}$	Levine C^{6}	ⒻLilac	89-14	Merrydown,RinbowSekr,HstyMort	10
1May85-9StP	6f	:22^{2}	:45^{3}	1:11^{1}ft	*3-2	107^{5}	1^{1}	1^{2}	2^{nk}	6$^{5\frac12}$	Jumpsen N^{7}	ⒻAw6530	85-16	PlenumBee,RinbowSkr,SndHoppr	10
20Apr85-9StP	6f	:23	:47^{2}	1:15^{3}sy	*9-5	116	1^{3}	1^{5}	1^{3}	2^{hd}	TurcotteYA^{7}	ⒻAw6800	69-29	RinbowSeekr,SonoitMly,Nl'sFshion	7
3Nov84-8StP	6f	:22^{4}	:46	1:11^{4}ft	*2$\frac12$	113^{5}	1$^{1\frac12}$	1$^{2\frac14}$	1$^{2\frac14}$	1$^{1\frac12}$	Mayo K^{4}	Ⓕ 16000	88-15	SonoitMley,PlenumBee,Nle'sFshion	9
21Oct84-8StP	6f	:22^{2}	:46	1:11^{3}ft	8$\frac14$	116	1^{1}	1$^{2\frac14}$	1^{4}	1^{3}	Ferris A S^{6}	Ⓕ 16000	89-12	SonoitMley,Geno'sAngle,PlenumBe	7

Aug 14 Cby 3f ft :38 b

Arctic Angel — **BASS S H** — **1155**
Own.—Lloyd Lucie

Ch. f. 4, by Another Double—Miss Bonmire, by Mountain Fire
Br.—Alexander Lucie D (Ky) — 1985 12 2 4 1 $12,638
Tr.—Van Berg Jack C — **$10,000** — 1984 0 M 0 0
Lifetime 12 2 4 1 $12,638

31Jly85-6Cby	6f	:223	:462	1:113ft	*8-5	1155	53	43½	2½	22¼	Bass S H6	Ⓕ 10000	88-14	SheWillTll,ArcticAngl,GimmiATip	10
18Jly85-7Cby	5½f	:223	:47	1:063ft	2½	1105	58	48	22½	12	Bass S H2	Ⓕ 12500	— —	Arctic Angel, Texoma, Trulinka	7
29Jun85-7Cby	5½f	:232	:471	1:06 ft	8-5	115	54	53¼	55½	55½	HansenRD4	ⒻAw11000	— —	FinalDancer,Adptble,ApricotCreme	5
18Jun85-9CD	6f	:213	:461	1:123ft	*2-3	1155	54	31½	12	14	Bass S H4	ⒻM10000	82-16	Arctic Angel, Hai Sun,VirtualLady	11
4Jun85-2CD	6½f	:232	:473	1:204gd	3	1175	32½	34	23½	23	Bass S H8	ⒻM10000	73-23	BoldndFlsh,ArctcAngl,BrdwyKtty	11
25May85-3CD	6f	:22	:461	1:122ft	2	1175	33½	24	23	22	Bass S H1	ⒻM10000	81-14	Dollmaker,ArcticAngel,WorkNMyrn	8
17May85-1CD	6f	:212	:453	1:121gd	5	119	54½	78¼	811	812	Melancon L9	ⒻM15000	72-14	Livittothelimit,GreyAllure,RlFmin	11
8May85-2CD	6f	:221	:462	1:114ft	3¼	122	43½	34½	36	26	Melancon L5	ⒻM10000	80-16	Lon'sDlght,ArctcAngl,Nncy'sBlssng	7
14Apr85-2FG	5½f	:23	:472	1:064ft	7	121	31½	54¾	45½	35¼	Ardoin R1	ⒻMdn	79-21	LilliBeth,BestThoughts,ArcticAngl	11
22Mar85-1FG	6f	:224	:471	1:124ft	6½	115	73¼	85¾	1113	1117¼	Melancon G8	M15000	64-20	Cakewalk,LavishLady,OuiskiBayou	12

●Jly 13 Cby 4f ft :471 h

Irish Lora — **SMITH M E** — **109**
Own.—Steinmann H

Dk. b. or br. f. 3, by The Irish Lord—Nori O, by McTavish
Br.—Steinmann H (Cal) — 1985 12 1 0 1 $13,115
Tr.—Pappalardo John W — **$10,000** — 1984 0 M 0 0
Lifetime 12 1 0 1 $13,115

11Aug85-1Cby	6f	:221	:452	1:121ft	15	115	42¼	44	43½	51¾	Kaenel J L3	Ⓕ 12500	85-12	Buckpasser'sGl,TruLdyRed,Trulink	9
11Jly85-3Hol	1	:453	1:101	1:362ft	19	116	610	616	617	618½	Estrada J Jr3	Ⓕ 25000	72-07	Don A Top,VitalScore,RockCanyon	6
19Jun85-6Hol	6f	:221	:453	1:111ft	80	115	912	711	64¾	53¾	Estrada J Jr11	Ⓕ 25000	87-05	‡Wlker'sLdy,FireMissLedr,AnniLis	11
22May85-4Hol	6f	:222	:454	1:104ft	37	118	96¼	77½	75¼	77	Meza R Q4	Ⓕ 25000	86-08	TammyLu,FireMissLeder,AnnieLis	11
25Apr85-7Hol	1	:451	1:104	1:37 ft	24	115	88¾	88¼	812	817½	Sibille R2	Ⓕ 25000	70-09	Iva'sRich,Clearway,FireMissLeder	10
18Apr85-7SA	6½f	:213	:45	1:164ft	60	118	76¼	66½	59	310	Estrada J Jr6	Ⓕ 32000	76-16	Proud Doll, Ritzy Chick, IrishLora	11
5Apr85-1SA	6f	:214	:451	1:102ft	11	120	56½	911	99¼	88¼	Pincay L Jr11	Ⓕ 25000	78-14	QuitKid,ProudDoll,Perfction'sGift	12
5Apr85—Lugged out, wide final 3/8															
28Mar85-3SA	6½f	:22	:462	1:214sl	4¼	117	63½	52½	3½	12	HawleyS12	ⒻSM32000	61-31	IrishLora,KimStep,MentlBnkMgic	12
22Feb85-3SA	6½f	:213	:443	1:18 ft	5e	115	710	712	712	65	Hawley S8	ⒻSM35000	75-18	Sntequos,SusnnRose,KpStorming	10
6Feb85-4SA	1 1/16	:462	1:112	1:444ft	8	117	612	716	1026	1024	McHrguDG6	ⒻM32000	53-15	StksTWn,SnstnlDrm,MntlBnkMgc	11
6Feb85—Lugged out															

Partner's Express — **LAGRANGE D L** — **114**
Own.—Axline C

Dk. b. or br. f. 4, by Partner's Hope—Miss Snow Nose, by Nashua Chip
Br.—Axline W & C (Kan) — 1985 10 0 1 1 $2,165
Tr.—Dickey George — **$10,000** — 1984 4 1 2 0 $1,583
Lifetime 14 1 3 1 $3,748

31Jly85-6Cby	6f	:223	:462	1:113ft	40	114	96¾	96¾	74½	812¼	Hoverson C2	Ⓕ 10000	78-14	SheWillTll,ArcticAngl,GimmiATip	10
21Jly85-3Cby	6f	:221	:46	1:113ft	27	116	64¾	64½	77½	710	Baze D7	Ⓕ 16000	— —	DrlingDorothy,DiboloRinbow,St.Trs	7
12Jly85-7Cby	6½f	:233	:464	1:18 ft	23	116	74¼	77	67	59¾	Baze D3	Ⓕ 25000	— —	JtullhMid,AxetheOdds,BettieBGood	8
2Jun85-5Aks	6f	:224	:461	1:121ft	31	116	65	78	98½	911	Frazier DL1	ⒻAw14400	65-27	Chocolate Kisses, Real Carri, Pool	9
19May85-10Ato	6f	:231	:464	1:133ft	2½	118	76	711	62¾	65¾	JonsRV3	ⒻF Brown H	83-21	SchellyBo,SweetDr.,Stcey'sSidkick	8
13Apr85-5Fon	6f	:223	:47	1:12 ft	14	116	42	42	42	45½	Shepherd DR1	Ⓕ 25000	86-10	Bright N Sunny, Real Carri, Lusive	7
6Apr85-7Fon	6f	:223	:462	1:121ft	58	114	2hd	22	23	27	Frazier D L7	ⒻAw5300	84-16	GentleGil,Partner'sExpress,RelCrri	7
30Mar85-6Fon	6f	:232	:48	1:134m	38	116	42	79½	619	725¼	Beck D L6	Ⓕ 32000	58-21	Gentle Gil, Lil Happy, Eilsel	9
16Mar85-9Fon	6f	:232	:472	1:121ft	27	115	63½	76¼	813	819	Frazier D L8	ⒻAw5618	72-16	Racing Jet, Bright NSunny,Tamyon	8
1Mar85-7Fon	4f		:224	:47 ft	14	114	2	2½	2½	3hd	Frazier D L8	ⒻAw5300	90-08	LilHppy,SilingJupon,Prtner'sExprss	8

Jly 30 Cby 3f ft :36 b   Jly 11 Cby 3f ft :372 b   Jly 6 Cby 4f ft :524 b   Jun 30 Cby 4f ft :52 b

Class Counts — **HAMILTON M** — **118**
Own.—Bogges L & FalconFarmsLtd

B. m. 5, by Turn And Count—Turner's Class, by Circle
Br.—Turner S A (Ky) — 1985 10 1 1 1 $6,046
Tr.—Boggess Lee — **$10,000** — 1984 3 0 0 0
Lifetime 19 2 1 1 $13,696

16Aug85-9Cby	5½f	:223	:461	1:054ft	14	118	86¼	79	66	46¾	LaGrange DL2	Ⓕ 12500	84-09	Sotetta, La Liz, Porch Cat	8
4Aug85-6Cby	5½f	:222	:461	1:053ft	23	116	52¼	74¼	67	56½	LaGrange DL6	Ⓕ 14000	85-10	DiboloRinbow,DrlingDorothy,Chtell	8
6Jly85-10Cby	1 1/16	:48	1:122	1:461ft	10	113	56½	54½	34	47	LaGrange DL6	Ⓕ 14000	— —	Mrzi'sHollow,SwtOlShri,FinnwyLdy	6
28Jun85-4Cby	1 1/16	:501	1:151	1:474ft	4	115	1½	2hd	42½	44	LaGrange DL5	Ⓕ 12500	— —	BnnerStone,CorrelKim,SweetOlShri	5
20Jun85-6FP	6f	:223	:464	1:133ft	*2-3	122	73¾	53	4¾	1nk	Louviere G E6	Ⓕ 15000	75-23	ClssCounts,AfridtoEntr,DinWithWn	7
7Jun85-8FP	1 1/16	:472	1:13	1:464m	7¾	117	41½	41¼	31½	22	LouviereGE1	ⒻAw4900	75-20	Dicentra, Class Counts, High Three	9
2Jun85-8FP	6f	:224	:462	1:112gd	10	117	52½	64¼	54½	34	LouviereGE2	ⒻAw4200	82-17	LdyChlee,JstrsonsHony,ClssCounts	7
25May85-6FP	6f	:224	:463	1:121ft	8	122	53½	55½	65¼	55¼	LouviereGE9	ⒻAw4200	77-23	AlottWmpum,Betty'sMist,LittlBss	10
24Apr85-9TuP	6f	:214	:44	1:083ft	8	114	52½	65¼	711	712½	LaGrngeDL5	ⒻAw6000	80-18	Cuervo, DronesFirefly,BlueSmokey	7
13Apr85-8TuP	6f	:212	:454	1:094ft	15	114	1011	1010	95¼	65	LaGrngeDL5	ⒻAw4000	82-14	WllBStnnng,DronsFrfly,FshonFrst	10

●Jly 24 Cby 5f sy 1:002 h

Race Description and Conditions

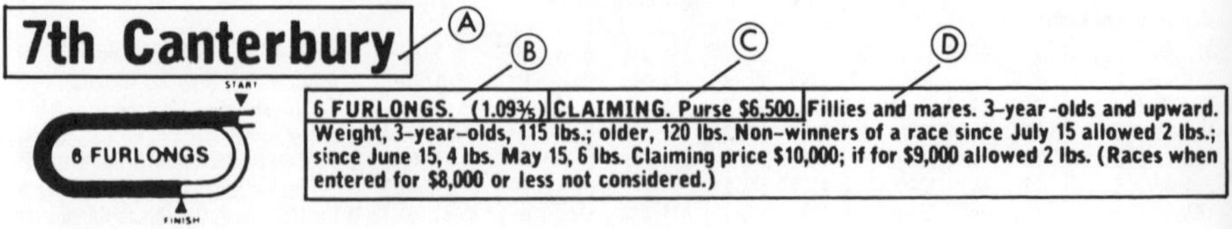

7th Canterbury
Ⓐ
Ⓑ
Ⓒ
Ⓓ
START
6 FURLONGS
FINISH
6 FURLONGS. (1.09⅗) CLAIMING. Purse $6,500. Fillies and mares. 3-year-olds and upward. Weight, 3-year-olds, 115 lbs.; older, 120 lbs. Non-winners of a race since July 15 allowed 2 lbs.; since June 15, 4 lbs. May 15, 6 lbs. Claiming price $10,000; if for $9,000 allowed 2 lbs. (Races when entered for $8,000 or less not considered.)

At the beginning of each race's Past Performances, there is a track diagram, indicating the start and finish, followed by a full description of the race ...

Ⓐ Race number and track name

Ⓑ Distance and track record for that distance

Ⓒ Type of race (e.g. claiming, allowance or maiden) and gross purse

Ⓓ Eligibility and Conditions of the race

Although frequently overlooked by some handicappers, the conditions of a race are extremely important. You can't handicap a race without knowing what kind of race it is and what kind of horses belong in it. The conditions of each race are set forth in a "Condition Book" (sample on facing page) published every two weeks by the track's Racing Secretary.

Trainers read these books like most men read *Penthouse.* It's their bible and guide, and they read it thoroughly — searching for races where the conditions best suit their horse. Trainers will look for races where ...

1) the distance to be run is appropriate,

2) the competitive level or "class" is a level where his horse has a chance of winning,

3) his horse will be required to carry the least amount of weight, and

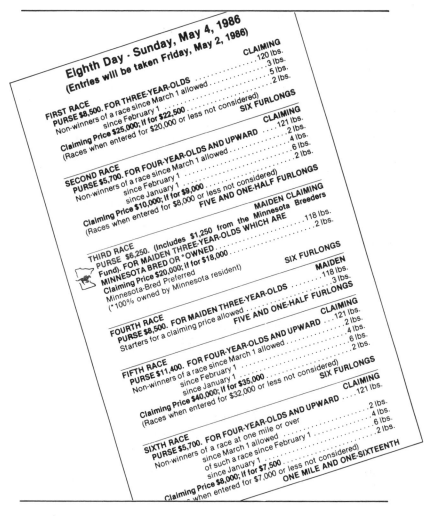

Eighth Day - Sunday, May 4, 1986
(Entries will be taken Friday, May 2, 1986)

FIRST RACE — **CLAIMING**
PURSE $8,500. FOR THREE-YEAR-OLDS .... 120 lbs.
Non-winners of a race since March 1 allowed .... 3 lbs.
since February 1 .... 5 lbs.
Claiming Price $25,000; if for $22,500 .... 2 lbs.
(Races when entered for $20,000 or less not considered)
SIX FURLONGS

SECOND RACE — **CLAIMING**
PURSE $5,700. FOR FOUR-YEAR-OLDS AND UPWARD .... 121 lbs.
Non-winners of a race since March 1 allowed .... 2 lbs.
since February 1 .... 4 lbs.
since January 1 .... 6 lbs.
Claiming Price $10,000; if for $9,000 .... 2 lbs.
(Races when entered for $8,000 or less not considered)
FIVE AND ONE-HALF FURLONGS

THIRD RACE — **MAIDEN CLAIMING**
PURSE $6,250. (Includes $1,250 from the Minnesota Breeders Fund). FOR MAIDEN THREE-YEAR-OLDS WHICH ARE MINNESOTA BRED OR *OWNED .... 118 lbs.
Claiming Price $20,000; if for $18,000 .... 2 lbs.
Minnesota-Bred Preferred
(*100% owned by Minnesota resident)
SIX FURLONGS

FOURTH RACE — **MAIDEN**
PURSE $8,500. FOR MAIDEN THREE-YEAR-OLDS .... 118 lbs.
Starters for a claiming price allowed .... 3 lbs.
FIVE AND ONE-HALF FURLONGS

FIFTH RACE — **CLAIMING**
PURSE $11,400. FOR FOUR-YEAR-OLDS AND UPWARD ... 121 lbs.
Non-winners of a race since March 1 allowed .... 2 lbs.
since February 1 .... 4 lbs.
since January 1 .... 6 lbs.
Claiming Price $40,000; if for $35,000 .... 2 lbs.
(Races when entered for $32,000 or less not considered)
SIX FURLONGS

SIXTH RACE — **CLAIMING**
PURSE $5,700. FOR FOUR-YEAR-OLDS AND UPWARD .... 121 lbs.
Non-winners of a race at one mile or over
since March 1 allowed .... 2 lbs.
of such a race since February 1 .... 4 lbs.
since January 1 .... 6 lbs.
Claiming Price $8,000; if for $7,500 .... 2 lbs.
(Races when entered for $7,000 or less not considered)
ONE MILE AND ONE-SIXTEENTH

4) where he can take full advantage of the "conditions", e.g. a race for "non-winners of two" for a horse who was nosed-out in his last start by better animals than would be found in this field.

The trainer's objective is to enter his horse against the weakest possible field at the proper distance and class level.

At this point, let's briefly define the most common types of races you will be handicapping ...

Maiden Races — Maiden races are limited to horses who have never won a race, and are usually contested by two and three-year-olds. (Don't be misled here ... *Secretariat* was a maiden once). There are two types of maiden races — "Maiden Special Weight" (or maiden allowance) and "Maiden Claiming".

Claiming Races — Claiming races are the most common type of race, constituting approximately 70% of all races run. In these races, horses are entered for a specific price and can be purchased or "claimed" by any licensed owner at that track. Because of this, owners will usually run their horses at a price that is equal to the horse's value. Clearly a $25,000 horse would demolish a field of $4,000 horses. Equally probable is that another owner would claim the horse. As such, the element (or threat) of claiming tends to equalize the class or competition among lower and medium quality horses.

Allowance Races — An allowance race is a non-claiming race for better quality horses. These races generally offer higher purses than claiming races. Eligibility requirements and conditions are similar to those of claiming races, and weight allowances are given based on earnings and/or number or type of victories.

Stakes & Handicap Races — These races offer the largest purses and attract the best horses — both on the grounds and from other tracks.

Starter Races — These races are limited to "claimers" who have started for a specific minimum claiming price since a certain date. Generally they are a series of route or distance races which increase in length as the season progresses.

We'll discuss each of these types of races in greater detail in subsequent chapters. Now let's get back to deciphering the PPs.

The Horse and His Connections

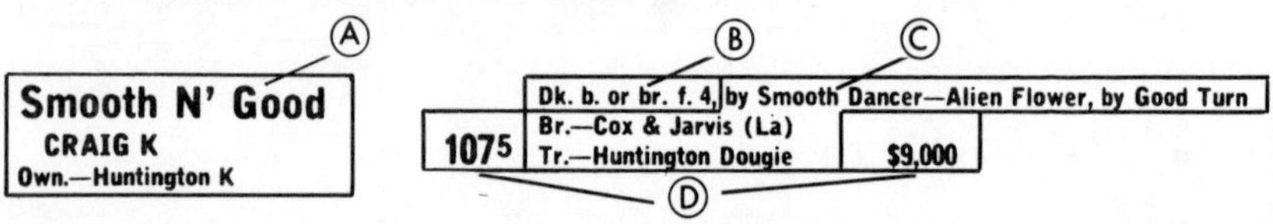

This block of information identifies:

- Ⓐ The Horse's Name, Jockey and Owner
- Ⓑ Color, Sex and Age
- Ⓒ Pedigree (Sire — Dam, Broodmare Sire), Breeder (Br.) and Trainer (Tr.)
- Ⓓ Assigned Weight and Claiming Price (when applicable)

Earnings Box

	Starts	1sts	2nds	3rds	
Lifetime	30	6	5	5	$32,564

	Starts	1sts	2nds	3rds	
1985	11	2	3	2	$12,216
1984	18	4	1	3	$19,448
Turf	1	0	0	1	$770

This useful tabulation provides the number of starts, wins, seconds and thirds — plus dollar earnings for the past two years and the lifetime. It further breaks down the horse's record on the turf. These dates are important when evaluating horses in terms of both Condition and Class. (Note: an "M" appearing in the Win column signifies that the horse was or is a maiden, i.e., a non-winner.)

Running Lines

ug85-10Cby	1	:48^2	1:13^2	1:39^{1}ft	6¾	116	3^2	43½	55½	79¼	Melancon G^6	c6250	76-11	Adobe Chief, SpeedSpy,TonicMajor	9
ug85-10Cby	1 1/16	:48^3	1:13^4	1:47^{4}ft	*2¾	114	21½	2½	1^{hd}	1^3	LaGrange D L^8	Ⓕ 6250	77-10	SmoothN'Gd,EnglshWzrd,Dwnsflng	8
y85-1Cby	1 1/16	:47^4	1:12^4	1:46 ft	*1	109^5	4^2	3^1	2^{hd}	11½	Bass S H^7	Ⓕ c5000	— —	SmoothN'Gd,MystclSng,SlvrStrshn	7
y85-9Cby	1	:48^4	1:13	1:39 ft	7¾	107^5	3^{nk}	3^{nk}	3^{nk}	3¾	Bass S H^1	Ⓕ 7500	— —	Snderell,SheWillTll,SmoothN'Good	8
un85-3CD	1	:46^3	1:11^3	1:38^{2}ft	2½e	116	6^6	45½	46½	4^8	Montoya D^5	Ⓕ 7500	69-18	TwinHerts,JestersJoy,TrojnGoddss	9
ay85-5CD	6f	:21^2	:45^1	1:11^{4}ft	3¾e	116	7^{15}	79¼	78¾	66¼	Melancon G^4	Ⓕ 10000	80-14	Countess Suzie, PorchCat,IronGold	7
ay85-1CD	1	:47^3	1:14^4	1:41 ft	*8-5	116	72¾	4¾	3^3	3^3	Fox W I Jr^6	Ⓕ c7500	61-14	She Will Tell, Joby, SmoothN'Good	8
ar85-11FG	1 1/16	:47^1	1:13	1:47^{4}ft	*2	112	8^{10}	8^{11}	3^4	2^{hd}	Fox W I Jr^4	Ⓕ 8500	73-20	JestersJoy,SmoothN'Good,TiffyK.	10
ar85-7FG	6f	:22^1	:46^2	1:12^{2}ft	*7-5	116	10^{13}	8^{14}	66¼	46¼	RomeroRP^4	ⒻS 12500	77-19	ClrCrkCt,Mg'sBlossm,HnrAndGlry	10
eb85-8FG	6f	:22^3	:47^1	1:13^{1}ft	16	114	7^9	8^{13}	5^6	2^{hd}	Faul J H^1	ⒻS 15000	79-21	Dr.PrttyFst,SmothN'Gd,LdyL.AndL.	9

15Feb85—Steadied to avoid tiring horse

The running lines are the guts of a horse's Past Performances — providing a detailed history of the horse's most recent (8-10) races. These running lines show the date, track, distance, position and times of the horse at various stages of a race plus a lot more ...

Explanation of Running Lines

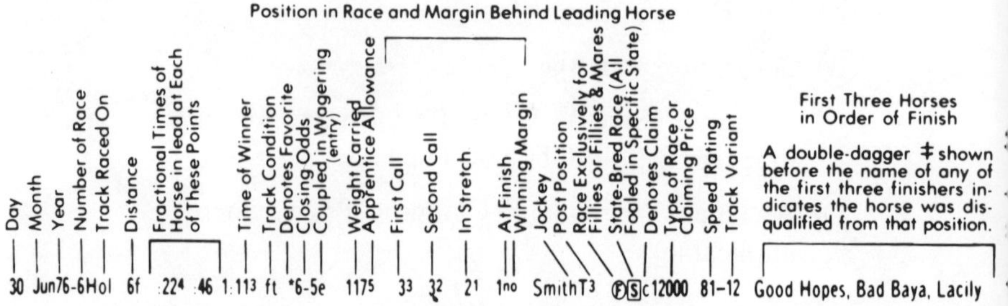

Note: In past performances the position in the race for "first call" is as follows: In races less than 5 furlongs the first call is the start; at 5 furlongs the first call is the three-sixteenths; from 5½ to 7½ furlongs the first call is the quarter mile; at 1 mile or more the first call is the half.

There is a Key to the Symbols used in the Past Performances and a list of Track Abbreviations contained in the Appendix. (If you are new to the game, you might want to turn to these exhibits now and become familiar with them to help you understand subsequent discussions.) These guides are also contained in every edition of the *Daily Racing Form* at the beginning of the Past Performances section. When just beginning, it's a good idea to clip these guides and put them in a cellophane sleeve for ready reference.

Workouts

Jly 30 Cby 3f ft :36 b **Jly 11 Cby 3f ft :37² b** **Jly 6 Cby 4f ft :52⁴ b** **Jun 30 Cby 4f ft :52 b**

The most recent workouts for each horse are listed beneath the running lines. This information reports the date, track, distance, track condition, time and type of workout, e.g. "breezing" versus "handily." (See "Condition" for more on Workouts.)

Okay, now that we have a rough idea of what all these symbols mean, let's examine the fundamentals — the basic handicapping factors — so that we can interpret the Past Performances and select the probable winner ...

III. Composite Handicapping

Most handicappers fall into specific categories such as "Speed", "Class," "Pace" or "Trip" handicappers. Their approach to selecting winners is "keyed" to a single factor, and they evaluate each and every race according to this measure. I recommend a broader approach — an approach I call "Composite Handicapping". The "Composite" approach enables you to identify the probable "impact factors" in each race and then to focus your analysis accordingly. It recognizes that:

1) There is no single factor that will predict the outcome of every race.

2) Certain factors will impact on other factors (e.g. Speed affects Pace) and these relationships must be understood and considered.

3) Horses must be evaluated in the context of the race and not separately, independent of the field, and

4) The physical condition of the horse — immediately before the race — must be considered.

"Composite Handicapping"is based on having a good grasp of the fundamentals of the game. Once these are understood, you will be able to predict — with some confidence — the outcome of most races.

To select winners, you must approach each race differently. Each race has its own personality and requires an open and comprehensive approach. There are at least a dozen "factors" to consider in each race. The following chapters will help you understand these factors, and then identify which factors to concentrate on to determine the probable winner. In some races, Pace might be the critical factor, and in others, it may of little consequence. The same applies to Speed, Class and the other popular "key" factors.

Each race is a canvas about to be painted. You must have a broad overview and understand the texture of the race before sharpening your pencil. The "Composite" approach will produce an informed "opinion," not decimal-pointed numerical dogma. For those of you who insist on precision and rules, don't despair. There is an area in this book — a critical area — where data, rules, percentages and statistics come together into hard and fixed rules. And that area is "Principles of Equine Investment" (also known, in some circles, as betting shrewdly).

Now let's examine each of the fundamental "impact factors" in detail ...

IV. Track Conditions

The first thing to consider is the track itself — both its configuration and natural "biases." Additionally, it's important to understand how weather will affect the running surface. Sound boring? It is, but bear with me ...

Track Configuration

Racetracks come in a variety of shapes and sizes, and these differences are important to note, especially when you are evaluating horses coming in from other tracks. The three major differences relate to circumference, angle of the turns and length of the stretch.

1) **Circumference —** A track's circumference is measured on a path approximately three feet off the inner rail. Most tracks are one mile to 1 1/8 miles in circumference. There are also some tracks, such as Sportsman's Park in Chicago, that are only 1/2 or 5/8 of a mile. These smaller tracks or "bull rings" tend to have

slower comparative times because almost every race — even the sprints — are run around a minimum of two turns.

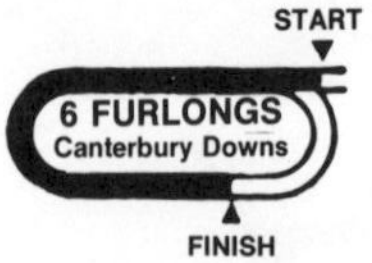

Horses lose velocity in turns, hence the slower times. Despite the slower times, these tracks definitely favor speed or front-runners who can get to the lead and then "save ground" along the rail in the turns.

A track's circumference also determines where the starting gate is positioned and the distance to the first turn. At one mile tracks, such as Canterbury Downs, the starting gate will be positioned on the finish line for races run at a mile, and the horses will run around two turns. At 1 1/8 mile tracks, such as Aqueduct, the starting gate for a mile race is positioned in a chute leading onto the straightaway of the backstretch, and the horses negotiate only one turn.

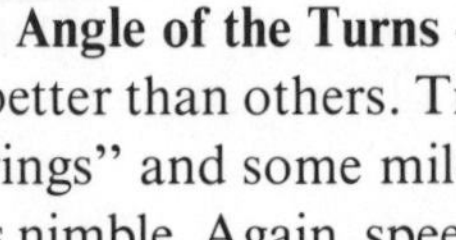

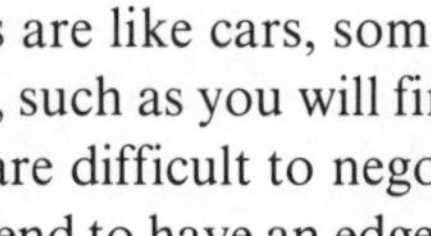

2) **Angle of the Turns** — Horses are like cars, some handle turns better than others. Tight turns, such as you will find at the "bull rings" and some mile tracks, are difficult to negotiate for the less nimble. Again, speed horses tend to have an edge on such tracks because they can get to the lead and not be forced wide in the turns.

3) **Length of the Stretch** — The position of the finish line varies from track to track. Generally speaking, the longer the

stretch, the better it is for horses who come from "off the pace" or "stretch runners". The added real estate can frequently make the difference for horses who make a late charge.

Track Surface and Biases

Most racetracks have a "bias" which will favor either "speed" horses or horses that come from behind or "off the pace." Speed-bias tracks are in the majority, and Canterbury Downs — based on its inaugural meeting — falls into this category.

The running surface of tracks differs according to the composition (sand and soil combinations) and depth of the upper or "loose" cushion. This running surface is subject to a great deal of fluctuation traceable to both weather and maintenance. Hard or firm surfaces tend to favor speed horses as these horses are able to bounce right along without sinking in. Generally speaking, the West Coast tracks have a harder surface than tracks in the Midwest and East. As a consequence, you will see faster times run on these western "parking lots." Deeper or softer tracks tend to be more tiring and sometimes will favor the stretch-runners. The depth of the upper cushion is controlled by the track maintenance crews. They determine both the depth of the cushion and the settings on the harrows of the large grooming rakes which are dragged across the track daily.

Another maintenance factor is how much water is put on a track before and between races. Very dry tracks tend to be "loose" and will break away from underneath a horse, making it difficult for the horse to "grab" onto the track. On a "dry" fast track, the more water, generally the faster the track will get. These "sprinklings" reduce the dust and tighten the surface much like surf will do to sand on a beach.

Weather & Track Conditions

Rain can change a track's condition quickly and sometimes dramatically. The *Daily Racing Form* determines the track condition prior to the running of each race, and the public is advised of the track's condition by a sign on the tote board. Dirt tracks are rated:

ft	fast
sy	sloppy
m	muddy
gd	good
sl	slow
hy	heavy
fr	frozen

Any surface other than "fast" is referred to as an "off track." During and immediately after a solid rainfall the track will go through a cycle of changes. Right after a heavy rain, tracks are usually rated sloppy when there is water standing on the surface. This type of surface is usually quite fast as the undercushion is still firm, and "speed" horses tend to skip right along.

As the moisture seeps deeper into the track, the condition will change to "muddy." Again, these surfaces tend to favor the front-running types. One reason is that they don't get the mud thrown back in their faces. And getting pounded by mud affects a horse in two ways, a) it adds significant weight as the mud sticks to both rider and horse, and b) it makes some horses quit or duck away from the onslaught. Quite understandable when you consider it.

As the track begins to dry, it tend to become tiring and thus may favor horses who run from behind or "stretch-runners." This drying out process produces track ratings of "good," "slow" or "heavy" before returning to "fast."

There is one other type of surface that the *Daily Racing Form* does not rate, and that is a "dead" track. A "dead" track is when the track is rated "fast," but the times are slower than normal. This condition may develop when the track is unusually dry or when the bottom cushion is holding moisture. It also occurs when the harrows cut deeper into the cushion. A "dead" track favors neither speed nor late comers. Its most significant impact is on the running times and resultant speed ratings (more on this later).

Lastly, you should recognize that on any given day, certain parts of the track may be better than others — sometimes the rail may be lightning fast, and on other days, it may be "dead". These differences create certain paths or "grooves" on the track, and the jockeys will try to place their mounts in these grooves where the footing is better. (More on this in "Trip Handicapping".)

Mud Marks

The *Daily Racing Form* rates horses in terms of their performance on "off tracks" and assigns "mud marks" to those horses who excel on an this type of footing. The symbols used are:

* **Fair Mud Runner**

X **Good Mud Runner**

⊗ **Superior Mud Runner**

Unfortunately, these marks are less meaningful today because they are neither assigned nor maintained as well as they were in the past. Years ago, these marks were changed — up and down — after careful review. There is less attention paid to this nowadays. The burden, therefore, is on the handicapper to identify which horses can handle or even excel on "off tracks." I look at the PPs and pay particular attention to horses who actually run better when the track is wet.

In 1985, I had a horse named *Bristling Blade* who had an X mud mark. After several disappointing efforts on a fast track, we got lucky. It started to rain one day when he was entered. By post time, it was coming down in mega-buckets and the track was a sea of mud.

Bristling Blade took one look at the track, giggled and then ran off and won easily by almost 5 lengths in 1:11^2 — a full second faster than he was able to run on a "fast" track! More importantly, he paid $9.60 to his supporters. A rather liberal reward, given his past efforts on "off tracks". Note his two previous victories, especially the race on 24Oct84 which was obviously run in a comparable downpour.

Bristling Blade ✕
BASS S H **112^5**
Own.—Pritchard T

Dk. b. or br. g. 5, by Blade—Southern Belle, by Drone
Br.—Clinkinbeard J E & R M (Ky)
Tr.—Gabriel Leo **$6,250**
Lifetime 32 7 3 4 $31,787

1985	8	2	0	2		$7,816
1984	8	2	1	0		$6,526
Turf	1	0	1	0		$720

1Aug85-1Cby	6f	:22^3	:46	1:12 ft	2¼	113^5	$7^{6\frac{3}{4}}$	6^7	$5^{2\frac{3}{4}}$	$3^{1\frac{1}{2}}$	Bass S H^8	Ⓡ 5000	86-12	Wltz'sShdow,FlgSeven,BristlingBld	9
24Jly85-9Cby	5½f	:23	:46^4	1:05^{4}m	3	110^5	$5^{3\frac{3}{4}}$	6^7	$6^{4\frac{3}{4}}$	$4^{2\frac{1}{4}}$	Bass S H^5	Ⓡ 8000	— —	PrivtRoom,Mt.TborRd.,RockingMn	6
30Jun85-6Cby	6½f	:23^3	:46^2	1:18^{2}ft	2¼	119	$3^{3\frac{1}{2}}$	$4^{3\frac{3}{4}}$	4^5	4^9	Hansen R D^5	c6250	— —	Icectrope,RoguePrince,AdobeChief	8
12Jun85-4Aks	6f	:22^3	:46	1:12^{1}ft	*3	120	$3^{1\frac{1}{2}}$	$3^{4\frac{1}{2}}$	$3^{2\frac{1}{2}}$	$4^{3\frac{1}{2}}$	Doocy T T^3	6500	72-25	Brazen Ego,Vitrion,SpaghettiTree	12
27May85-1Aks	6f	:22^4	:46	1:13^{1}m	*2½	116	2^2	$3^{2\frac{1}{2}}$	$3^{2\frac{1}{2}}$	$1^{\frac{1}{2}}$	Doocy T T^{10}	6500	71-32	BrstlngBld,Mchodoon,CutosDcson	10
12May85-10Aks	6f	:22^3	:45^4	1:11^{1}ft	8	116	$8^{7\frac{3}{4}}$	$9^{9\frac{1}{2}}$	$5^{5\frac{1}{2}}$	4^5	Doocy T T^8	11000	76-21	Namletk,PromiseMeReb,Woodbrir	12
2May85-6Aks	6f	:23	:46^3	1:12^{3}ft	*4¼	118	1^1	1^{hd}	$3^{\frac{1}{2}}$	3^{nk}	Doocy T T^{12}	8500	74-31	IndinPrince,Flgellte,BristlingBlde	12
17Mar85-8TuP	5½f	:21^4	:44^2	1:02^{1}ft	11	114	$2^{1\frac{1}{2}}$	2^2	2^1	$1^{1\frac{1}{2}}$	Dittfach H^6	8000	97-13	Bristling Blade,Recline,PersianDeal	7
24Oct84-8StP	6f	:22^3	:46^1	1:12 gd	13	115	1^{nk}	1^2	—	1^5	Seymour D J^8	10000	87-28	BristlingBlde,SqudCr,CelestilReson	8
24Oct84—Running positions omitted because of weather conditions															
3Oct84-8StP	6f	:22^4	:46^1	1:11^{3}ft	6¼	121	$7^{5\frac{1}{2}}$	$7^{7\frac{3}{4}}$	$8^{5\frac{1}{2}}$	5^4	Malgarini T M^3	c8000	85-18	Kid Klown, Hail Cloud, Old Sim	9

SIXTH RACE
Canterbury
AUGUST 9, 1985

6 FURLONGS. (1.09⅘) CLAIMING. Purse $5,850 (includes $1,350 from MBF). 3-year-olds and upward, Minnesota-bred or owned. Weight, 3-year-olds, 116 lbs.; older, 121 lbs. Non-winners of two races since June 1 allowed 2 lbs.; of a race since then, 4 lbs.; of a race since May 1, 6 lbs. Claiming price $6,250. (Races when entered for $5,000 or less not considered.) (Minnesota-bred preferred.)

Value of race $5,850; value to winner $3,510; second $1,170; third $643; fourth $351; fifth $176. Mutuel pool $53,603. Exacta Pool, $43,828.

Last Raced	Horse	Eqt.	A.	Wt	PP	St	¼	½	Str	Fin	Jockey	Cl'g Pr	Odds $1
1Aug85 ^{1}Cby^3	Bristling Blade	b	5	112	5	4	$3^{\frac{1}{2}}$	$3^{1\frac{1}{2}}$	1^1	$1^{4\frac{1}{2}}$	Bass S H^5	6250	3.80
25Jly85 ^{7}Cby^3	Raised Proud		3	114	8	2	2^2	1^{hd}	$2^{1\frac{1}{2}}$	2^{hd}	Adkins R M	6250	5.60
24Jly85 ^{9}Cby^2	Mt. Tabor Rd.		7	115	2	5	5^{hd}	$5^{2\frac{1}{2}}$	$3^{1\frac{1}{2}}$	$3^{1\frac{1}{2}}$	Montoya D	6250	4.20
27Jly85 ^{2}Cby^1	My Kind		6	115	9	1	9	8^1	7^3	$4^{1\frac{1}{2}}$	Smith M E	6250	8.20
1Aug85 ^{1}Cby^1	Waltz's Shadow	b	4	115	3	8	$8^{\frac{1}{2}}$	$6^{\frac{1}{2}}$	$4^{2\frac{1}{2}}$	$5^{1\frac{1}{2}}$	Orona W	6250	3.40
5Jly85 ^{1}Cby^3	Royal Dude		4	111	6	9	7^2	$7^{2\frac{1}{2}}$	6^{hd}	6^2	Medero F^5	6250	25.40
1Aug85 ^{1}Cby^2	Flag Seven		4	115	4	6	4^{hd}	4^{hd}	5^{hd}	$7^{5\frac{1}{2}}$	Rashall R D	6250	14.50
16Dec84 ^{4}Lat^2	Angel of Battle	b	3	110	7	3	1^{hd}	$2^{\frac{1}{2}}$	$8^{2\frac{1}{2}}$	$8^{3\frac{1}{2}}$	Moyers L	6250	4.60
2Aug85 ^{1}Cby^1	Charmin Bug	b	3	113	1	7	6^2	9	9	9	Martino M	6250	19.90

OFF AT 6:28. Start good. Won handily. Time, :22, :45⅘, :58, 1:11⅕ Track muddy.

$2 Mutuel Prices:				
	5–BRISTLING BLADE	**9.60**	**4.20**	**3.80**
	8–RAISED PROUD		**5.00**	**3.80**
	2–MT. TABOR RD.			**3.60**

$2 EXACTA (5–8) PAID $58.40.

Dk. b. or br. g, by Blade—Southern Belle, by Drone. Trainer Gabriel Leo. Bred by Clinkinbeard J E & R M (Ky).

BRISTLING BLADE, never far back, drove to the lead outside horses entering the stretch and won going away. RAISED PROUD set or forced the early pace outside ANGEL OF BATTLE and continued well in the drive. MT. TABOR RD. went to the inside going into the far turn, angled outward for the drive and finished willingly. MY KIND passed mostly tired horses. WALTZ'S SHADOW, slow to find his best stride, stayed to the inside for the drive but lacked the needed rally. ROYAL DUDE broke a step slowly. FLAG SEVEN carried wide into the stretch, weakened. ANGEL OF BATTLE was finished after a half. CHARMIN BUG steadied, then clipped MT. TABOR RD.'S heels going into the far turn almost falling.

Owners— 1, Pritchard T; 2, Hauptman Trudy; 3, Leyda C; 4, Newcomb L; 5, Silver Ring Bloodstock; 6, Frost J L & Green J; 7, Thomas J; 8, Johnson L & Doris ; 9, Strom Kathleen & G.

Trainers— 1, Gabriel Leo; 2, Wismer Glenn; 3, Lammers Jim; 4, Ingram Steve; 5, Rhone Bernell; 6, Poincelet Michael R; 7, Bethke William; 8, Van Berg Jack C; 9, Estenson Marlyn.

Overweight: Royal Dude 1 pound; Angel of Battle 5; Charmin Bug 2.

Angel of Battle was claimed by Story B; trainer, Story Blaine.

Scratched—Princely Rock (31Jly85 ^{7}Cby^6); Milaca (14Jly85 ^{1}Cby^8).

Turf Races

Turf or grass courses are also rated and subject to changes in condition. Generally, they don't run races over a wet turf course. These races are switched to the main (dirt) track. This switch is necessary for both safety considerations and to prevent the turf course from being torn up (golfers who occasionally hit behind their chip shots can readily embrace this reasoning).

Turf courses are rated on the basis of firmness ranging from:

hd hard

fm firm

gd good

sf soft

yl yielding

The condition of a turf course is affected by four factors:

1) Moisture content
2) Density and texture of the grass
3) Length of the grass
4) Degree of traffic or activity

Typically, a turf course will be softer and denser during the spring and early summer months. By late summer, however, the course dries out and the grass density is reduced by normal wear and tear. As such, the surface tends to harden and become faster as the season progresses.

As in races run on the dirt, certain horses will perform better under different track conditions. Speed horses (especially West Coast horses) usually run better on firmer courses. European horses, on the other hand, are more familiar with, and consequently prefer a softer footing.

Summary

The expression "horses for courses" is quite accurate. A

track's configuration and running surface will either suit an individual horse or it won't. Some horses who win repeatedly at large tracks can't handle the smaller "bull rings" and vice versa. Recognizing the differences between tracks will be extremely helpful in evaluating "shippers" and new arrivals. (In the Appendix, I have indicated which tracks are less than a mile in circumference. See "Track Abbreviations.")

When faced with an "off track," you should focus your pre-race analysis on the Track Condition factor and each horse's ability to handle this type of footing. You are safe in eliminating horses who have demonstrated an inability to handle an "off track," and then focus on those who can. Further, you should be sensitive to the cycle of changes that occurs as the track dries out. And these changes frequently happen from race to race.

V. Distance

"The distance suits" is an apt phrase because most horses are best suited for running a very specific distance where their speed and stamina are both maximized. A few exceptional horses are able to compete effectively within a broader range of distances. Even these horses, however, have difficulty jumping back and forth from sprints to routes without a change in their training programs.

After determining track conditions, the distance factor is a good starting point when evaluating a field. The is a process of either qualifying or eliminating horses based on their Past Performances relative to today's distance. Further, by starting with distance, you can approach the Condition, Speed and Pace factors within the proper context.

Definitions

Before launching into this discussion, let's establish some definitions ...

> **Sprint races** — races run at a distance of 6 1/2 furlongs or less.
>
> **Middle-distance Sprint races** — races from 7 furlongs to a 1 1/16 miles.
>
> **Routes or Distance races** — races at 1 1/8 miles and longer.

Another definition states that any race which goes around a single turn is a sprint race, and those races run around two or more turns are routes. At Canterbury Downs, you are safe in viewing races of 6 1/2 furlongs or less as being sprints and races of a mile or longer as being routes.

Key Considerations

There are a number of factors that determine what distance best suits a horse. The most important considerations are breeding, conformation, condition and past performances.

Breeding — For most handicappers, breeding is a perplexing mystery. Breeding does, however, have a definite bearing on a horse's ability to run either long or short. When evaluating maidens and younger, lightly-raced horses, pedigree may be the only clue you have as to whether or not the horse will like the distance. Breeding may also influence a horse's predisposition for running well on the grass versus dirt and whether the horse can handle an "off track." Although the top sires are rated in terms of their offspring's ability to run various distances, most sires aren't. (I've included abbreviated listings in the Appendix for Speed, Distance, Grass and "Off Track" sires which may be helpful in this regard.)

Another aspect to consider is the effect breeding has on trainers. If a horse is bred to run all day, the trainer is likely to train the horse to go a route. As such, pedigrees may produce self-fulfilling prophecies.

Conformation — Horses are very similar to track athletes when it comes to distance. There are natural sprinters, and there are natural distance runners (routers). And like their two-legged counterparts, basic physiology or conformation frequently determines whether a horse is better suited for sprints or distance running.

Equine sprinters are usually stocky individuals with well-developed hind quarters, large girths and compact physiques. Routers tend to be long and lanky with longer backs and legs. (Studies have been done recently where muscle tissue has been analyzed to determine whether a horse has long or short-twitch muscle fibers. These studies have shown a strong correlation to muscle type and distance abilities.)

Condition — Current condition or fitness also affects a horse's ability to effectively compete at various distances. Routers must have both stamina and good wind. A router coming back after an extended layoff usually requires more time and training to recapture "distance form" compared to sprinters getting back into "sprint form."

Past Performances — For the most part, however, a horse's track record or Past Performances will indicate whether or not a horse is well-suited for the distance he will be running. An examination of past races will generally indicate a horse's preferred distance. Moreover, these "histories" will indicate at what point the horse will be ready to compete effectively (more on this in "Condition").

Qualifying Horses at the Distance

This is a relatively simple process. Horses who have recently won or been in the money (i.e. 1st, 2nd or 3rd) at the distance qualify for further consideration. Horses who have shown little or nothing at the distance — when competing against the same class of horses — can also be eliminated for the most part. So far, so good. This is easy, you say. Then you encounter a horse that is either switching from a sprint to a route or vice versa, or a horse coming off a layoff or the horse who is moving up or down in class. Now life isn't so simple.

Sprinters Going a Route

Younger Horses — Determining a young horse's best distance requires some experimentation by the trainer. Young horses start in sprints ranging from 3 to 5 1/2 furlongs. Once they graduate from the maiden ranks, they will attempt longer distances, being "stretched out" until the horse demonstrates the distance it prefers.

Route races for younger horses are tough to figure. Generally, these fields include a number of entrants who are trying a distance for the first time. As an owner, I can tell you that nobody knows with certainty if a young horse can carry his speed or be rated until you try him under race conditions. Consequently, these races are sometimes better watched than wagered on. If you are intent on playing such races, you should consider the following ...

1) **Breeding** — Is the horse by a proven Distance sire?

2) **Conformation** — Is the horse built like a router? Is he a lanky, long-legged individual versus a short, stocky type?

3) **Trainer** — Does the trainer have a history of successfully "stretching out" his stock? Does the trainer do his training in the morning and not on the racetrack?

4) **Running Style** — Has the horse shown an ability to run alongside other horses? Can he be "rated" or relaxed during the early going of a race based on past efforts? Has the horse been coming from off the pace, closing in the final 1/4 mile, indicating a desire to go further?

Older Horses — Any change in distance for older horses is a more difficult assignment than it is for younger horses, particularly when the horse is going from a sprint to a route. Whenever an older horse changes distance, current form/condition, class, jockey etc. must be considered. If a horse appears to warrant consideration based on those factors, then look for sprinters who have shown signs of wanting to go on. Examine the running lines and look for a strong "late move" where the horse gains 3-5 lengths on the leader in the stretch.

14Aug85 Cby 6f :22³ :45⁴ 1:13 10⁹ 6⁷ 3⁴ 2¹

Another situation which might favor a sprinter in a route is when the expected "pace" (i.e. the speed at which the early part of the race is run) is slow. A slow pace will develop if there is an absence of "early speed" or front-running horses. If you encounter such a race, then it is possible for a sprinter to use his speed tactically and "steal" the race. A speedball, who looks like he'd need a taxi to go longer than seven furlongs, ridden by an experienced jockey, may be able to carry his speed wire-to-wire. To do so, the horse must get an easy and early lead, then be relaxed or "rated" by the rider, save ground along the rail and ideally have enough left in the stretch to hold off the late-comers.

Another type of horse to consider is the older horse that is "raced into shape." Some trainers elect to put an older "router" in a series of sprint races after an extended layoff. When examining the Past Performances, look for a horse who has run routes in the past, was laid up and returns in sprint races. If the horse was running at a distance prior to the layoff, you can assume that his recent sprints were "tune-ups." As such, his finish in those races is not that critical. Rather, look at these races versus each other; has the horse shown a modest improvement (e.g. speed rating) race-to-race? If so, he may be rounding into form and ready for a good effort going a distance.

Routers in a Sprint

Generally speaking, these horses are not a good bet. In the case of older horses, such efforts may be "tune-ups" after a layoff where the objective is conditioning versus winning. Another situation to be wary of is when you see an older router in a sprint accompanied by a sharp drop in price, this is usually a strong signal that the horse has major physical problems.

There are some exceptions to these guidelines, and like most exceptions, they offer huge mutuel payoffs. You might give consideration to a router dropped into a sprint race if there is a ton of early speed in the race. If all the main contenders are front-running types with a lot of speed, the early pace may be suicidal. Such a scenario may enable a router to capitalize on his stamina and even running style to catch the early leaders as they gasp for breath at the sixteenth pole.

Summary

Most horses are best suited for a specific distance, and this distance is usually evident by examining its Past Performances. Older horses are less likely to be successful when changing distances. Trainers will experiment with horses that are not running well. Aside from equipment and rider changes, trainers have only two choices with a losing horse — drop it down in price or change the distance. Consequently, you are better off waiting for a horse to demonstrate that he can successfully handle a new distance before plunging at the mutuels.

VI. Condition

Thoroughbreds are exquisite athletes, and their current physical condition or form is a critical handicapping consideration. A horse's form or fitness varies throughout his life and during each racing season.

Until recently, racing was limited to the warm weather months. During the winter, horses were usually turned out on farms while a small percentage would race at the southern and western tracks. This pattern has changed with the advent of virtually year-round racing in the northern states. The desire to keep the state's coffers filled has prompted state racing commissions to extend racing dates. This fact coupled with the ever-increasing cost of maintaining racehorses has resulted in many horses, especially claimers, being over-raced. Consequently, identifying good current form has become an even more important handicapping consideration.

Training

Horses are put through various training and exercise programs to develop and maintain fitness. The typical training program consists of walking, restrained gallops and workouts. These activities vary according to trainer, animal, time of year, objectives, etc. All horses need daily exercise of one type or another — not only for physical reasons, but also to ease the boredom that comes from confinement in a racetrack environment. Boredom can deaden a horse's competitive drive almost as much as overwork. Consequently, periodic "turn-outs" (60-120 days) and "fresheners" (40-60 days) are beneficial, if not required, to maintain good form.

Bringing a horse into form after an extended layoff generally starts with daily gallops (restrained), gradually increasing the distance and speed of these outings. A horse is usually given one day off every four to five days. On these days, he will be walked for about 45 minutes. During this period, the horse's ration is changed, adding more grain for protein. Once the "hay belly" is gone and the muscle tone and wind return, the horse is ready for more serious work to restore his quickness and speed. This is done through "breezes," i.e. wide open gallops over short distances. These are called workouts and are recorded by the track clocker and reported in the *Daily Racing Form.*

Published Workouts

The *Daily Racing Form* publishes workout clockings daily, highlighting the fastest "work at the distance" by printing that work in bold face (such workouts are subsequently indicated in the horse's Past Performances by a (•) bullet preceding the date and time). These logs also contain "Clocker Comments" which contain noteworthy workouts and other information such as "worked in company," meaning that the horse worked out with one or two other horses. (See sample on page 5.)

The *Daily Racing Form* employs a number of symbols to describe each workout. The most common of which are:

b — "breezing," where the rider has a light hold on the horse

h — "handily," where the rider urges the horse with his hands, rolling his knuckles across the horse's neck

g — signifies that the workout was from the starting gate

d — means that rubber cones or "dogs" were on the track off the inner railing. The track puts the "dogs" out after rain or when the inner going along the rail is a little treacherous.

Trt — indicates that the workout was over the training track as opposed to the main track

In terms of evaluating workout times, there is a reference chart for Canterbury Downs included in the Appendix. These figures, however, should be used only as a general guide. There are some horses who are better timed with a calendar than a stopwatch in the morning. Yet these same horses run a hole in the wind in the afternoon. And the reverse is also true. Some "morning glory" horses impress the clockers and never run back to their workouts. Furthermore, different trainers work their stock differently. Some will push their horses in the mornings and others won't. Some horses may be ridden by 150 pound exercise riders, while others may have a 85 pound jockey on board. Some horses may work right off the rail, while others might work in the middle of the track. All of these unknowns affect the recorded times. Another factor to consider is that some trainers condition their horses off the track on the farm or at private training facilities, and these drills are not reported in the DRF.

The primary considerations with regard to workouts are currentness, frequency and acceptability. A regular pattern of workouts in acceptable times is a positive sign, indicating fitness or a well-defined training regime. In terms of higher quality animals, especially stakes horses, the times of their works are more important. These horses are usually drilled fast. And on some occasions, too fast. More than once, a jockey has worked a top horse too fast before a race, and the horse "leaves his race on the training track."

A final caution regarding workouts ... "nobody's perfect," especially clockers.

Form Cycles

When horses are racing they go through a regular exercise program. Different trainers employ different techniques to maintain form. The most traditional approach employs a combination of gallops, walks and workouts.

Horses that are running more frequently (e.g. lower-priced claimers) may not be worked out between starts as the proximity of their races will keep them sharp. Horses with over 12 days between races generally benefit from a workout in the middle of this period. Some horses, however, can be kept on edge simply through morning gallops.

Like other athletes, thoroughbreds are subject to cyclical changes in their physical condition or form. Intertwined with these physical cycles are "emotional" cycles which also influence their performance. Over-raced horses and horses who have been at the track for extended periods go dead flat. They lose their enthusiasm and perform accordingly.

"Private Files"

In that the *Daily Racing Form* only lists a horse's last eight to 10 races in the Past Performances, you should save your old DRFs right from the start of the season. By so doing you will have, by mid-season, each horse's last 20+ races. Although a little time-consuming, these "private files" will give you an excellent profile or "form-curve" on most of the horses — files that the general public has no access to. (Further benefits of keeping such files will be discussed in subsequent chapters.)

Factors Affecting Form

In general, horses are capable of maintaining peak form for 2 to 3 months. This peak period is usually preceded by a 30-45 day period where they are rounding into form — followed by a 45-60 day period where their form declines. These cycles or curves vary somewhat by animal and are influenced by the following:

1) Number of starts
2) Intervals between races
3) Running distance
4) Basic soundness/Injuries
5) Class/Age
6) Training regime

We can determine a horse's condition in two ways — by analysis of his Past Performances and by physical inspection (more on this aspect in "Paddock Handicapping"). In terms of Past Performances, we should consider the following ...

Number of Starts — Every horse has a limit in terms of "winning efforts." The "Earnings Box" for each horse provides the number of starts for the current year, the previous year and lifetime. Cheaper horses are usually run more frequently. The average low-end claimer may start as many as 20+ times a year. The number of starts becomes a factor as the season progresses. In the fall, you are likely to find many horses who have campaigned since the beginning of the year. These horses are usually tapped-out. As such, look for "fresh" horses late in the season versus horses who have been raced for months without a break.

When a horse passes peak form, his efforts show definite signs of "dullness," apathy or fatigue. You should eliminate horses competing at the same price/class level which have:

1) finished fifth or worse in their last start,
2) finished six lengths or further behind the winner, or
3) failed to make a "move" (gain three to five lengths) on the leader at any point during the race.

Unless these horses take a sharp drop, i.e., two to three notches, in price — they are likely to continue to disappoint their loyal supporters who remember the horses' better days.

Interval Between Races — A horse is more likely to maintain good form if his racing activity is properly scheduled with adequate intervals between races. The length of such intervals depends on the horse and a number of other factors. A good guideline, however, is 10 days for sprinters and 14 days for routers. These intervals can be adjusted depending on the effort a horse puts out in any given race. If a horse has a tough race where he is fully extended throughout the entire race, he may need a little extra time between races. On the other hand, a horse who puts in a "conditioning" race or wins easily, may be ready to run back in five to seven days.

On the flip side of the interval question is when a horse has not raced in the past 20-40 days. Such a gap is not really long enough to be considered a "freshener" or "therapeutic layoff" and may, in fact, take a horse off his edge. To determine whether or not such a gap should eliminate a contender, you must consider a number of other factors. Among "acceptable" reasons are:

1) **A horse claimed in his last race.** The new trainer will usually do a number of things after a claim, including diet changes, reshoeing and the like. He will also want some time to learn the horse's likes and dislikes, what works and what doesn't. And lastly, a trainer may not want to race the horse while he is "in jail" (the thirty day period following a claim whereby the new owner must race the horse at a price no less than 25 percent higher than the price at which the horse was claimed).

2) **A recent arrival at the track.** When a horse is moved from one track to another, he may need some extra time to acclimate and adjust to his new environment. Moreover, the trainer may want to train the horse over the track several times in the morning to get the horse familiar with the running surface.

3) **Competitive Cripples.** There are some older horses who can't run as frequently due to chronic leg

problems, and these horses require more time between starts. If their Past Performances show such a pattern, without loss of form, such horses should be considered. (These competitive "cripples," hampered by chronic injuries, are capable of two or three winning efforts when competing. Their trainers run them cheap — where they can win — with little fear of anyone claiming the horse because it's bad-legged.)

Evaluating Horses After A Layoff

If a horse is returning to competition after an extended layoff, he is unlikely to connect at first asking. Most horses will require two or three races to recapture previous good form. Consequently, some handicappers will automatically eliminate any horse who has been away from the races for over 45 days. While this practice is basically sound, I'm not so rigid in this regard. There are some positive signs to look for when evaluating these horses . . .

1) **In sprint races,** the horse being considered should have a) one race in the past thirty days, or b) a regular pattern (every four to five days) of workouts, including one of 1/2 mile or longer.

2) **In route races,** the horse should have a) one race and a minimum of two workouts in the past month, with one work at 5/8 mile or longer, or b) one race and one workout within the past ten days.

There are exceptions to these guides, and these horses offer big payoffs if you can spot them. Look for horses who have a history of winning in their first race after a layoff.

An important element to consider when evaluating "returnees" is the trainer. Certain trainers are noted for bringing horses back to competition dead fit, while others are more likely to race their stock back into form. Knowing the various trainers and their patterns will give you a big edge in this regard.

Age and Class

Age and class should be considered when determining current form. Different types of horses are trained and raced differently. In order to determine fitness or condition, let's look at horses in terms of age and class ...

Two-Year Olds — Many trainers (and owners) rush young horses and race them "before their time." It requires a great deal of patience and money to wait on young horses. Many owners lack both, and their horses are frequently thrown into competition too soon. Many established racing operations will keep their 2YO's off the track until mid-summer or early autumn. This makes good sense for a number of reasons. First, 2YO's are still growing. Horses don't begin to mature until late in their three-year-old year. Young horses need time for their bones to form and to develop their respiratory capacity and muscle groups. And this process of bringing a horse "up to the races" usually takes several months.

Some trainers will shortcut this program and throw an unfit horse into his first race. Big mistake. Frequently, the first race or two will form lasting impressions on a young horse. Consequently, if a horse has a bad first trip, he is unlikely to be enthusiastic in subsequent efforts.

When evaluating the fitness or readiness of 2YO's (especially first-time starters), look for signs of speed and "education." Young horses tend to run as fast as they can for as long as they can. It's unusual for a young horse to be "rated," i.e. reserved off the pace. Restraining an anxious youngster might discourage him. Consequently, trainers usually "send" their youngsters in their initial outings. After a number of unsuccessful efforts, however, the trainer might change tactics and keep the horse off the early pace or try him at a longer distance. Both approaches are accompanied by changes in the training program.

Given the above, you should look for the following positive signs when evaluating first-time starters:

1) At least three published workouts in the past 30 days;

2) One workout from the starting gate;

3) A workout of five furlongs or longer;

4) A workout "in company," i.e. with one or more other horses, is another good sign. Horses must be able to run alongside of other horses and be accustomed to their presence during a race. Horses that only work out by themselves might react quite poorly when they find themselves surrounded by other horses.

Claimers — These horses are the hardest worked horses at the track and, consequently, are more vulnerable to shifts in condition. Many claimers make 20 to 30 starts each year. They are rarely turned out for extended periods unless injured. Again, the economics dictate that claimers run, not vacation. Larger stables tend to turn over their claiming inventory regularly. When horses turn sour, the trainer will drop them sharply in price, hoping they will be claimed.

Generally speaking, claimers round into form and are able to maintain that good form for five to six races. Aside from a series of recent good performances, there are other positive signs to look for, e.g. workouts between races. This indicates fitness because fit horses have to either run or workout regularly, otherwise they'll kick down their stalls. Many trainers will keep their horses on edge by brisk gallops. These efforts are not considered "workouts" by the clockers and, as such, are not reported. Consequently, the absence of workouts between races is not necessarily a negative sign.

Allowance/Handicap/Stakes Horses — Better quality horses race less frequently and are able to maintain good form for longer periods. Allowance horses run less frequently for two reasons. First, there are fewer allowance races scheduled. Secondly, the trainer is always looking for the right "spot" where he can maximize his horse's "conditions" or eligibility. He won't waste a race just for the sake of running a horse. Consequently, better quality horses may only run once every 12-20 days. They maintain their form, however, through a regular training program, usually consisting of gallops and at least one solid workout every six to nine days.

Better quality horses are usually given periodic breaks in training. They are turned out on farms and allowed to unwind and put on weight. Once rejuvenated, these horses return to competition. Many of the considerations applied to evaluating the fitness of claimers applies to allowance horses. The major difference is that trainers are more likely to train an allowance or stakes horse versus racing him into shape. Therefore, these horses will usually come back to competition more fit than claimers. In many cases, top form will return after only one or two prep races. And some horses can be brought back on workouts alone. A perfect example of the latter was *Greinton's* return to action in 1986. This Charlie Whittingham-trained stakes-winner was turned out in early November 1985 after the Breeders Cup. *Greinton* made his 1986 debut four months later in the million dollar Santa Anita Handicap going a mile and a quarter. He won the race, beating an exceptional field. And he did it strictly off workouts without a prep race.

Negative Factors

There are a number of negative factors to watch for, regardless of class or age. You are well advised to eliminate any horse that:

1) Bled in its last start (see "Medication" for more information on "bleeders");

2) Came back "lame" in any of its last three races;

3) Was "eased" in its last start with no excuse;

4) "Bore out" or "bore in" in its last race; or

5) Was "fractious" (unruly behavior) in either the paddock or the starting gate.

Any of the above situations indicate that the horse in question has a physical problem, an emotional disorder or both. In any case, you should eliminate such a horse from further consideration.

You should also take a close look at the running lines of recent winners who have engaged in "wars" in their last race or two. If a horse is pressured for the lead by another horse(s) throughout most of the going — particularly during the stretch run — that horse will be weakened. Head-to-head stretch battles take quite a bit out of a horse, and they are unlikely to come right back and win. Frequently, a trainer will freshen a horse who has endured two consecutive battles for a couple of weeks. If he doesn't, look for that horse to come up "short" in his next start.

Another negative sign is when a horse wins a race but loses ground in the stretch. These "winners of their last" frequently come back as eminently beatable "false favorites" as they may have rounded the turn on their "form curve" and are tailing off.

There are some past races that you should ignore. Many handicappers look only at a horse's last start and eliminate that horse because of a dismal showing. Check the Results Chart to see if that race was a true race, and that the horse didn't have an "excuse." Races to be ignored or thrown out include the following:

1) Races on an "off track" if the horse's prior race on a fast track was a good effort.

2) Races where the horse was clearly outclassed, running "in jail" or going the wrong distance.

3) Races where the horse experienced some kind of trouble, e.g. "stumbled at start," "lacked racing room", etc.

22Mar85-3SA 1 1/16 :46 1:11² 1:45 ft 6 109⁵ 9¹⁷10¹² 4⁷½ 3⁶ DomngzRE² ⒻM28000 70-17 RcklssMss,DonATop,GdnghtMyLv 12
22Mar85—Very wide into stretch, bumped at 1/8
22Feb85-3SA 6½f :21³ :44³ 1:18 ft 20 110⁵ 10¹⁹10²⁴ 9¹⁶ 7⁵½ DmngzRL⁵ ⒻⓈM35000 74-18 Sntequos,SusnnRose,KpStorming 10

This information appears in the PPs as "trouble lines" under the running line of the race in many cases, but is omitted just as frequently. Therefore, you should go back to the Results Chart of any unusually bad race to determine whether the horse had an "excuse." (More on this in "Trip Handicapping.")

Darkened Form

Occasionally a longshot will pop up and win a race despite apparently bad current form. This may occur when a stable is looking to "steal a purse" or cash a bet. It's accomplished by "darkening" or disguising a horse's true form through bad races and/or workouts. It's usually done to capitalize on a recent bad race. Here's a typical scenario ... A fit horse puts in a bad race for any number of reasons — bad start, traffic problems or whatever. The trainer then enters the horse in another race where either the distance or the class level is inappropriate, and the horse again runs poorly. Or else, the trainer might give the jockey instructions that are contrary to the horse's natural running style. For example, he might tell the jockey to take a stretch-running horse to the lead right from the gate. The jockey complies, and the horse burns out and finishes out of the money. Next, the trainer gives the horse a miserable workout, e.g. 1/2 mile in :54. Now he's "darkened" the horse's form and is ready to make the score. The trainer then drops the horse down a notch or two in price and wins the race at long odds. It doesn't happen too often, and sometimes it even backfires on the culprits. But it's still fun to try to spot these plays.

Summary

Horses aren't machines — they're athletes. They have their physical and emotional ups and downs just as we do. And these cycles are influenced by a number of factors. The key is recognizing a horse's current form, i.e. how fit is the horse today! If you are able to plot a horse's "form curve" and know when he is "right," you will be rewarded at the mutuels.

VII. Class

You will frequently hear a horse referred to as being the "class of the field." Thoroughbred class or quality is an important, yet somewhat elusive characteristic to define. There are those who believe that class comes with a horse's registration papers from the Jockey Club. Others point to certain attributes such as consistency, stamina, gameness and "heart" as being measures of class.

Although class may be an inherent attribute in some thoroughbreds, it is not a constant measure. Like other athletes, horses go through cyclical changes in terms of performance, and this "form" curve generally is followed or paralleled by a "class curve." This is particularly true when evaluating claimers. Even a high-quality or "classy" animal is subject to these shifts. The horse may be willing, but his body won't cooperate.

Class Advantage

When evaluating a field, look for a horse who has an edge in class. Unfortunately, it's not as simple as looking to see if there's Perrier in the horse's water bucket. Detecting a class advantage is not an easy task because most horses do race "where they belong" or against horses of comparable quality. A significant class advantage, however, can offset a number of other factors. Frequently, a higher quality horse will defeat a cheaper horse, even though the latter appears to have a significant advantage in other respects.

To determine the relative class of horses in a given field, you should consider the following:

1) Breeding
2) Earnings
3) Claiming Price/Purse Values
4) Track Class
5) Competition
6) Consistency
7) "Heart"

Now let's examine the class factor by type of race ...

Maidens & Two-Year-Olds

Establishing class differences in young or lightly-raced horses is difficult in that they have limited, if any, Past Performances to evaluate. Consequently, you must rely on the following:

Breeding — Look for well-bred horses, particularly in maiden claiming races. Pedigree may be the only clue you have when evaluating a batch of first-time starters. There have been quite a few fashionably-bred youngsters who couldn't outrun a mailbox, but generally, these horses are the exception. To help you in this regard, I've included a list of prominent sires in the Appendix.

Connections — Another subtle indicator of class may lie in a horse's "connections" — his ownership and trainer. A knowledge of the stable often provides a good clue as to the value of their younger horses. The bigger operations and better trainers usually have better bred, higher quality horses to work with.

Attitude/Demeanor — Sometimes you can get an indication of class by examining the horses in the paddock before the race. Classy horses look classy and carry themselves differently than cheaper horses. (This area is covered in greater depth in "Paddock Handicapping.")

Claiming Horses

On the surface, these races would appear to be the easiest to handicap in terms of class because each horse is entered for a specific price and has a history competing at that and other levels. Unfortunately, it isn't that simple. There are differences, and some are quite subtle. So when evaluating a field, we should ask ourselves the following questions:

1) Is this a level or claiming price where the horse has been competitive recently or in the past when at the same point in his "condition/form curve"? The key here is competitive.

2) Is the level of competition or "class of the field" representative of the stated claiming price? Is it a "soft" or tough field?

3) Is this a "restricted" race, in terms of state-bred horses, sex or age?

4) Are there other conditions in the race that restrict the entrants in terms of performance, e.g. "non-winners of the year" or "non-winners of two races"?

5) If the horse has been competing at a different track, is that track of the same "class?"

6) Was the horse claimed recently?

Let's look at each of these questions more closely ...

Claiming Price — Horsemen, for the most part, run their horses where they "belong" or are competitive. Running a horse over its head is bad for the owner's bankroll and the horse — it can break a horse's spirit if the horse is repeatedly placed against better quality horses. Both winning and losing are habit-forming.

Frequently, you will spot a horse who has been running for $16,000 and finishing up the track. Finally, the trainer drops the poor animal down to $12,500. To the casual observer, this horse might appear to have an edge in class when, in fact, he's back where he belongs. Moreover, this horse might have developed a "confidence problem" and may require an even sharper drop before returning to the winner's circle.

Examine the PPs and determine if the horse can be competitive at this price. Has the horse won or been in the money recently at this level or were his most recent efforts showing strong signs of improvement (gaining three to four lengths on the leader between calls, especially in the stretch)? Or has he been competitive at this level in the past when at the same point of his "condition curve." The later comparison can't always be determined if you don't know the horse from past seasons, or if you don't have a "private file" on the horse.

For example, a horse's PPs might show that it had placed second in a $12,500 claiming race 10 races back, then started to fall off in form and was steadily dropped in price during the year, ending at $6,250. The horse was then turned out, and when he returns he is again entered for $6,250. After one or two starts, he wins at that level and is raised to $8,000. After two more races, he wins at $8,000 and is then jumped up all the way to $12,500. By now, however, the running lines in his Past Performances don't show that he was a legitimate $12,500 caliber horse eight months ago — those races have dropped off the bottom of his Past Performances. To the average player, this horse may appear to be in over his head against $12,500 company, despite his excellent current form and speed ratings, and these players eliminate the horse on the basis of class.

An example of this occurred last year at Canterbury Downs with a horse named *Funny Secret.* Take a look at the following sets of Past Performances for *Funny Secret.* Set "A" appeared when he made his first start at Canterbury Downs on June 28, 1985 in a $5,000 claiming race. Set "B" appeared later in the season (September 8th, 1985) when *Funny Secret* was entered for $20,000.

(A)

une 28th

'unny Secret — Ch. c. 3, by Foreign Power—Step Out Funny, by Funny Fellow

HANSEN R 114 — Br.—Devries Dorothy (Fla) — 1985 6 0 0 0 $345

Tr.—Van Berg Jack C — $5,000 — 1984 6 2 0 2 $11,995

wn.—Opstein K — Lifetime 12 2 0 2 $12,340

Jun85-5Aks	6f	:22^4	:46	1:12^{1}ft	7$\frac{3}{4}$	116	3$^{\frac{1}{2}}$	6^6	8^{11}	9$^{13\frac{1}{2}}$	Masters T A^5	11000	62-23	Psychitrst,MyBuddyDon,Abomnton	9
May85-6Aks	6f	:22^2	:46	1:13 gd	13	116	10^{13}	10^{12}	9^{10}	9$^{10\frac{1}{4}}$	McGurn C^8	18000	62-24	UnitedCopy,He'sASplsh,TkeOnTot	10
Mar85-5Hia	6f	:22^1	:45^4	1:11^{2}ft	17	115	3^1	3^3	3^2	5$^{4\frac{3}{4}}$	Breen R^9	16000	79-16	SugarWho,CraftyBeu,SilverDrling	10
Feb85-2GP	6f	:22^3	:46^2	1:11^{3}ft	11	117	6^5	8^{12}	10^{16}	8^{18}	Breen R^8	20000	63-24	HckryHllFlyr,DncngSpdr,RgntsPrd	12
Jan85-3GP	6f	:23	:46^3	1:11^{3}ft	9	115	3^{nk}	6$^{6\frac{1}{4}}$	7^9	7$^{13\frac{1}{2}}$	Breen R^1	27500	67-19	PrideofPortr,UpperGrde,WilesRod	10
Jan85-8Crc	6f	:22^2	:46	1:12^{4}ft	4$\frac{1}{2}$	116	1^{hd}	2^1	7^6	6$^{6\frac{3}{4}}$	Breen R^8	30000	80-16	UpperGrde,StrtegyTlk,PridofPortr	10
Nov84-10Crc	6f	:22	:45^2	1:12^{2}ft	8$\frac{1}{2}$	118	2^{hd}	1^{hd}	2^{hd}	3^1	Breen R^6	25000	88-18	Upper Grade, Alaco, Funny Secret	12
Nov84-10Crc	6f	:22^4	:46^2	1:13 ft	13	114	1$^{1\frac{1}{2}}$	3$^{\frac{1}{2}}$	1$^{\frac{1}{2}}$	1$^{\frac{1}{2}}$	Breen R^1	20000	86-20	FunnySecret,HezPro,TexolticTom	11
16Nov84—Came out, drvng															
Nov84-8Crc	6f	:22^3	:46^3	1:13^{2}ft	84	114	2^{hd}	2^{hd}	3^3	3$^{3\frac{1}{4}}$	Breen R^8	25000	81-18	Valatory, O. K. Amy, Funny Secret	9
Oct84-10Crc	6f	:22^1	:45^4	1:12^{2}ft	34	114	7$^{4\frac{1}{2}}$	7$^{7\frac{3}{4}}$	9^{14}	9$^{12\frac{1}{4}}$	Breen R^3	25000	77-22	Vltory,GloriousReserv,TxolticTom	11

Jun 12 Aks 5f sl 1:06^1 b **May 11 Aks 5f m 1:07 b**

(B)

eptember 8th

'unny Secret — Ch. c. 3, by Foreign Power—Step Out Funny, by Funny Fellow

BASS S H 110^5 — Br.—Devries Dorothy (Fla) — 1985 12 5 0 1 $15,540

Tr.—Van Berg Jack C — $20,000 — 1984 6 2 0 2 $11,995

wn.—Opstein K — Lifetime 18 7 0 3 $27,535

Aug85-6Cby	6f	:22^3	:46^1	1:11^{2}gd	*9-5	110^5	5$^{3\frac{3}{4}}$	5$^{3\frac{1}{2}}$	4$^{1\frac{1}{2}}$	1$^{1\frac{3}{4}}$	Bass S H^4	16000	91-13	FunnySecret,SilverAccent,SpdyPln	9
Aug85-1Cby	6f	:22^2	:45^1	1:11 ft	*3-2	109^5	2^1	1^{hd}	1^1	1$^{1\frac{1}{2}}$	Bass S H^6	12500	93-12	FnnyScrt,ColorMGon,Groton'sMstr	7
Aug85-6Cby	6f	:22^2	:45^3	1:11^{2}ft	*6-5	112^5	7$^{4\frac{1}{2}}$	6^4	1^{hd}	1$^{2\frac{1}{2}}$	Bass S H^7	8000	91-10	FunnySecrt,CrusdrDn,WorthyDriftr	9
Jly85-7Cby	6f	:22^3	:45^4	1:11^{4}ft	*3-2	110^5	6$^{2\frac{1}{4}}$	4^5	3^2	1$^{1\frac{1}{2}}$	Bass S H^1	8000	— —	FunnySecrt,AsidofPlsur,RisdProud	8
Jly85-6Cby	6$\frac{1}{2}$f	:23^3	:46^4	1:18^{4}ft	*8-5	115	7$^{3\frac{1}{4}}$	6$^{4\frac{1}{4}}$	5$^{3\frac{1}{2}}$	3^2	Hansen R^7	8000	— —	Suvge'sImg,Mrty'sGift,FunnyScrt	10
Jun85-1Cby	5$\frac{1}{2}$f	:22^4	:47^1	1:06 ft	*6-5	114	3$^{4\frac{1}{2}}$	3$^{3\frac{1}{2}}$	1^1	1$^{7\frac{1}{2}}$	Hansen R^5	5000	— —	FunnyScrt,SonotRd,Stomp'N'Smsh	7
Jun85-5Aks	6f	:22^4	:46	1:12^{1}ft	7$\frac{3}{4}$	116	3$^{\frac{1}{2}}$	6^6	8^{11}	9$^{13\frac{1}{2}}$	Masters T A^5	11000	62-23	Psychitrst,MyBuddyDon,Abomnton	9
May85-6Aks	6f	:22^2	:46	1:13 gd	13	116	10^{13}	10^{12}	9^{10}	9$^{10\frac{1}{4}}$	McGurn C^8	18000	62-24	UnitedCopy,He'sASplsh,TkeOnTot	10
Mar85-5Hia	6f	:22^1	:45^4	1:11^{2}ft	17	115	3^1	3^3	3^2	5$^{4\frac{3}{4}}$	Breen R^9	16000	79-16	SugarWho,CraftyBeu,SilverDrling	10
Feb85-2GP	6f	:22^3	:46^2	1:11^{3}ft	11	117	6^5	8^{12}	10^{16}	8^{18}	Breen R^8	20000	63-24	HckryHllFlyr,DncngSpdr,RgntsPrd	12

Sep 5 Cby 5f ft 1:02^2 b **Jly 9 Cby 4f ft :47^4 h**

You will note that *Funny Secret's* previous races at higher levels no longer appear in the September PPs, and to the casual observer he may have appeared outclassed; he wasn't and won handily.

EIGHTH RACE
Canterbury
SEPTEMBER 8, 1985

6 FURLONGS. (1.09$\frac{3}{5}$) CLAIMING. Purse $7,500. 3–year–olds. Weight, 120 lbs. Non–winners of a race since August 1 allowed 3 lbs.; since July 1, 5 lbs. Claiming price $20,000; if for $18,000 allowed 2 lbs. (Races when entered for $16,000 or less not considered.)

Value of race $7,500; value to winner $4,500; second $1,500; third $825; fourth $450; fifth $225. Mutuel pool $61,910. Exacta pool, $65,484.

Last Raced	Horse	Eqt.	A.	Wt	PP	St	¼	½	Str	Fin	Jockey	Cl'g Pr	Odds $1
24Aug85 ^{6}Cby^{1}	Funny Secret		3	110	3	5	$5^{1\frac{1}{2}}$	$3^{\frac{1}{2}}$	$3^{1\frac{1}{2}}$	1^{2}	Bass S H^{5}	20000	1.20
27Jly85 ^{4}Cby^{5}	Amabeauty's Joy		3	115	1	7	$6^{\frac{1}{2}}$	$5^{1\frac{1}{2}}$	2^{hd}	$2^{\frac{1}{2}}$	Melancon G	20000	9.10
24Aug85 ^{8}Aks^{2}	Dial Home		3	113	4	2	$2^{1\frac{1}{2}}$	$2^{2\frac{1}{2}}$	1^{hd}	3^{4}	Pettinger D R	18000	4.70
15Aug85 ^{5}Cby^{1}	The Grocery		3	113	6	3	4^{hd}	4^{hd}	5^{1}	$4^{1\frac{1}{4}}$	Smith M E	18000	14.70
16Aug85 ^{4}Cby^{7}	Smooth Shine		3	115	8	1	$1^{1\frac{1}{2}}$	1^{2}	$4^{2\frac{1}{2}}$	$5^{\frac{3}{4}}$	Orona W	20000	20.70
2Aug85 ^{2}Cby^{5}	Bold Genius		3	117	7	6	$7^{1\frac{1}{2}}$	8	7^{3}	$6^{1\frac{1}{2}}$	LaGrange D L	20000	7.10
24Aug85 ^{6}Cby^{6}	Thoroly Crow	b	3	113	2	8	8	$6^{1\frac{1}{2}}$	$6^{1\frac{1}{2}}$	7^{6}	Martinez N C	18000	13.40
4Aug85 ^{10}Cby^{7}	Timber Road		3	117	5	4	3^{1}	$7^{\frac{1}{2}}$	8	8	Hansen R D	20000	4.50

OFF AT 5:38. Start good. Won ridden out. Time, :22$\frac{4}{5}$, :46, :58$\frac{3}{5}$, 1:11 Track fast.

$2 Mutuel Prices:

3–FUNNY SECRET	4.40	3.20	2.60
1–AMABEAUTY'S JOY		10.20	5.60
4–DIAL HOME			3.20

$2 EXACTA (3–1) PAID $46.60.

Ch. c, by Foreign Power—Step Out Funny, by Funny Fellow. Trainer Van Berg Jack C. Bred by Devries Dorothy (Fla)

FUNNY SECRET, unhurried early, moved to contention along the inside on the far turn, went outside the leader for the drive, was bumped by AMABEAUTY'S JOY in the upper stretch, then finished strongly to drive to the lea in midstretch. The latter, bumped hard and carried far inside by THOROLY CROW passing the gap, rallied toward the leaders while wide on the stretch turn, lugged in in the upper stretch bumping with FUNNY SECRET, the continued well. DIAL HOME gained a brief lead nearing the furlong pole but could not sustain his drive. THE GROCERY, outside horses to the stretch, lacked the needed rally. SMOOTH SHINE sprinted clear early, but tired i the stretch. THOROLY CROW ducked in badly at the start forcing his rider to take up sharply. TIMBER ROAD wa finished early.

Recent Claims — After a horse is claimed, he must be entered at a price no less than 25 percent higher than the claiming price for a 30 day period. During this period, a horse is referred to as being "in jail." You should not view those races run while "in jail" as being reflective of a horse's true level of competition. Frequently, such horses perform poorly when they're moved up the ladder, and then promptly return to winning form when returned to their proper level. (More on moving up and down in class later).

Competitive Level — If a horse appears to properly placed in terms of price, we then consider the competitive level of the race. Not all $10,000 claiming races are true $10,000 races. Sometimes the race will come up "soft" or easy. And conversely, sometimes these races will come up tough. Horses are entered 48 hours in advance, and trainers have no idea as to who their competition will be. Further, there may be 20 horses entered in a given race, and the 10 toughest or the 10 weakest horses may be "scratched" or withdrawn. Consequently, all $10,000 fields are not equal. To determine the competitive level of a given field, consider the class of the top four horses entered and compare the company they've running with. To do so, study the "company line" in the PPs.

Another factor with regard to comparative claiming prices is the price range that occurs in many claiming races. The running lines in the Past Performances show the price at which horse was entered and not the top price of other horses in that race. For example, the conditions of a claiming race may state that the claiming price is "$12,000 down to $10,000". Should a horse be entered for a lower price, that horse is granted a weight concession (e.g. two pounds off for each $500 off the $12,000 down to $10,000). As such, you may see a horse whose last race is listed Clm10000, when in fact he was taking the weight concessions and was competing against $12,000 horses. When in doubt, refer to the charts of past races or consult your "private files."

Restricted Races

There are a number of claiming races that restrict the entrants by one or more of the following conditions ...

State-Bred or Owned — In recent years, there has been an increase in the number of "restricted" races which limit the entrants to those horses that are either "state-bred or owned." Such races are designed to encourage local breeding and ownership and are indicated in the Past Performances by either an Ⓢ or an Ⓡ preceeding the claiming price. Restricted races are generally not as competitive as "open" or non-restricted races at the same price because the fields are limited. As a general rule, I discount state-restricted races one or two notches when comparing those races to races against "open company." For example, if a horse ran in a Ⓡ1000, I'd peg the horse to have run in a $8,000 race against "open company."

Filly Races — Another type of "restricted" race are those races limited to fillies and mares indicated by a Ⓕ preceeding the claiming price. On occasion, you will see fillies running against colts. Not to sound "unenlightened" or chauvinistic, but colts usually have an edge over fillies. Consequently, such fillies must be discounted when competing against mixed company. On the other, watch for fillies who have been running (with limited success) in mixed company and then return to filly races at the same price level. This apparent lateral move is, in fact, a drop in class.

3YO's vs. Older Horses — Many claiming races are written for "three years and upwards." In such races, especially during the first nine months of the year, 3YO's are usually at a disadvantage when competing against older horses. This edge diminishes later in the year, but should be considered in all cases. These 3YO's & Up races are not indicated in the running lines, except in the Eastern edition of the *Daily Racing Form.* Consequently, when in doubt about a past race, you should check the Results Chart for the conditions.

"Conditioned" Claiming Races — Another type of "restricted" race is a claiming race where entrants are qualified according to their race records. There are claiming races limited to "non-winners of two races," "non-winners of the year," "non-winners at a mile or longer," etc. Again, many of these races should be discounted when being compared to races with few or no restrictions.

Track Class — The class of horses varies greatly from track to track. As a result, there are meaningful differences between horses that might appear to have been competing at the same level. These class differences are more significant when evaluating allowance/handicap/stakes races, but do exist when trying to compare claimers, especially recent arrivals at your track. When comparing claiming levels, using just the claiming price can be misleading.

Each meeting takes on its own class level, depending on both how many horses are on the grounds and the quality of the horses competing. Certain class levels may be quite competitive, while some may not be. For example, there may be a large number of mid-range, older sprinters at a meeting, making the fields very competitive. As such, trainers may have to drop $10,000 horses down a notch to be competitive. On the other hand, there may be only a few mid-range fillies and mares that can go a route, and therefore, they may compete at artificially higher levels.

To deal with such individual nuances, one has to keep track of how well horses do when arriving from other tracks. You can also determine class differences by studying Par Times and Class Ratings analyses. An excellent source for these data is Woodside Associates in Millerton, NY. (An abridged table of Par Times for Canterbury Downs and "source" tracks is included in the Appendix).

Competition — In racing you are known "by the company you keep." Since quality horses usually put out just enough to win and no more, it's important to know whom a horse has been running against — whom he's beaten and who's beaten him. You should also monitor other tracks, especially those tracks which send horses to your meeting. Study and save the charts from other tracks. Horses have names ... remember them.

The running lines in the Past Performances list the top three finishers in each of a horse's past races ("company line"). Here's where a good memory and files are important. You have to know the quality of the horses a horse has run against. Thoroughbred racing is very much like other sports in this regard. A Big Ten team can run up the score and post impressive stats against East Overshoe in non-conference play — then get their socks knocked off when playing in the conference. The same is true with horses.

Consistency — Consistency is a quality found in some claimers, but is generally associated with allowance-caliber horses. Better horses are more likely to run "to form." One mark of consistancy is a high "in-the-money" percentage (50+ percent). But when looking at these figures in the Earnings Box, eliminate horses who are consistently second or third. Some horses are afraid to pass the final horse. These "bridesmaids" would rather visit than win.

"Heart" — "Heart" is that special quality that separates two physically comparable horses at the wire. It's an intense competitiveness that drives horses to their fullest extension. These horses are the type who will win even if they encounter bad trips or bad racing luck. Horses with "heart" refuse to quit and frequently run beyond their pedigree. There is no symbol in the Past Performances for such horses, but when you see them compete, you'll remember them.

Allowance Horses

Many of the class measures discussed in the preceeding apply to allowance-caliber horses as well. Additional factors to consider include:

Purse Value — For years, determining class in allowance races was a frustrating task. In recent years, however, the *Daily Racing Form* has included the purse value of all allowance races in the running lines of the Past Performances. It appears in the race description, for example, as AW14000 which translates to "an allowance race with a gross purse of $14,000." The value of the purse is an excellent measure of class/value when comparing allowance horses.

Track Class — The Daily Racing Form publishes a "Purse Value Index" (PVI) based on the average net purse, and these ratings are particularly valuable when comparing better quality horses from other tracks or when evaluating earnings records. (The 1985 PVI is contained in the Appendix.) The PVI, however, can be misleading on occasion.

A good example of this would be to compare horses racing at Turf Paradise in Phoenix versus horses running at Sportsman's

Park in Chicago. Both tracks are usually running during the late winter/early spring. The Purse Value Index for Turf Paradise is four compared to a 13 for Sportsman's Park. A statistician might conclude that the horses at Sportsmen's Park are three times better than those competing at Turf Paradise. Not true. The reality is that Sportsman's Park offers higher purses than Turf Paradise. Purses are directly related to each track's "handle" (the total amount bet) in that a fixed percentage of the overall handle constitutes the amount of money available for purses. Consequently, the higher the handle, the better than purses. Going back to our Sportsman's Park and Turf Paradise comparison, the Chicago track has a higher handle/purse structure than Phoenix, but many horsemen choose to run in the pleasant climate than compete for better purses in snow storms and below freezing weather. Consequently, horses running at Turf Paradise may be "depressed" in true value, whereas Sportsman's Park horses may be "inflated" in value.

Determining Class Differences — The underlying principle is that trainers will run allowance horses for the highest purse value at which the horse is competitive. The range in allowance purses at a typical track will run from $8,000 up to $22,000 with the average purse being in the $11,000 — $14,000 range. As in claiming races, dollars generally equal value, so this is your basic point of departure when evaluating an allowance field.

There are certain exceptions to this rule, and they relate to those races where the conditions of the race restrict the entrants based on Past Performances. The same principles discussed previously with regard to claiming races apply to allowance races.

Conditions — You should study the conditions of an allowance race to identify the probable contenders. Allowance races have very specific entry requirements and allowances. The "allowances" granted certain horses are in terms of weight reductions. There are allowances for sex (fillies carry less weight than colts), age (3Y0's carry less weight than older horses) and past performance (predicated on either earnings or distance).

Allowance races are also restricted by certain performance-related conditions. The most notable of these conditioned races are those for "limited winners," e.g. "non-winners of two (or three) races," "non-winners of the year" or "non-winners at a mile or over". You will frequently find these types of races with younger and lightly-raced horses. Good trainers will try to maximize the conditions available for their horses — placing them in the least competitive environment that offers the highest possible purse.

Maintaining a good Results Chart file is helpful when trying to determine the specific conditions of past races. However, you can frequently speculate as to the conditions of a past race by checking a horse's Earnings Box. For example, if a horse has had 10 lifetime starts and two wins, it is probable that his first victory was in a maiden race and his second score was in a race limited to "non-winners of two races".

Once a horse exhausts his "lifetime conditions," the trainer will then explore conditions that relate to either distance or current year performance/earnings. Horses that are coming back after an extended layoff will be placed where they can use their absence to an advantage. If a horse is properly placed and maximizes his "conditions," he should be successful and that will be reflected in his earnings stats.

Earnings — Gross earnings are an excellent measure of class. The horse's Earnings Box details earnings for the past two years, turf versus dirt and lifetime. Further, it reports the number of starts, wins, seconds and thirds which produced these earnings.

A quick and easy way to establish a "class rating" is to calculate each horse's earnings-per-start by dividing the number of starts into total earnings for each horse in a given field. The age of the horse and the time of the year should dictate which numbers to use. A rough guide is as follows:

2YO's — use their lifetime earnings and starts

3YO's — use both the lifetime and the current year

earnings (minimum of six starts) indices and weigh them equally.

Older horses — use the past two years, with only nominal consideration given to lifetime stats.

One must be cautious when employing earnings figures in class calculations. Earnings figures can be either inflated or depressed by several factors including ...

1) Horses that regularly compete in state-bred or owned restricted races have inflated earnings. On average, these purses are inflated by 20 to 30 percent compared to allowance races written for "open company." In addition to this inflation, one must remember that those earnings were generated against lesser competition.

2) On the other side of the coin are those horses that have generated their earnings at "depressed" tracks such as Turf Paradise where the purse structure frequently belies the class of the competition. As such, all earnings figures must be adjusted by a "Track Class" factor.

Stakes & Handicap Horses

Horses competing in the major races should be measured much in the same fashion as allowance horses. Competition, Earnings and Track Class head the list of class measures. Also worth noting is the horse's ability to ship well and win on all types of running surfaces and conditions. Additionally, the "classiest of the classy" are able to carry higher weight assignments.

Moving Up/Down in Class

Class or value is not a constant in most horses. Horses will move up and down depending on a number of considerations. Recognizing when these moves are warranted will pay off at the mutuel windows.

Class/Condition Relationship — As stated earlier, there is an undeniable relationship between a horse's condition or fitness and his ability to compete at different class levels. Just as there is a seasonal "form curve," there is a "class curve" for each horse. The two curves, for the most part, mirror each other. This is particularly true for claimers who go up and down the claiming ladder according to their form.

Moving Up In Class — Most jumps in class are traceable to normal improvement in condition or form. In terms of age, younger horses are constantly learning and improving. As such, they are capable of rather dramatic improvement and resultant rises in class. Further, these improvements can come race-to-race. Consequently, don't be shy when it comes to supporting a rapidly improving youngster who might appear to be in "over his head." Wait until such a horse disappoints before you get off its bandwagon.

A sharp move upwards in class for older and cheaper horses, however, is quite another story. These horses generally find a very specific level where they are comfortable and competitive. Raise them a notch or two and you'll need a search party to find them at the end of the race. You'll see horses taking these big rises after a win when they are owned by smaller outfits who are afraid of losing the horse by running him where he belongs. Big outfits aren't concerned about losing horses through the claiming process. In fact, they get concerned if they don't lose a couple of horses during a meeting. The key is to keep a horse at a level where it is competitive and can bring home a check. Then as the horse's form starts to decline, drop it down, hope it's claimed — then go back and claim a new, fresher replacement. That's how the successful stables go about it when it comes to claimers.

There are some legitimate reasons for dramatically moving up an older or cheaper horse. One such case is when a claimer that has been plugging along in $6,500 middle distance sprints (e.g. 1 1/16 mile) is entered in a Starter Handicap race at 1 1/2 miles against horses that have been running for $10,000. Such a horse may only fire going a long route, e.g. 1 1/2 to 2 miles.

Another situation is when horses switch from the dirt to turf or vice versa. Some horses that win stakes races on the grass couldn't beat $8,000 claimers on the dirt.

Dropping Down In Class — Aside from normal drops in class/price relative to form. one should be suspect of any horse taking a sharp drop in class, particularly claimers. Granted, there are occasions when trainers will drop a horse way below his value to either "steal the purse" or cash a bet, but these situations are in the minority when compared to those horses dropping down because of injury. Sharp "drop-downs" look too good to be true — and they usually are! One exception might occur at the very end of a meeting, when trainers are looking to reduce rather than increase their stables because of shipping costs.

Knowing the various trainers and stables will be helpful in speculating as to the probable cause for a horse taking a dramatic drop. A better solution to this dilemma is to skip the race when the soundness of your choice is in question.

Moving From Claiming to Allowance — Generally speaking, this reflects a move upwards in terms of class. The exceptions come in two circumstances — recent maiden winners and high-ticket claimers.

Some horses with lesser pedigrees are entered in maiden claiming races and they score impressive wins. Based on this performance, a trainer might move the horse into allowance company running against other "limited winners." This may or may not be a rise in class depending on a) the speed rating and fashion in which the horse won its maiden race, and b) the experience level of the competition. Horses who have already run credibly against winners have an edge over recent maiden winners. This is generally true regardless of the level at which the maiden victory was registered — claiming vs. allowance.

When evaluating a claimer moving into an allowance race, the key is the purse. For example, a $35,000 claiming race may offer a purse of $12,500 while an allowance race may offer a purse of only $11,000. Consequently, a move from the claiming ranks into an allowance race may not necessarily be a rise in class. Knowing the purse structure at your local track will help you in evaluating crossovers by high-ticket claimers.

Another favorable situation is when an experienced, winning claimer in top form switches to allowance company — especially against limited winners. An example might be a 4YO sprinter running for $20,000, who has just registered two consecutive victories at six furlongs — posting speed ratings of 88+ entered in a race restricted to "3YO's and upwards who have not won a race other than maiden or claiming." In a spot such as this, a high-ticket claimer in top form might run away from a soft allowance field of limited winners.

Summary

Class is an elusive, yet critical handicapping factor. In order to determine accurate class ratings and comparisons, you will be well served by keeping good files and chart books. Class is closely connected to a horse's current form. And this condition/class relationship is more pronounced in the claiming ranks.

VIII. Speed

Speed is obviously a key factor when evaluating contenders. After all, they give the cigar to the horse who travels from point A to point B the fastest. As important as speed is, it is equally misunderstood and mis-used by some handicappers.

Speed is a commodity, much like fuel, that all thoroughbreds possess. This speed can be used in bursts or can be metered out over a distance. It is generally accepted that a thoroughbred can maintain peak speed or velocity for about three furlongs or 3/8 mile. It follows that since most races are considerably longer than three furlongs, it is the deployment of that speed which must be considered. Consequently, the elements of Distance, Pace and Condition are closely related to speed and must be considered.

Speed Ratings

The most common measure of speed is a horse's final running time at a specific distance. The *Daily Racing Form* expresses this estimated time by the use of speed ratings. I say "estimated" because the final running time is electronically timed only for the winner — and then estimated for those horses that finish behind the winner. The *Daily Racing Form* considers one length to be equal to one fifth of a second when making these estimates.

Each horse is assigned a "speed rating" for every race he runs, and this figure appears in his Past Performances in the running line.

A speed rating is essentially an index versus the track record. It's calculated by comparing a horse's final running time to the track record for that distance (as it existed at the start of the meeting). The track record is assigned a speed rating of 100 — and one point is subtracted for each fifth of a second over the track record time. For example, let's say that the track record for six furlongs is 1:09 1/5. A horse wins a race and posts a final running time of 1:11 3/5. This time is 12 fifths slower than the track record and thus would be assigned a speed rating of 88. In the same race, a horse that finished 4th, six lengths behind the winner would be given a speed rating of 82.

It should be noted that track records and the resultant speed ratings are greatly influenced by the quality of horses that compete on each track and how long that track has been in operation. You can't equate a speed rating of 88 set at Belmont Park with a 88 speed rating at Canterbury Downs. The greatest horses that ever raced have competed over the prestigious New York track and, as such, their standards are much higher than those at Canterbury Downs. To help the reader compare running times and speed ratings for horses from other tracks, I have included in the Appendix an abridged Par Time comparison chart for the primary or "source" tracks (tracks that appear in the majority of the Canterbury Down's horses' PPs). This chart will be helpful when comparing running times and speed ratings for horses that arrive at Canterbury Downs from other tracks. (You can purchase an updated, complete set of Par Times charts prepared by William L. Quirin, Ph.D. from Woodside Associates in Millerton, NY.)

Track Variants

Immediately following the speed rating in the Past Performances is the "track variant" figure. This figure is generated by averaging all of the winners' speed ratings on that day and subtracting that number from 100. For example, if the average winning speed rating for a nine race card was 84, the track variant for that day would be 16. The higher the variant, therefore, the slower the races were run on that particular day.

This figure can be terribly misleading because it reflects either a) the quality of the horses who ran that day or b) the condition of the racing surface, or c) a combination of both. Consequently, the term track variant is really a misnomer in that the quality of the horses competing influences this measure. For example, you will have higher quality (and faster) horses competing on a Saturday than you will on a Thursday and consequently a lower track variant. As such, I use the DRF's track variant in a rather casual fashion — I rate tracks fast, normal or slow.

Track Variant	Pritch's Rating
0 - 12	Fast
13 - 24	Normal
over 24	Slow

I do consider the track variant when a race was run on a wet track, especially when the surface was rated "good", "muddy," "slow" or "heavy." On these occasions, you may see significant differences, with variants ranging from 18-30. The higher variants indicate that the surface, and hence the horses, were affected by the moisture. The DRF variants, I believe, should be used directionally, not religiously.

Speed Handicapping

"Speed handicappers" focus on final running times and speed ratings. They will adjust these "figures" with respect to lengths behind the winner, weight carried and track variants.

More sophisticated "speed handicappers" go beyond these figures and make further adjustments with respect to class, pace, weight, track condition and their own daily "variant" figures. All of these efforts are designed to produce a final, single numerical rating for each horse in a race.

Fundamental to this basic approach are the following principles:

1) Final running times are determined by adding 1/5 second for each length a horse finishes behind the winner.

2) Adjustments to equalize horses coming from another track or for a horse going a different distance are predicated on standard par time and parallel time tables or similar general formulas. These figures may then be further adjusted depending on pace or other considerations.

I must interject at this point that I am not a devoted speed handicapper. I recognize that one must qualify each horse in terms of his capability to go a certain distance within a specific time standard. However, I don't believe that speed "figures" can be used with absolute reliability any more than you can rely totally on any other single factor. Without diving into an in-depth debate on the reliability of speed figures, I will simply point out a few of the obvious difficulties ...

1) Horses run at various velocities during a race. Generally, they start off faster than they finish. Using "1/5 of a second equals one length" is convenient because running times are reported in fifths of a second. However, most horses are traveling at a rate of perhaps six to seven lengths per second in the opening quarter mile and five to six lengths per second in the final furlong. Consequently, the "lengths behind" formulas require considerable adjustments.

2) The distance behind the leader is influenced by how hard the jockey/horse are trying at the end of a race.

Obviously if a horse is beaten by only one length, he is still trying at the end. However, another horse — who is eight lengths behind and is not going to win — may be hand ridden or "wrapped up" in the final furlong to save the horse, thus depressing its speed for that effort.

3) A speed horse that is pressed hard during the early going and becomes a victim of his own fast early pace, finishing far behind the leader, will also earn an artificially low and non-representative speed rating for that effort.

4) Speed figures decrease in reliability as the distance increases. With each "adjustment" required, the margin for error increases geometrically. And since most races are won or lost by no more than a length or two, these "adjusted" figures are frequently outside an acceptable confidence level.

How to Use Speed Figures

Despite my casual regard for "speed handicapping," I always consider speed when making selections. The following are some of the ways I use speed figures ...

1) After estimating a final running time for a given race, I eliminate horses that have demonstrated that such a running time is far beyond their reach.

2) Race-to-race improvement in speed ratings is a positive sign and should be considered as opposed to where the horse finished. Such improvements are signs that a horse is coming into form.

3) I place more emphasis on speed figures when looking at sprint races. The shorter the race, the more reliable the speed rating.

4) Older horses establish more reliable upper limits on their speed ratings and are less likely to improve on past efforts when compared to young horses.

5) Speed ratings tend to be a less reliable indicator for better quality horses because these horses usually run "just fast enough" to win. (It's not the rider's objective to set track records. He will try to "save" his mount for future races, rather than push him to the limit in each race.)

6) Be cautious when using speed ratings when the early pace is unusually fast or slow. This is particularly true when there is a "false" or slow early pace.

Summary

Speed figures are imprecise measurements and should be used directionally. I use speed ratings to "qualify" a horse as a contender. The shorter the race, the more importance I assign to the speed factor. Lastly, you must understand the element of pace and be able to evaluate and interpret speed in this context.

For those of you who would like to learn more about speed handicapping, I can recommend several books on the subject — "Winning at the Races" and "Thoroughbred Handicapping — State of the Art" by William L. Quirin, Ph.D and "Picking Winners" by Andrew Beyer. Further, I recommend that you subscribe to Henry Kuck's Speed Figures and Par Times, available through Woodside Associates, P.O. Box 798, Millerton, NY 12546.

IX. Pace

Simply put, pace is the measure of how fast the first part of a race is run, i.e. the fractional times for the first quarter mile or half mile in a sprint and the first half mile or three quarters of a mile in a route race. Pace is influenced by several, independent factors:

1) Track bias and condition

2) Running styles of the entrants

3) Distance

4) Post positions

5) Race strategies employed by the trainers and jockeys.

Let's examine each of these factors ...

Track Bias and Condition

Each racetrack develops a particular bias that favors either speed horses or horses that come from behind. Speed-bias tracks are in the majority. There are a number of elements that influence a track's bias — the composition and depth of the upper cushion, moisture content, configuration of the track, angle of the turns and length of the stretch. And when a track gets wet, these apparent biases can change dramatically. The effect of these changes is discussed in detail in the chapter "Track Conditions."

Running Styles:

Thoroughbreds can run full out for approximately 3/8 mile. Certain horses tend to use their speed early in a race and are known as "front-runners" or "speed" horses. Others reserve themselves during the early going and come on strongly in the final phases. These horses are referred to as "stretch-runners" or "closers." There are a few horses that can run either way. These horses are in the minority and generally are higher quality allowance, handicap or stakes horses.

The pace of any race will be fast if there are a number of front-runners in the field. They will instinctively go for the lead and draw off right from the gate. When you encounter a field with a lot of "early speed" or "early foot," you can be assured of a fast or "honest" pace. Assuming there is no change in either the class level or current form, I will generally take the fastest half mile time that any of these horses has run in their past three races and establish that figure as the expected time for the race being evaluated. I then look to see if that horse will be seriously challenged if he goes out in that time. If so, I then look to see if he will be able to withstand the pressure on the lead and whether he can go on after being challenged during the early going. Then I examine the other front-runners to determine who will still be in contention after a half mile run at this estimated time. This will usually eliminate the "quitters" and those horses who are successful only if they get the lead, or are not pressured during the early going.

After determining which of the front-runners will "survive" a brisk early pace, you should then evaluate the closers to see if they will be able to benefit from the early pace and outrun the front-runners in the stretch. Again, you must establish projected fractions for both the early quarters and an estimated final time. Then examine the late comers to see if they will be able to overtake the leaders.

You must be cautious when evaluating stretch-runners to eliminate "phony closers." These are horses who appear to be making strong closing moves when in fact all they are doing is passing tired horses who have stopped running in the final furlong. To determine whether a horse's late charge is a legitimate move, examine his time for the last quarter mile and how many lengths he gained on the leader in the final quarter. In some races where the early fractions are brisk, several of the lesser front-runners will stop badly in the stretch and be easily passed. As such, you might see a horse who was seventh after the first half mile who finishes third (an apparent improvement of four positions) who in fact made little or no headway against the leader. He may have been seventh by eight lengths after a half and finish third by six lengths.

9^{10} 7^{8} 5^{7} 3^{6}

Conversely, a horse may be seventh by eight lengths after a half mile who finishes fourth by two lengths. That is a move of note in that the horse gained six lengths on the leaders in the final quarter mile.

9^{10} 7^{8} 5^{5} 4^{2}

Another aspect in evaluating "closers" is to identify horses that "catch, but don't pass" the lead horse. Some horses show a definite pattern of coming on boldly at the end of their races, yet never seem to pass the last horse. These characters are quite frustrating. They appear to prefer "visiting" with other horses rather than beating them. I call this trait "terminal politeness." A similar situation prevails when these horses are stretched out from a sprint to a distance. On paper, it would appear that all they need is "a little more distance." But more often than not, what they really need is a little more "heart" as they end up the perennial bridesmaid, irrespective of distance. These horses generally have a disproportionate number of seconds and thirds compared to wins in their Earnings Box.

A final word on the horse that comes from off the pace. As a general rule, front-runners tend to win more often than closers. And this pattern is even more pronounced on tracks that favor speed, as was the case with Canterbury Downs during its inaugural meeting in 1985. Consequently, when selecting a horse that comes from off the pace, look for that horse to a) have an edge in class, b) be in top condition and c) have a shrewd, experienced rider on board. Without these plus factors, the closers generally come up short, despite the pace.

Distance

Although pace is an important factor in all races, it is frequently more important in the sprint races where speed and the deployment of speed are primary considerations. Route races are influenced more by relative condition/stamina, class, jockey and weights.

There are, however, some excellent betting opportunities in route races which are influenced by pace. The most common example is when a sprinter is placed in a route race where that horse is the only speed in the race. On paper, there may not be any evidence that this horse can go a route, but in a race where he can control the pace by being on the lead, the rider can set a "false pace," i.e. get to the lead by three to four lengths, then hold the horse back, setting very slow fractions during the early going. If the other riders don't sense the slow pace, they may continue to run behind the leader until the stretch. Then when they make their late charge, they discover that the horse on the lead has plenty of gas in reserve and can hold them at bay down to the wire.

Post Position

The post position becomes a factor in analyzing pace when evaluating both sprints and route races. In both types of races there are certain races where the distance to the first turn is quite short. Front-runners are frequently at a disadvantage when coming from the outside post positions in that they must use a lot of their speed to get out in front, then move into good position close to the rail before they hit the turn. If they are unsuccessful in this attempt, they are frequently forced to run wide on the turn and lose a lot of ground and calories in the process. Conversely, speed horses coming from the inside post have a big edge in such races. The post position advantage is even more pronounced in races with cheaper horses. "Cheap speed" horses usually have to have everything their own way or they'll quit. As such, if they can't get to the lead by the turn and are forced to drop in behind horses, they will frequently pout and not run a lick. In those races where the run to the first turn is a furlong or longer, the importance of post position diminishes.

Given the above, you must consider post position when estimating pace. The post position of the "pace-setters" will influence the race strategy of the rider and, consequently, how the first quarter mile will be run.

Race Strategies

The pace of a race is one of the few handicapping factors which can, to some degree, be controlled by humans. Trainers will study the Past Performances of the horses he is running against and then develop a strategy for his animal. This strategy is relayed to the jockey prior to the race (usually in the paddock). The basic question is whether to: a) "send" a horse to the lead or be close to it, or b) to "lay back" off the pace. The trainer's estimate of what the pace will be and knowledge of his own horse and its running style determines this pre-race strategy. But like most "well-laid plans," things can change dramatically when the gate springs open.

How a horse breaks from the gate as well as how the field breaks, forces the jockey to make some quick decisions. If his mount breaks on top and the horses he expected to be in front break poorly or choose not to go for the lead, a jockey might take the lead, rather than following the game and laying off the early pace. This is where an experienced jockey can determine whether or not your mutuel ticket gets cashed or lines the bottom of your parakeet's cage.

Pace Formulas/Ratings

Pace is a close neighbor to Speed and Speed Ratings. As such, many arithmetic pace formulas and ratings are generated by enthusiasts. And many of these are quite helpful given one very important consideration — all of the contenders must be comparable in terms of class and condition.

Since we are rarely treated to a race where "all other things are equal," we must be sensitive to differences in class and condition when utilizing pace figures. A horse with a definite edge in class may be the type of horse that runs only as fast as is required to win, thus making his speed/pace ratings difficult to assess. And a horse who is in top form may outlast "better" horses that are not fit — particularly when they're running a route. As such, pace should be a directional factor and not be used with unwarranted reliance.

Summary

"Pace makes the race" is a revered racetrack axiom, and one that hasn't changed much in the past fifty years. When analyzing any race, you must determine what the expected pace will be. This will dictate how much emphasis you place on other factors such as speed, fitness, post position, etc. If the anticipated pace is slow to normal, then you can usually immediately eliminate the stretch-runners from further consideration.

Pace is particularly important when evaluating cheaper horses. Cheap horses are not as versatile in their running styles and thus less likely to be rated. And when considering horses with "cheap speed," i.e. horses who run fast when and only when they have an uncontested lead — these horses can usually be eliminated if the expected pace is fast or if they are in against "classier" horses.

X. Weight

The "weight factor" is probably the most over-rated and misused factor in thoroughbred handicapping because it rarely, by itself, determines the outcome of a race. It can, however, be the "tie-breaker" you need to select between otherwise comparable contenders. (Sorry, you can't skip the chapter.)

Before examining weight as a handicapping factor, let's get some definitions and principles on the table ...

"Weight" — refers to the total amount of weight a horse is required to carry in a race. Weights are specified by the conditions of each race and the allowances offered. For example, a race may be written as follows ...

> "Six furlongs for 3YO's. 120 pounds. Fillies 117. Non-winners of three races allowed 2 pounds. Non-winners of two races allowed 4

pounds. Claiming price $12,500. 2 pounds allowed for each $500 down to $11,500"

Under these conditions, a 3YO colt who has won five races and is entered for $12,500 would be required to carry no less than 120 pounds. A 3YO filly who had only one win and is entered for the bottom claiming price of $11,500 would be required to carry only 109 pounds.

Trainers are always looking for an edge in the conditions of a race. And all trainers believe "the less weight, the better". This is especially true for smaller horses (particularly fillies) and horses who are leg sore.

Another way of reducing the weight burden on a horse is to employ apprentice jockeys or "bug boys." Apprentice jockeys are granted a special allowance starting at 10 pounds until his first victory, seven pounds until his fourth win and five pounds for a period of a year following his fourth win. This apprentice allowance is in addition to other weight concessions. When a horse has an apprentice rider aboard, his weight in the program will be preceded by an asterisk (*) or "bug." Hence, the name "bug boy."

The average thoroughbred weighs about 1000 pounds, and the average jockey "rides" at 110 pounds. The jockey's riding weight includes the weight of his attire and saddle. In the event that a horse is required to carry a weight higher than a jockey's riding weight, the difference is made up by placing lead weights in pockets on the saddle. These added weights are referred to as "dead weight." A high percentage of dead weight (e.g. 12+ pounds) is not desirable because a jockey ("live weight") can move or work with the rhythm of the horse — the dead weight can't.

Overweights — Every day the track announcer proclaims that certain horses are "x pounds overweight", meaning that the jockey has weighed in that day at a weight higher than the minimum weight that horse is required to carry. (I listen to these announcements with the same level of attention I pay to a stewardess' emergency procedures). One or two pounds over rarely will have much, if any, effect on the outcome of most races. One or two pounds over has the same effect as adding a deck chair to the Queen Mary. Overweights of four pounds or more, however, get my attention. Any trainer who is going to ride a jock 4+ pounds over is either lobotomized or is not trying in the race. An exception might be if the overweight is tied to a rider change where a top jockey is on board. The edge in rider ability might justify the overweight, particularly if the absolute weight is not excessive. For example, if a horse gets in light because of the conditions and is required to carry only 109 pounds, the trainer may use a leading jockey who rides at 113 despite the overweight of 4 pounds. The absolute weight of 113 pounds is a weight that most horses can manage easily, particularly in sprint races.

When Weight Counts

As stated earlier, weight is rarely the single factor that determines the outcome of a race. Generally speaking, there is not much of a spread in weights in any given race. Usually this range is no more than four to six pounds between the top and low weights. Secondly, horses are granted weight concessions because they are at a disadvantage in other regards, be it sex, age or recent form. Consequently, most weight concessions are meant to equalize horses rather than to give one horse an edge. And generally speaking, a few pounds off isn't going to help a horse who is not in good form. Said another way, adding a lot of weight may slow down a better horse, whereas taking off weight will not make a lesser horse run appreciably faster.

The importance of weight grows in direct proportion to the distance the horse must carry that weight (a rather obvious concept to embrace). I seldom even bother to consider minor weight differences in races under a mile, where speed is more of a consideration than stamina. However, when evaluating horses running a mile and an eighth or longer, I check the weights. There's an old "rule of thumb" used by racing secretaries and handicappers which establishes the following "weight to distance" ratios:

five pounds equals 1/5 second or one length in races of six furlongs

three pounds equals 1/5 second or one length in races at a mile

two pounds equals 1/5 second or one length in races at a mile and an eighth

one pound equals 1/5 second or one length in races at a mile and a half

The above formula is "neat" but not very useful because it assumes that all the horses are equal in class, condition, weight-carrying ability, etc. The only time these "guidelines" might prove useful is in Handicap races.

Handicap Races

These races are usually contested by better quality, older allowance/stakes caliber horses. In an effort to "equalize" each horse's chance of winning, the Racing Secretary will assign weights or handicaps to each of the horses entered, assigning the high weight to the best horse. Weight assignments are an important consideration for the trainer. If the assigned weight is too high (either in absolute or relative terms), a trainer may not start his horse and select another race where the weight assignments are more acceptable. As a consequence, today's racing secretaries — in an effort to get the best horses to run at their respective tracks — will be "kind" to the top horse by assigning a "low" highweight assignment, usually a weight that the horse was able to win at in the past. Then he scales down the remaining assignments in proportion to a scale such as presented above. The net effect of these assignments is that the better horse usually wins because the absolute weight is a manageable bundle.

A favorite expression heard around the track is "weight can stop a train" — usually uttered by the frustrated trainer of the highweight (within earshot of the racing secretary). And it's true, but the frequency of having a "crushing weight" assigned, much less carried, is very uncommon in today's competitive racing environment.

Weight Shifts are the Key

What I look for, particularly in allowance races and in races going a route is a shift in weight between the top contenders. For example, horse "A" beats horse "B" by two lengths in their last encounter. In that race, horse "A" carried 113 pounds and horse "B" carried 120 pounds.

In today's race, because of the conditions of the race or perhaps the switch to an apprentice rider, there is a shift of weight between the two horses. Horse "A" now carries 119 and horse "B" carries 111. Horse "A" has added six pounds since their last encounter and horse "B" has dropped nine pounds for a net shift in wieghts of 15 pounds. Now we're talking about something. A shift such as this may well reverse the outcome from their last encounter. You won't always find such a dramatic shift, but carefully consider any weight shift over eight pounds if the contenders were close in their last race.

Summary

When considering weight as a factor, its importance is usually subordinated by other differences such as class or condition. In those races where all other factors appear to be equal, it might be considered as a tie-breaker. But in races that hard to peg, you are better off watching the race and keeping your wallet in your pocket.

The keys to look for are high absolute weight assignments and significant weight shifts between two otherwise equal horses. Finally, the importance of weight is in direct proportion to the distance it must be carried. As such, weight becomes a more important factor in route races.

XI. Jockeys & Trainers

The "people factor" in selecting winners provides a edge to the experienced handicapper — especially those who keep track of jockeys and trainers beyond their own local track. There is one consideration you must keep in mind when utilizing the "people factor." And that is the better trainers get the owners with better horses. And the more experienced, competent riders get to ride better horses. These combinations are more of a result than a cause. I've never yet seen a jockey or a trainer carry a thoroughbred across the finish line. However, different trainers and different jockeys have certain skills and certain habits or patterns. Knowing these will help you know their horses.

Although jockeys are greatly restricted by the ability, class and condition of the horses they ride, they do play an important role in many races. And certain trainers seem to be better at training one type of horse versus another. Owners, on the other hand, are of no real consequence in the people equation. All we do is pay the bills, complain and sometimes go to the winners circle to get our picture taken.

The Jockey Factor

Qualities — At any given racetrack, the jockey colony has a broad range of talent — from jocks who win consistently on all kinds of horses to jockeys who couldn't ride a bus. The good riders possess common attributes: intelligence, courage, physical strength, good judgment, quick reflexes and competitiveness. They have an inner clock and are excellent judges of pace. They have courage and are fearless in splitting traffic or ducking into a small opening. These jockeys study each race and know the other riders and horses they are up against. A good rider uses the whip sparingly and never abuses his mount when soundly beaten nor drives a winner beyond a safe margin of victory. He follows the trainer's instructions. In short, he is a professional.

And because of this, the best jockeys usually get the best mounts. As a consequence, they tend to lead the jockey standings each year. Apprentice riders and riders with lesser ability tend to ride less frequently and generally on lesser horses. This simple fact tends to create an illusion that there are great differences in jockeys' abilities. These differences, however, are not as great as they might appear. At any given meeting, there are usually eight to ten top jockeys who possess nearly equal skills. Their relative rankings are influenced more by how good their agent is and luck than it is by their abilities as a rider.

The more important considerations center around a jockey's riding style, his "fit" with a particular horse and his current "form." Let's deal with each of these separately ...

Riding Styles — Jockeys tend to develop very distinct riding styles or talents that can be broken down into a number of categories. There are good "gate" riders who have a knack of getting their mounts out of the gate quickly and to the lead. These riders tend to be aggressive and are best suited on front-running style horses. There are also "finesse" riders who have "soft" hands and are very good at relaxing horses and rating their speed. These riders are well-suited for stretch-runners and horses that don't like strong handling. Then there are "strong finishers." These jockeys have good strength and use their strength to bring their mounts home in tough stretch battles. There are also "stick" riders who are adept at using their whip and switching hands.

A Good Match — Regardless of riding style or special talents, the key is finding a good match between rider and horse. Sometimes a good fit comes from the jockey working with the horse in the mornings. Good jockeys are always on the "backside" early in the morning to work horses they will be riding later in the week. It may take some time for a jockey to learn how to handle a certain horse. The good rider will learn from each ride. He gets to know the horse and what the horse will respond to. As a consequence, I am more comfortable when my selection has his "regular rider" aboard.

Current Form — Jockeys, like other athletes, have slumps and spurts. Keeping track of who's hot and who's not is a worthwhile activity for handicappers. You must, however, avoid betting jockeys "blind." When a jock is really hot, he may be able to improve a marginal horse, but he can't boot home a total bum.

When a jockey hits a slump, it usually affects his riding. He may lose his confidence or try too hard. His judgment gets clouded and, as a result, he may ride poorly. When you see a leading rider in a slump, be cautious. A "hot" rider can't make a bad horse win, but a rider in a slump might hurt the chances of a good horse. As one turf sage once commented, "Jockeys lose more races than they win."

Jockey Changes — As stated previously, I prefer to have a horse's regular rider on board if the combination has been doing well in the past. You should take note, however, when you see a top jockey put on a horse who hasn't been showing much of late. These rider changes can produce an immediate reversal in the horse's form — and do so at a big price. Keep in mind that a jockey gets a flat fee of about $40-$50 per mount. However, they get 10 percent of the winner's share. If they win which translates to about $500 in the average race. As a consequence, a top rider, who generally has his pick as to which horse to ride in any given race, wouldn't take a mount unless he thought he could win with him. Before you rush out and bet on every longshot with a leading rider on board, you must first determine why he took the mount:

1) Was it as a favor to a trainer he rides for regularly? Many jockeys have deals with trainers whereby they get to ride the good horses if they ride the bums as well. Therefore, it is important to know which jockeys are "stable riders," i.e. ride regularly for certain trainers.

2) Did the top choices have their regular riders and this mount was the "best of the rest?"

3) Or is it because the horse is a legitimate "live horse?" To answer this, look for other clues such as: a) a change in equipment or medication, b) a "shipper" from another track whose recent form was "darkened" by bad racing luck, c) a sharp workout since the horse's last start. Frequently these workouts were posted with the new rider in the irons.

Apprentice Riders — An apprentice rider is a rider who is just starting out in the game. As explained in the chapter on "Weight," apprentice riders are granted weight allowances ranging from ten to five pounds for a period of about a year. After which time they are considered "journeyman" riders and are no longer grated weight concessions.

For the most part, you are taking a slight chance when you bet on an apprentice rider. By definition, he lacks the experience of other riders and is still learning his trade. They are safer bets when aboard front-running sprinters going short. In these races, they have little to do but to go for the lead, make left turns and not fall off. In route races, however, where pace, judgment and experience loom more important, apprentices may be at a disadvantage versus more seasoned riders. The exception to this is when there is a "hot" apprentice. They frequently get good mounts when they're on a roll.

Jockeys & the Odds — The leading or "hot" riders have a decided effect on the odds. Many racing fans who have yet to discover the *Daily Racing Form,* bet on jockeys — not on horses. And there are enough of these "jockey handicappers" to drive the odds below what they would be if another rider were on board. This presents both problems and opportunities for the knowledgeable player. Sometimes it will depress the odds on the horse you wanted to bet, and other times it will draw money away from your choice and produce a generous payoff.

First-Time Starters — Young horses go through a long training process prior to making their first start. Horses who show a lot of promise in the mornings are noted by jockeys and their agents. Additionally, a horse showing promise will generally be breezed by a good jock before its first race. If a top jockey likes the horse, he'll take the mount. Consequently, I pay more attention to the "jockey factor" when evaluating maidens and first-time starters.

For reference, I have included in the Appendix a list of the leading riders — both nationally and at Canterbury Downs for 1985.

The Trainer Factor

Just as there are differences in riders, there are significant differences in trainers. Although they too are limited by the talent of their charges, better trainers are more adept at getting the most out of a horse. It is important that you follow trainers closely and keep track of their percentages. In this regard, don't look only at a trainer's ranking based on total wins at a meeting. Rather, look at his percentage of winners and "in the money" percentages. A trainer with only eight horses will never lead the trainer rankings, which are based on total number of winners, but he may have twice the winning percentage.

Aside from tracking trainers in the win/lost column, you should get to know their "style" and their particular strengths. Some trainers are very good at bringing young horses up to the races. Last year at Canterbury Downs, A.J. Foyt, III started 10 2YO first time starters. Six of these won at first asking (including *Rare Brick*) and three others won in their second or third start. Quite an impressive record. But by studying these horses, you could see that they were dead fit and well-schooled when they made their first start. Moreover, Foyt placed them where they could win. Some ran in Maiden Special Weights, others (with lesser pedigrees) were entered in Maiden Claiming races.

Certain trainers have a special knack when it comes to claiming horses and winning with their new acquisitions in their first start, despite the mandatory rise in price. And the list goes on of special areas where certain trainers tend to excel. Equally important is knowing how a trainer conditions his stock. Some trainers race their charges into shape, while others will bring their horses into top form in the mornings through a well-defined training program.

Another factor to consider is stable size and the owners a trainer works for. Big stables usually run their horses at a competitive level and are less concerned about losing a horse or two to claims. Smaller operations coupled with less experienced owners are frequently too conservative and put horses in over their heads — afraid of losing the horse or because they are unrealistic in terms of evaluating the abilities of their "pets." Knowing the trainer, his connections and his operating style will be invaluable when making your selections.

Summary

Although greatly restricted by the talent and abilities of the horses they ride or train, jockeys and trainers should be tracked and considered when making your final selections. Pay particular attention to their percentages, especially among the "lesser knowns." Lastly, study their "styles" and patterns — knowing that will help you know their horses better.

XII. Trip Handicapping

"Trip" handicapping is essentially an analysis of how prior races were run in terms of a) obstacles each horse may have encountered during the race, b) how well the jockey rode the horse, c) track bias, and d) what "path" the horse traveled in that race. In some respects, it could be considered a study of "racing luck." Trip handicapping has grown in popularity with the advent of the video replay. In the old days, handicappers had but one opportunity to view the running of a race —the actual running of that race. Subsequent analysis could only be made by referring to the *Daily Racing Form's* Results Chart for that race — and these charts were usually generated after a single viewing by the DRF chart-maker.

Now that video replays are standard fare at most tracks, the handicapper can watch the race immediately after the running of the race and again the following day. In some cities, these replays are run that evening on local TV stations. As a result, you have several opportunities to review races and make notes regarding the "trips" each horse experienced. The first thing you must learn. however, is how to watch a race.

Watching a Race

If you are really serious about his game, you should have a good set of binoculars and not rely on the naked eye or a TV monitor to watch a race. The track cameraman has one job — and that is to follow the lead horses. As a consequence, you frequently miss out on a lot of the real "action" back in the pack — and many of the eventual winners come from this second flight of horses. Moreover, the horses on the lead rarely experience any "trouble." They are usually clear of traffic and don't experience the obstacles which frequently confront horses clustered in the second flight.

Try the following approach and see what you've been missing ...

At the Gate — Watch the horses as they are loaded into the starting gate. Note if any horse is reluctant to enter his stall or is "fractious" in the gate, e.g. rearing up. When a horse is a "bad actor" in the gate, it may indicate one of the following:

1) He is anxious or reluctant about running — frequently symptomatic of a sore horse who knows that he's going to hurt when asked to run. Recent "bleeders" are also bad actors in the gate for the same anticipatory reason.

2) He is a young, inexperienced horse who lacks adequate schooling in the starting gate. Frequently, owners rush younger horses and start them before they are properly schooled in both the paddock and the gate.

3) He is just a headstrong animal who dislikes the confinement or the presence of other horses.

When you spot a "bad actor," watch how he runs. Does he break alertly? Does he tire or stop suddenly in the stretch? If his performance is below expectations, watch for the horse to return with one or both of the following: a) a change in equipment, e.g. the addition of blinkers, or b) a workout from the starting gate since his last race. Either might be considered a positive sign.

The Start — The start is a critical part of every race, particularly sprint races because a horse who breaks poorly usually doesn't have the time or distance to overcome a bad start. Watch the video replays, particularly the head-on angles and note which horses break cleanly and which horses have problems, e.g. break sideways, break in the air, get bumped by their neighbors, stumble or get pinched back.

The First Quarter Mile — The first quarter of a mile is used to get position. Speed horses will shoot out and try to get to the lead and the rail. Horses who come from off the pace will look for a "spot" somewhere behind the lead horses where they will experience a minimum of interference. All horses try to get in a favorable "groove" or path — usually as close to the rail as possible to save ground.

After the horses have traveled the first furlong (1/8 mile), pan back from the leaders and watch the second flight of horses. You can keep track of the leaders by listening to the track announcer.

Entering the Turn — As the horses enter the far turn, note their position and whether or not the jockey is asking the horse to run or whether he is still "saving" his mount. Note horses that are out of position and are forced to run wide going into the turn. Other jockeys might "take up" their mounts and drop them down towards the rail rather than be forced wide and lose ground. Note any traffic problems that might occur.

In the Turn — Many races are won or lost in the far turn. This is where horses on the lead try to stretch out and lose the field. And horses who come from off the pace split traffic and move into a striking position to mount their stretch drive. It's in this turn that jockeys make critical decisions — when to move their horse, whether to stick on the rail, split horses or swing to the outside — and in this turn, traffic can be a problem as cheap speed begins to back up and everyone is looking for a clear path to the wire. You should note which "path" each horse is traveling. (Trip handicappers are quite specific in this regard, noting P-1 as being on the rail and P-6 as being six paths off the rail.)

Head of the Stretch — Watch the leaders as they round the turn at the head of the stretch. Note if they go wide (frequently caused by being tired or sore) or whether they hold close to the rail. Compare paths they assume for the final drive. Lastly, watch for horses to "change leads," i.e. switch their stride by changing their lead foreleg.

The Stretch Run — During the run through the stretch, watch for the lead horses to show signs of fatigue. They will shorten their stride and raise their heads — collectively this action is referred to as "climbing." Also some pooped ponies will arch their tails — another sign of fatigue — but it is also signifies that they are still trying!

Watch for the horses that run late. See if the jockey has put them into a position where they will have a clear lane to the wire. Sometimes a jockey will get into his stretch-runner only to get stuck behind dying speed. He then must "check" or pull-up the horse, swing him to the outside and refire him. This type of "start/stop/start" ride usually kills any chance the horse might have unless he is a super horse. Once the rider gets a stretch-runner rolling, he has to keep him rolling.

When viewing the head-on video replay of the stretch run, note any horse who drifts in or out. This "bearing out" or "bearing in" is very common among 2YO's and lightly raced horses who are still learning how to run straight. But when you note such behavior in older horses, this may be a sign of fatigue or soreness. Further, such behavior can frequently get a horse disqualified for interfering with other horses. Also, if a horse does start to drift, the jockey has to pull him in and this "reining" can stop a horse or, at a minimum. break his rhythm in the final drive.

Importantly — during the actual running of a race — quickly check the trailing horses in the stretch run. These horses are usually out of camera range in the replays and this will be your only opportunity to watch these horses.

The Finish — Too many horseplayers make the same mistake — they stop watching a race the minute the winner crosses the wire. As a consequence, they miss a lot of important notes for future reference. I watch the riders of the horses who are back in third through seventh place to see what they are doing with their mounts. Are they still driving them? Are they just hand riding or have they "wrapped them up" or eased the horse. This is important because their Past Performances will show how many lengths they finished behind the leader — but not how hard they were trying in the final furlong or 1/16 mile. And for those of you who rely on "speed ratings," your figures can be thrown off totally if a jockey wraps up his horse when he realizes he can't catch the leaders.

Pulling Up — Generally, when the horses turn around and return to the unsaddling area, most fans are either heading for the cashier, the bar or rechecking the DRF to see "what they missed." You have plenty of time for postmortems and celebration later. Watch the horses as they return, are unsaddled and led off the track by their grooms. Note their general appearance and how they walk. Sore horses stick out to even the novice observe as they are led off the track after a race.

Video Replays — Once the result of the race is official, position yourself in front of a TV monitor and watch the replay — noting on your program any observations. You can transfer these notes later, but I like to have all my my preliminary notes in the program as I save these for future reference. All of these notes are important when you update your "private files."

Key Factors in Trip Handicapping

Trip handicappers concentrate primarily on two elements in each race — track biases and whether or not a horse experiences any "trouble" during the running of the race.

Track Biases — On any given day, the track can develop certain biases or grooves. Some days the inside path or groove along the rail is lightning fast, and on other days, the rail might be "dead." Biases are the result of traffic, weather/track conditions and track maintenance. At most tracks, the inside favors speed because it gets the most traffic and gets "pounded down," so to speak. The exception to this is when the track is wet. Then the inside is frequently a bad spot to be in because the water runs off the track towards the infield.

Track maintenance can also affect a track's bias. How they set the harrows can dramatically impact on the relative quickness of the running surface. Setting the harrows as little as 1/8th inch deeper can throw off running times by as much as a second or more. And these settings may vary from one tractor to another. The amount of water the trucks put on the track can also affects these grooves. Consequently, you must note biases and realize that they can change from day to day — and even from race to race.

When not able to actually witness a race, you can still determine grooves by studying the relative success of different post positions during that racing day.

Trouble Lines — As discussed earlier on, there are an infinite number of ways a horse can get into "trouble" during a race. When these incidents are flagrant and apparent to all, they usually appear in the comment section of the Results Chart and subsequently beneath the running line in the Past Performances.

22Mar85-3SA $1\frac{1}{16}$:46 1:11^2 1:45 ft 6 109^5 9^{17}10^{12} 4$^{7\frac{1}{2}}$ 3^6
→ 22Mar85—Very wide into stretch, bumped at 1/8

It is important that you study Results Charts carefully and circle horses who experience any trouble. For the most part, the DRF is good at noting these problems in the charts. Unfortunately, these problems do not always appear in the running lines. Because of this, trip handicappers, who keep a Chart File and good notes, have a big edge when a horse returns to competition after experiencing a "bad trip." These horses are frequently the best betting opportunities you will have all season.

A good example of this occurred at Canterbury Downs in 1985 with a maiden filly named *Security Anthem.* The following Past Performances appeared in the DRF When she was making her fifth start.

Security Anthem B. f. 3, by Allegiance—Rocka Dilly, by Eskimo Prince
FERNANDEZ A L **116** Br.—Bell Bloodstock Co (Cal) 1985 4 M 1 1 $1,635
Own.—Drakos & Taliaferro Tr.—Taliaferro Charles L $10,000 1984 0 M 0 0
Lifetime 4 0 1 1 $1,635

23Aug85-3Cby	6f	:22^3	:46^2	1:13^{3}ft	4½	115	65¼	53¼	42¼	42¼	Fernandez AL^7	M10000	78-15	RoringBr,DinWithDv,RikiNikWldmn	9
15Aug85-3Cby	5½f	:23	:47	1:06^{2}ft	4½	115	41¼	42	32½	33¼	FernndezAl^7	ⒻM10000	85-12	Brbrnero,RoringBer,ScurityAnthm	10
3Jly85-6Cby	6f	:23^2	:46^2	1:13^{1}ft	*2-3	117	43	44½	43	45	FernandezA^2	ⒻM16000	— —	Galarob,Barbarnero,JoyfulProspect	7
26Jun85-3Cby	6f	:22^4	:47^3	1:12^{1}ft	2½	117	21	21½	21½	24½	FernandezA^6	ⒻM16000	— —	I'mSpy,SecurityAnthem,ByForNow	8

Aug 4 Cby 4f ft :48^3 b Jly 29 Cby 5f ft 1:02^3 b Jly 17 Cby 5f ft 1:01 h

Looking at her past races, we see that she ran a credible second in her first start for $16,000. That effort was followed by three apparently even efforts running for $10,000. However, what is not shown in the Past Performances is what happened to this poor filly in each of her four starts. Here are the Results Charts for each of these races ...

THIRD RACE
Canterbury
JUNE 26, 1985

6 FURLONGS. MAIDEN. CLAIMING. Purse $4,000. Fillies. 3–year–olds. Weight, 117 lbs. Claiming price $16,000; if for $14,000 allowed 2 lbs.

Value of race $4,000; value to winner $2,400; second $800; third $440; fourth $240; fifth $120. Mutuel pool $80,273.

Last Raced	Horse	Eqt.	A.	Wt	PP	St	¼	½	Str	Fin	Jockey	Cl'g Pr	Odds $1
20Jun85 ^{5}CD^{11}	I'm a Spy		3	117	5	1	1^1	1^{1½}	1^{1½}	1^{4½}	Hansen R	16000	1.70
	Security Anthem		3	117	6	3	2^{hd}	2^{hd}	2^{1½}	2^{nk}	Fernandez A	16000	2.30
3Apr85 ^{3}TuP^2	Bye For Now		3	115	1	7	5^{1½}	3^{1½}	3^{½}	3^3	LaGrange D L	14000	3.10
18Apr85 ^{2}Fon^4	Ken Smoke	b	3	117	3	4	4^{hd}	4^{½}	4^{3½}	4^7	Hoverson C	16000	6.80
7Jun85 ^{1}Aks^8	Galarob	b	3	117	2	8	6^{hd}	5^2	5^3	5^{4½}	Oldham J	16000	17.50
8Mar85 ^{1}Fon^7	Kelly Diane		3	117	7	6	7^1	7^{½}	6^2	6^{½}	Orona W	16000	26.50
	Gypsy Jovan		3	110	4	5	8	8	7^{½}	7^{½}	Bergsrud S A^5	14000	22.20
20Jun84 ^{1}HP^6	Old Time Saying		3	115	8	2	3^{½}	6^1	8	8	Kaenel J L	14000	23.20

OFF AT 5:11. Start good. Won ridden out. Time, :22⅘, :47⅗, 1:00⅖, 1:12⅕ Track fast.

$2 Mutuel Prices:			
5–I'M A SPY	5.40	3.20	2.40
6–SECURITY ANTHEM		3.20	2.60
1–BYE FOR NOW			2.60

B. f, by Graustark Lad—Head Spy, by Chieftain. Trainer Van Berg Jack C. Bred by Iandoli Mrs Lewis (Fla).

I'M A SPY outsprinted rivals for the early lead, turned back a bid from SECURITY ANTHEM on the far turn, then was kept to intermittent pressure to the final sixteenth. SECURITY ANTHEM was hard ridden to press I'M A SPY on the far turn, then continued with good courage in the drive. BYE FOR NOW broke outward to bump with GALAROB, lodged her best bid ont he stretch turn and finished evenly. KEN SMOKE lacked a rally. GALAROB, bumped at the start, was fanned wide into the stretch. KELLY DIANE tired in the drive. OLD TIME SAYING showed only brief speed.

In her first race, she hooked a tough filly, yet "continued with good courage in the drive." She was then dropped down to $10,000.

SIXTH RACE **6 FURLONGS. (1.12) MAIDEN. CLAIMING. Purse $4,000. Fillies. 3-year-olds. Weight, 117 lbs. Claiming price $16,000; if for $14,000 allowed 2 lbs.**

Canterbury

JULY 3, 1985

Value of race $4,000; value to winner $2,400; second $800; third $440; fourth $240; fifth $120. Mutuel pool $45,183. Exacta pool $32,071.

Last Raced	Horse	Eqt.A.Wt	PP	St	¼	½	Str	Fin	Jockey	Cl'g Pr	Odds $1
26Jun85 ^{3}Cby^{5}	Galarob	b 3 117	6	3	2^{1}	$1^{1\frac{1}{2}}$	$1^{1\frac{1}{2}}$	1^{2}	Oldham J	16000	18.90
20Jun85 ^{3}FP^{3}	Barbaranero	3 117	4	4	1^{hd}	$2^{2\frac{1}{2}}$	$2^{1\frac{1}{2}}$	$2^{1\frac{1}{2}}$	Hamilton M	16000	6.10
28Jun85 ^{3}Cby^{4}	Joyful Prospect	(b 3 115	5	2	3^{2}	$3^{\frac{1}{2}}$	3^{hd}	$3^{1\frac{1}{2}}$	Warhol V L	14000	3.70
26Jun85 ^{3}Cby^{2}	Security Anthem	3 117	2	6	4^{hd}	$4^{2\frac{1}{2}}$	$4^{2\frac{1}{2}}$	4^{3}	Fernandez A	16000	.70
26Jun85 ^{3}Cby^{4}	Ken Smoke	b 3 117	7	1	6^{5}	$5^{\frac{1}{2}}$	$5^{2\frac{1}{2}}$	5^{3}	Hoverson C	16000	10.10
	Pritchett	3 117	3	7	7	7	6^{2}	6^{6}	Montoya D	16000	16.90
9May85 ^{3}Spt^{10}	Fortunate Eagle	3 115	1	5	5^{hd}	6^{2}	7	7	Kaenel J L	14000	13.00

OFF AT 6:27. Start good. Won driving. Time, :23⅖, :46⅖, :59⅖, 1:13⅕ Track fast.

$2 Mutuel Prices:			
6-GALAROB	39.80	26.40	4.80
4-BARBARANERO		7.40	4.20
5-JOYFUL PROSPECT			3.20

$2 EXACTA (6-4) PAID $493.80.

B. f, by No Robbery—Gala Lassie, by Galanomad. Trainer Gardes Jack H. Bred by Kuster Mr-Mrs Theodore (Ky).

GALAROB moved to the lead outside BARBARANERO on the far turn, drew clear and held the advantage. BARBARANERO continued well once headed by the winner. JOYFUL PROSPECT raced inside of SECURITY ANTHEM into the stretch, was brushed several times with that one in the upper stretch and finished willingly for the show. SECURITY ANTHEM broke slowly, was asked to go after the leaders on the backstretch, lugged in brushing with JOYFUL PROSPECT in the upper stretch and flattened out. KEN SMOKE showed little. PRITCHETT broke slowly. FORTUNATE EAGLE was finished after a half.

In this race, she had some problems — "broke slowly" and was "brushing with *Joyful Prospect*" in the stretch. She came back in her next race at the same level and experienced more trouble.

THIRD RACE **5 ½ FURLONGS. (1.04) MAIDEN. CLAIMING. Purse $3,500. Fillies. 3 and 4-year-olds. Weight, 3-year-olds, 115 lbs.; 4-year-olds, 120 lbs. Claiming price $10,000.**

Canterbury

AUGUST 15, 1985

Value of race $3,500; value to winner $2,100; second $700; third $385; fourth $210; fifth $105. Mutuel pool $73,794.

Last Raced	Horse	Eqt.A.Wt	PP	St	¼	⅜	Str	Fin	Jockey	Cl'g Pr	Odds $
11Jly85 ^{1}Cby^{6}	Barbaranero	3 115	4	4	1^{hd}	$1^{\frac{1}{2}}$	$1^{\frac{1}{2}}$	1^{nk}	Hamilton M	10000	14.8
28Jly85 ^{1}Cby^{6}	Roaring Bear	b 3 115	1	1	3^{1}	$3^{\frac{1}{2}}$	2^{2}	2^{3}	Melancon G	10000	3.1
3Jly85 ^{6}Cby^{4}	Security Anthem	3 115	7	5	$4^{\frac{1}{2}}$	4^{hd}	3^{hd}	$3^{\frac{1}{2}}$	Fernandez A I	10000	4.6
28Jly85 ^{1}Cby^{4}	Dine With Dev	3 115	5	8	9^{2}	8^{2}	6^{2}	4^{nk}	Hansen R D	10000	1.5
14Jly85 ^{1}Cby^{6}	Virtual Lady	4 120	8	7	7^{3}	$6^{\frac{1}{2}}$	$4^{1\frac{1}{2}}$	5^{3}	Rubbicco P	10000	22.3
31Jly85 ^{1}Cby^{4}	Fox Of All Foxes	4 120	9	6	5^{1}	5^{2}	5^{1}	$6^{1\frac{1}{2}}$	Oldham J	10000	26.6
25Jly85 ^{2}Cby^{3}	Parade Lass	3 110	6	3	6^{hd}	7^{3}	7^{1}	$7^{1\frac{1}{2}}$	De La Cruz V5	10000	33.0
11Jly85 ^{5}Cby^{4}	Regalo Gratis	3 115	2	10	10	10	$9^{2\frac{1}{2}}$	$8^{1\frac{1}{2}}$	Woods C R Jr	10000	8.6
14Aug84 ^{4}Aks^{9}	Sway To The Music	b 3 115	10	2	2^{hd}	2^{1}	8^{2}	$9^{3\frac{1}{2}}$	Smith M E	10000	18.7
	Harem Pants	b 3 115	3	9	$8^{\frac{1}{2}}$	9^{hd}	10	10	Warhol V L	10000	18.8

OFF AT 5:02. Start good. Won driving. Time, :23, :47, :59⅗, 1:06⅖ Track fast.

$2 Mutuel Prices:			
4-BARBARANERO	31.60	10.00	5.40
1-ROARING BEAR		4.80	4.00
7-SECURITY ANTHEM			3.60

Ch. f, by Figonero—Call Barbara, by Tiltable. Trainer Boggess Lee. Bred by A Levy Thoroughbred Farm (Cal).

BARBARANERO, on the early pace between horses, disposed of SWAY TO THE MUSIC and drew clear on th stretch turn, then gamely held ROARING BEAR safe in the final furlong. The latter saved ground to the stretch lodged her bid outside the winner and finished well although unable to get up. SECURITY ANTHEM, bumped at th start, between horses into the stretch, continued willingly. DINE WITH DEV lacked early speed and was never factor. VIRTUAL LADY, slow to gain stride at the start, rushed up behind the early leaders, remained a factor to th upper stretch and flattened out. FOX OF ALL FOXES, well out from the rail to the stretch, weakened. PARADE LAS was bumped at the start. SWAY TO THE MUSIC, outside the winner for three furlongs, tired.

In this race, *Security Anthem* was "bumped at the start, between horses (in a box) in the stretch, continued willingly."

THIRD RACE Canterbury AUGUST 23, 1985

6 FURLONGS. (1.09⅗) MAIDEN. CLAIMING. Purse $3,500. Fillies. 3 and 4-year-olds. Weight, 3-year-olds, 115 lbs.; 4-year-olds, 120 lbs. Claiming price $10,000.

Value of race $3,500; value to winner $2,100; second $700; third $385; fourth $210; fifth $105. Mutuel pool $76,617.

Last Raced	Horse	Eqt.A.Wt	PP	St	¼	½	Str	Fin	Jockey	Cl'g Pr	Odds $1
15Aug85 ^{3}Cby^{2}	Roaring Bear	b 3 115	8	1	$3^{2\frac{1}{2}}$	2^{hd}	2^{2}	1^{hd}	Melancon G	10000	2.30
15Aug85 ^{3}Cby^{4}	Dine With Dev	3 115	2	7	$7^{\frac{1}{2}}$	$6^{2\frac{1}{2}}$	3^{hd}	2^{2}	Hansen R D	10000	2.80
31Jly85 ^{1}Cby^{3}	Riki Niki Waldman	b 3 115	6	8	5^{hd}	4^{hd}	$5^{1\frac{1}{2}}$	3^{nk}	Smith M E	10000	9.70
15Aug85 ^{3}Cby^{3}	Security Anthem	3 115	7	6	$6^{2\frac{1}{2}}$	5^{2}	$4^{1\frac{1}{2}}$	4^{1}	Fernandez A L	10000	4.60
9Aug85 ^{1}Cby^{7}	Tahari	b 3 115	1	5	1^{hd}	1^{1}	1^{hd}	5^{2}	Moyers L	10000	4.60
15Aug85 ^{3}Cby^{8}	Regalo Gratis	3 115	3	9	9	8^{5}	$7^{3\frac{1}{2}}$	6^{3}	Woods C R Jr	10000	19.40
15Aug85 ^{3}Cby^{5}	Virtual Lady	4 120	4	3	$2^{\frac{1}{2}}$	3^{2}	6^{2}	7^{4}	Rubbicco P	10000	14.80
9Aug85 ^{1}Cby^{9}	Rosy Outlook	3 115	9	2	4^{2}	7^{hd}	8^{8}	8^{13}	Kaenel J L	10000	15.40
1Aug85 ^{5}Bml^{10}	Sam's Sunny Cat	b 3 115	5	4	8^{hd}	9	9	9	Robley J J	10000	30.50

OFF AT 5:03. Start good. Won driving. Time, :22⅗, :46⅖, :59⅗, 1:13⅘ Track fast.

$2 Mutuel Prices:			
8-ROARING BEAR	6.60	3.40	3.00
2-DINE WITH DEV		3.80	3.20
6-RIKI NIKI WALDMAN			4.20

Ch. f, by Native Uproar—Tulle Bear, by Tom Tulle. Trainer Fires William H. Bred by Lofton Archie (Ark).

ROARING BEAR, prompted the early pace outside horses, lodged his bid outside TAHARI entering the stretch, gained the lead leaving the furlong pole, then lasted over DINE WITH DEV. The latter lacked early speed, then finished with a good run to be moving fastest late. RIKI NIKE WALDMAN finished evenly. SECURITY ANTHEM rallied along the inside in the drive, took up sharply in midstretch, swung to the outside and continued evenly. TAHARI, a bit slow to gain stride, moved to the lead along the inside on the backstretch but tired in the drive. VIRTUAL LADY, on the pace between horses for a half, tired. SAM'S SUNNY CAT tired badly.

In this fray, she was making a strong, and in my view, winning stretch run when another horse ducked out and forced her to "take up sharply in midstretch." I had bet the filly in this race and was convinced that her luck had to change. So I waited for her next start and brought my piggy bank to the track that day.

Going back to her PPs before her fifth start, you will note that none of the problems she encountered are noted in the running lines. As a consequence, she went off at 7-1 and generated one of the best returns of the meeting.

FOURTH RACE Canterbury SEPTEMBER 5, 1985

6 FURLONGS. (1.09⅗) MAIDEN. CLAIMING. Purse $3,500. Fillies. 3 and 4-year-olds. Weight, 3-year-olds, 116 lbs.; 4-year-olds, 120 lbs. Claiming price $10,000.

Value of race $3,500; value to winner $2,100; second $700; third $385; fourth $210; fifth $105. Mutuel pool $44,292. Exacta pool $49,831.

Last Raced	Horse	Eqt.A.Wt	PP	St	¼	½	Str	Fin	Jockey	Cl'g Pr	Odds $1
23Aug85 ^{3}Cby^{4}	Security Anthem	3 116	3	1	1^{hd}	$1^{\frac{1}{2}}$	$1^{2\frac{1}{2}}$	1^{2}	Fernandez A L	10000	7.00
22Aug85 ^{1}Aks^{2}	Sweet Alich	3 116	1	5	4^{hd}	$4^{2\frac{1}{2}}$	$2^{\frac{1}{2}}$	$2^{1\frac{1}{4}}$	Doocy T T	10000	2.30
23Aug85 ^{3}Cby^{2}	Dine With Dev	3 116	6	9	$6^{\frac{1}{2}}$	$6^{2\frac{1}{2}}$	4^{3}	3^{2}	Hansen R D	10000	2.80
6Aug85 ^{2}Atl^{5}	Beverly B. Good	b 3 116	5	3	$3^{1\frac{1}{2}}$	2^{2}	3^{1}	$4^{3\frac{1}{2}}$	Hamilton M	10000	10.00
21Aug85 ^{3}Cby^{5}	Gemara	3 116	7	7	7^{1}	$7^{1\frac{1}{2}}$	7^{4}	$5^{1\frac{1}{2}}$	Smith M E	10000	4.90
15Aug85 ^{3}Cby^{6}	Fox Of All Foxes	4 120	9	4	$5^{4\frac{1}{2}}$	5^{1}	6^{1}	6^{nk}	Kaenel J L	10000	19.70
29Aug85 ^{2}Cby^{3}	Sandy Connection	b 3 116	10	2	2^{hd}	$3^{\frac{1}{2}}$	5^{1}	$7^{2\frac{1}{4}}$	Melancon L J	10000	7.70
18Apr85 ^{5}Fon^{9}	Purely Innocent	3 111	4	10	10	10	9^{2}	8^{3}	Bass S H^{5}	10000	24.70
14Aug85 ^{2}Cby^{4}	Leslie Feels Lucky	3 116	2	6	9^{10}	$8^{1\frac{1}{2}}$	$8^{\frac{1}{2}}$	9^{4}	Warhol V L	10000	27.20
15Aug85 ^{3}Cby^{10}	Harem Pants	b 3 111	8	8	$8^{\frac{1}{2}}$	9^{4}	10	10	Craig K^{5}	10000	34.00

OFF AT 5:31. Start good for all but PURELY INNOCENT. Won ridden out. Time, :22⅗, :45⅘, :58⅘, 1:12⅕ Track fast.

$2 Mutuel Prices:			
3-SECURITY ANTHEM	16.00	5.60	4.80
1-SWEET ALICH		4.80	3.40
6-DINE WITH DEV			3.40

$2 EXACTA (3-1) PAID $45.60.

The above example is not an isolated case. There are many such bonanzas waiting for the astute "trip handicapper." Moreover, you don't have to have seen the prior races — it's all in the charts. So by studying and saving Results Charts, you will be rewarded.

Summary

The key to trip handicapping is to watch the whole race — not just the leaders or the horse you bet on. Secondly, you should keep good notes. Lastly, if you are like most people and can't be at the races every single day, then be sure to study and save the Results Charts in the *Daily Racing Form* or the daily newspaper.

XIII. Other Factors

The following hodge-podge of equine dogma includes some observations, pointers and angles that either didn't warrant a full chapter or were inconvenient to incorporate where they probably belong. Excuse my lethargy and read on — these pearls might help you recapture the money you squandered on this book ...

Post Position

Post positions are assigned randomly through a draw among those horses entered in a race. As was discussed in "Track Condition," "Distance" and "Pace," post position can influence the outcome of races, particularly those races with a short run to the first turn. Generally speaking, the inside post positions have an inherent advantage because they are closer to the rail and thereby shorten the distance a horse will have to travel. This is particularly true for "speed" horses who can quickly get to the lead from the gate and establish a position on or near the rail.

On the other hand, "closers" sometimes benefit from the outside post in that they are less likely to get caught in early traffic.

Another aspect of post position relates to the track's bias. Each racetrack develops its own "grooves." These so-called grooves may change from day to day and even more so after rain. Identifying these biases in a track can be an important consideration when evaluating future races. Frequently, you must watch the early races to see how the horses run on various parts of the track. Pay close attention to the jockeys. After several rides, they will know where the footing is the best and will direct their mounts accordingly.

Field Size

The size of the field — or number of horses in a race — is a frequently overlooked item in a horse's Past Performances. It appears as the last number in a race's running line. On some days, particularly at the beginning or toward the end of a meet, the fields are small. The Racing Secretary has trouble filling races because of a shortage of horses. In such cases he is likely to recruit some reluctant "volunteers" to get a race to go. In small fields, consequently, a horse's finishing position might greatly overstate his performance. For example, a horse finishing third in a field of six may have only beaten three horses — two of which were "volunteers."

Shippers

Horses are periodically arriving at your local track, and these "shippers" present a challenge to the the handicapper. It's impossible to follow every racetrack and know the exact level of competition a "shipper" has faced. And frequently it is difficult to evaluate his speed ratings without keeping current and detailed speed figures (Par Times) for every track in the country. I've included a "Par Times Chart" in the Appendix to provide some clues as to the relative speed figures for the various "source tracks" for shippers arriving at Canterbury Downs.

These are some steps to follow when evaluating "shippers:"

1) Determine "why" the horse is on the grounds. Is the horse just one of a string of horses that have shipped in after another track has closed its season, or is he a "single?" These "singles" or mystery horses frequently arrive because the track bias favors his running style — or because the race conditions suit the horse. In 1985, for example, Canterbury Downs offered a number of 5 1/2 furlong races for older horses. These races were very attractive to trainers who had sprinters that couldn't carry their speed a full six furlongs. Trainers like Jack Van Berg, who have several strings of horses at different tracks will move their horses around — placing them at the track which best suits his stock.

2) Does the new arrival get the riding services of a leading jockey? Or does the horse's regular rider come in for the race from another track? If either case is true, view these as positive signs.

3) Does the horse show an ability to win at first asking on a new track? Is he a good "traveler?"

4) Has the horse won at long odds in the past? Or does the trainer have the reputation of winning races at a price? If so, watch out.

5) Has the horse had a workout over the track? This is a good sign, irrespective of the time posted in the workout. If the trainer is looking to cash a bet, he will probably put a heavy exercise rider on board, and work the horse out in the middle of the track to depress the time.

6) Determine whether the horse is in form and placed competitively. Checking the Purse Value Index (PVI) and Par Times should provide a basis for this judgment. (See Appendix for tables.)

7) Lastly, watch the tote board closely in the final minutes to see if any "late money" goes down on the

> horse. When a horse is in for a bet, its connections usually wait until the last minute to make their bet. They don't want to draw attention to the horse until it's too late for the public to react. And if the horse is in an exacta race or part of the daily double, pay careful attention to the payoffs to see if the horse is getting a disproportionate amount of play versus the win pool. Frequently, the connections will wheel a "live" horse in the exotics rather than playing the horse to win in an effort to keep the public off the scent.

Generally speaking, horses need a trip over the track before posting a winning effort. And these races may not be terribly impressive in that their purpose is to acclimate the horse and possibly improve the odds for his next outing. Nevertheless, it costs money to ship a horse. And trainers usually do it for reasons other than a change in scenery. So pay very close attention to shippers — especially "drop-downs" and those "singles" that sneak in mid-season.

Weather

In addition to rain, other weather conditions can affect a horse's performance. Strong headwinds (over 15 to 20 mph) blowing into the face of horses out of the gate will tend to stop front-running sprinters. These front runners must "break" these headwinds, while those horses who run off the pace can "draft" behind the leaders, much like in auto racing. Headwinds tend to stop cheap speed more than quality horses.

Another weather factor is when it is unusually hot and humid. These conditions are difficult for all horses, particularly those horses using Lasix. Since Lasix is a diuretic, these horses can't afford additional fluid loss caused by excessive sweating. They can be weakened significantly on these "dog days."

Medications

The most frequent question I got last year in the Fans' Forum was about medications. There are two medications that are commonly given to thoroughbreds on race day — Bute (phenylbutazone) and Lasix (furosemide). Bute is an anti-inflammation medication used to reduce both pain and swelling in horses with minor soreness or arthritis. Lasix is a diuretic used to treat "bleeders," i.e. those horses that suffer from respiratory stress and consequent hemorrhaging. Both medications (at varying blood levels) are allowed at most tracks. These medications are not stimulants and will not make a horse run any faster. Their purpose is to allow horses to "play hurt" as they say in the NFL. From a handicapping standpoint, I pay little attention to the use of bute since about 80% of the horses use it. Lasix, on the other hand, becomes a factor in the following situations ...

1) **First-Time Lasix Horses —** Many horses can show an immediate reversal in form when given Lasix for the first time (indicated by an asterisk in the program). Look at the horse's Past Performances. When you see a horse who showed good speed, wire-to-wire, followed by a series of races where he quits or loses ground in the stretch or after a half mile — this is classic "bleeder form." A horse can travel a half mile before he starts to bleed. Once he detects the problem, the horse will slow down abruptly.

On some occasions, blood is discharged through the nostrils, but more frequently this problem can only be detected by "scoping" a horse who is suspect. First-time bleeders are required by the Racing Commission/state veterinarian to rest for a minimum of 14-21 days before racing back. Good trainers will rest bleeders (the best treatment for the problem) between races. They will also give the horse a workout of at least 5/8 mile (with Lasix) before running the horse again. This is important because the horse must know that he will be able to run down the lane without bleeding.

Properly cared for, the first-time Lasix horse can return to its prior good form in his first race — and do so at a big price. There were a number of such horses last season at Canterbury Downs. *Mr. Pistil* (who was also a "mystery" shipper) provides a good example of this form reversal ...

Mr. Pistil | **Dk. b. or br. c. 4, by Pocket Flower—Lanyons Lick, by Lanyon**
KUTZ D | **115** | **Br.—Truscott John (Neb)** | **1985 6 1 0 1 $4,624**
Own.—Truscott J | **Tr.—Glass Orin J Jr** | **$6,250** | **1984 5 2 0 1 $4,136**
Lifetime 11 3 0 2 $8,760

25Aug85-6Aks	6f	:22	:44 3	1:09 3 ft	16	114	1 2	1 hd	2 1	4 3¼	McGurn C 10	6000	86-10	J. Conway, FortdeGold, BrazenEgo	12
17Aug85-4Aks	6f	:22 1	:45 3	1:11 4 m	11	116	1 2	1 2	2 2	10 10½	McGurn C 10	6500	67-25	Namletak, BeBckShortly, OsgeBully	10
4Aug85-6Aks	6f	:23	:46 2	1:12 ft	12	116	2½	2½	5 3½	6 5¾	Walker B J Jr 6	8500	71-27	DevilHimself, BeBackShortly, Leckie	9
2[illegible]Jly85-9Aks	6f	:22 2	:45	1:11 ft	6¾	116	1 hd	2 3	2 2	3 6½	Compton P 1	8500	75-24	IndinPrince, DevilHimself, Mr.Pistil	10
14Jly85-4Aks	6f	:22 3	:45 2	1:11 ft	20	117	1½	1½	1 1	1 3	Compton P 3	Ⓢ 5000	82-20	Mr. Pistil, Par's Pal, Beau'sWinner	12
29Jun85-1Aks	6f	:22 2	:46	1:12 ft	33	117	2½	2½	5 2	8 8¼	Compton P 4	Ⓢ 6500	69-20	SmoothBow, GlssCrft, Admirl'sDrm	10
11Nov84-3LnN	6f	:24	:48	1:15 ft	2¾	117	1 hd	2½	1½	1 2½	Compton P 6	Aw3605	77-25	Mr.Pistil, IffenAPlesure, Prevl'sTss	10
31Oct84-1LnN	6f	:24 2	:48 4	1:15 2 m	3½	118	1 3	1 1½	1 2	1 7	Compton P 10	ⓈMdn	75-34	Mr.Pistil, DmximJunior, FrmrHrryB.	10
[illegible]Oct84-2LnN	1 70	:49 4	1:22 2	1:57 sl	2¾	118	2 hd	2 hd	2½	7 11½	Schaber D 4	ⓈMdn	— —	LuckyFella, LadyTiffany, V.Shooter	10
[illegible]20Oct84-2LnN	1 70	:50 1	1:17 1	1:48 ft	3½	118	1½	1 1	1½	3 3¼	Schaber D 10	ⓈMdn	61-29	EndlessSkies, LadyTiffny, Mr.Pistil	10

Aug 14 Aks 4f gd :49 b

FOURTH RACE
Canterbury
SEPTEMBER 26, 1985

6 FURLONGS. (1.09⅘) CLAIMING. Purse $4,500. 4-year-olds and upward. Weight, 121 lbs. Non-winners of a race since August 1 allowed 2 lbs.; since July 1, 4 lbs.; June 1, 6 lbs. Claiming price $6,250. (Races when entered for $5,000 or less not considered.)

Value of race $4,500; value to winner $2,700; second $900; third $495; fourth $270; fifth $135. Mutuel pool $38,442. Exacta Pool, $52,338.

Last Raced	Horse	Eqt.	A.	Wt	PP	St	¼	½	Str	Fin	Jockey	Cl'g Pr	Odds $1
25Aug85 6Aks 4	Mr. Pistil		4	115	6	2	1½	1½	1 1½	1 3½	Kutz D	6250	13.20
24Aug85 6Aks 2	Daneil's Precious	b	4	110	1	5	2 hd	3 1½	3 2½	2 1	Bass S H 5	6250	6.60
11Sep85 2Cby 2	Favored Mood	b	5	115	9	6	4 1½	2 1	2 hd	3 1¼	Orona W	6250	15.20
11Sep85 6Cby 5	J. A. Prince		6	115	4	7	7 1	6½	4 1	4 2¼	Baze D	6250	7.40
11Sep85 2Cby 3	G. Willie Coop		4	115	5	3	6½	7 1½	6½	5 no	Doocy T T	6250	23.00
15Sep85 6Cby 4	Granite Mountain		4	121	3	8	10	10	9 1	6 3¼	Hoverson C	6250	7.30
19Sep85 4Cby 10	Arriba Man	b	6	115	8	10	8½	8 1½	7½	7 hd	Robley J J	6250	24.10
15Sep85 6Cby 10	Haggins Choice		4	115	10	9	9½	9 hd	10	8 hd	Montoya D	6250	27.00
14Sep85 2Cby 3	Spring The Trap		5	121	2	4	5 2	5 2	5 1	9 1	Melancon G	6250	.80
11Sep85 6Cby 10	Ammo Pistol		4	119	7	1	3 1	4 1	8½	10	LaGrange D L	6250	16.10

OFF AT 5:29. Start good. Won driving. Time, :22, :45, :57⅗, 1:11 Track fast.

$2 Mutuel Prices:

6–MR. PISTIL	**28.40**	**11.20**	**6.20**
1–DANEIL'S PRECIOUS		**8.00**	**5.80**
9–FAVORED MOOD			**5.00**

$2 EXACTA (6–1) PAID $175.60.

Dk. b. or br. c, by Pocket Flower—Lanyons Lick, by Lanyon. Trainer Glass Orin J Jr. Bred by Truscott John (Neb).

MR. PISTIL set the early pace from between horses, drew clear in the upper stretch and was kept to steady pressure to the closing yards. DANEIL'S PRECIOUS saved ground to the stretch, lugged outward in the upper stretch and continued evenly. The rider of DANEIL'S PRECIOUS lodged an objection agaisnt MR. PISTIL for interference entering the stretch but after reviewing the videotape the stewards ruled that the incident did not warrant a disqualification. FAVORED MOOD lodged his best bid outside horses on the stretch turn and continued willingly. J. A. PRINCE raced outside horse in the drive. SPRING THE TRAP tired after a half. AMMO PISTOL prompted the early pace outside horses and tired.

This dramatic change in form is possible, however, only if the horse has shown good speed/form prior to bleeding. Lasix only restores form, it doesn't create it. Said another way, bad horses aren't going to improve just because they are given Lasix.

2) **Non-Lasix Tracks** — There are three major racing states that do not allow Lasix on race day — New York, Arkansas and Arizona. Consequently, you must consider this factor when evaluating the Past Performances of "bleeders" shipping in from these states. In the case of Canterbury Downs, horses coming in from both Turf Paradise and Oaklawn Park were competing without the benefit of Lasix. Consequently, their true form may be "darkened" by such races. A final note, once a horse has used Lasix for the first time, there is no indicator in the program when he is put back on the medication.

Equipment

There are a few items of equipment that the handicapper should be aware of including ...

Blinkers — Horses have incredible peripheral vision (320^0). In racing, this "gift" may work to the disadvantage of some horses. Blinkers are those hoods with eye cups attached that many horses wear. The addition of blinkers does different things to different horses (and in many cases, it does nothing at all). The most common desired effects include:

1) Increasing the horse's early speed

2) Reducing "fractious" behavior in the gate

3) Eliminating distractions

4) Preventing horses from stopping when other horses come up on them

5) Preventing horses from stopping when they get a clear lead

6) Making horses, especially young horses, run in a straight line (except around the turns, naturally)

While these are the desire effects, not all horses change one lick when blinkers are added. I give consideration to the addition of blinkers (noted in the program as "Blinkers On") in two cases ...

1) When a horse has had "trouble" in his past race, e.g. "bore out" or was "fractious."

2) When the horse has posted a workout, since his last race, that shows marked improvement. Many tracks require a work from the starting gate when a trainer adds or removes blinkers.

The removal of blinkers or "Blinkers Off," on the other hand, usually signifies that the prior addition did little to improve the horse's form or problem. Removing the blinkers sometimes benefits a sprinter who is going a route by taking away some of its early speed.

Mud Caulks — Mud caulks or "stickers" are special racing plates worn by some horses when competing on off-tracks or on the turf. These horseshoes have cleats attached (similar to those on a baseball shoe) to improve a horse's "grip" on a slick running surface. On some tracks, they can be very helpful In fact, on some tracks, horses can't stand up — much less run — without them. And there are other tracks, such as Canterbury Downs last year, where caulks were not necessary. It really depends on how "slippery" a track gets after a good soaking.

There are some horses who can't wear caulks because of their stride. Horses who have a propensity for "catching" themselves (front leg striking the rear leg) can be injured quite seriously when wearing caulks.

Shadow Roll — This is a cloth or sheepskin roll that's placed on the muzzle (nose) of a horse to block his vision of the ground. It's generally used on horses to prevent them from jumping over shadows, tire tracks, puddles and the like. It's also used by some trainers to force the horse to lower its head when running, thus extending its stride.

Entries

An entry is when two or more horses are entered in a race by either the same trainer or owner. These horses are coupled as an entry for betting purposes and will be listed in the program as number 1 and 1A, 2 and 2B etc. and will wear corresponding saddle clothes. (It should be noted that post positions generally do not correspond to saddle cloth numbers as they do in races without entries. A horse's post position will appear below his program number.)

When considering an entry, try to determine why a trainer is running two horses and basically competing against himself. The following are the most common reasons.

1) The trainer enters two horses in an effort to make the race "fill," i.e. have the minimum number of starters. In these cases, he is willing to "sacrifice" one horse because he feels the other horse has an excellent chance.

2) To ensure an "honest" pace. Let's say that a trainer has a very fit "closer" who can win only if the early pace is fast or "honest." To ensure a fast pace, the trainer will enter a speedster or "rabbit" to prompt the pace. This also prevents the race from being "stolen" by a speed horse who is not challenged during the early going.

3) On some occasions, a trainer may have two horses who fit the same conditions (usually with two different owners), and there aren't enough races written for this type of horse. The trainer is then forced to compete against himself simply because there are no other spots to place the other horse.

4) Uncertain track conditions might prompt a trainer to enter two horses, particularly when a race is carded to be run on the grass. If it were to rain, such a race would be switched to the main track. In these tactical situations, you will frequently see one part of the entry being scratched just before post time.

5) Some trainers may frequently enter two horses waiting to see how the field shapes up. The level of competition, track condition or expected pace will

then determine which horse is best suited for the race. Again, the second part of the entry will frequently be a late scratch.

Entries offer a number of excellent wagering opportunities. In a later chapter, we'll examine how and when to bet an entry.

Summary

The preceding were just a few of the many secondary factors that come into play when looking at a race. The list goes on and on — but the scope of this book is, by design, somewhat limited. If I were to list all the "angles," you'd get a hernia hauling this book home from the store.

We have plenty to work with, given the major "impact factors." Now let's put it all together and go back to the *Daily Racing Form* and apply this new knowledge to a real, live race.

XIV. Putting It All Together

Now that you have a handle on the fundamental handicapping factors and understand the symbols etc. of the Past Performances, let's analyze a race from last season at Canterbury Downs.

Marking *The Daily Racing Form*

Marking or highlighting the key information in the Past Performances facilitates the selection process and is a lot of fun to do. Once you have noted the most relevant information, you can then begin your analysis. Every handicapper develops his or her own system for reading and marking the DRF. The following is the approach I use when doing my preliminary read-through. (I suggest you use a ball point rather than a felt-tipped pen to avoid smudging the paper.)

For this tutorial, we will examine and mark a six furlong, $10,000 claiming race for fillies and mares. In this exercise, I will first describe the process, then look at each horse individually.

7th Canterbury

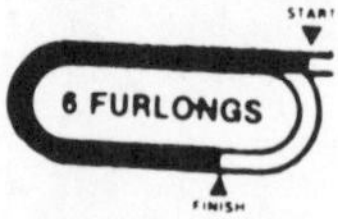

6 FURLONGS. (1.09⅗) CLAIMING. Purse $6,500. Fillies and mares. 3-year-olds and upward. Weight, 3-year-olds, 115 lbs.; older, 120 lbs. Non-winners of a race since July 15 allowed 2 lbs.; since June 15, 4 lbs. May 15, 6 lbs. Claiming price $10,000; if for $9,000 allowed 2 lbs. (Races when entered for $8,000 or less not considered.)

Coupled—Goodnight My Love and Irish Lora.

Smooth N' Good

CRAIG K **107^{5}**
Own.—Huntington K

Dk. b. or br. f. 4, by Smooth Dancer—Alien Flower, by Good Turn
Br.—Cox & Jarvis (La)
Tr.—Huntington Dougie **$9,000**
Lifetime 30 6 5 5 $32,564

1985	11	2	3	2
1984	18	4	1	3
Turf	1	0	0	1

1985 11 2 3 2 **$12,216**
1984 18 4 1 3 **$19,448**
Turf 1 0 0 1 **$770**

18Aug85-10Cby	1	:48^{2}	1:13^{2}	1:39^{1}ft	6¾	116	3^{2}	4^{3½}	5^{5½}	7^{9¼}	Melancon G^{6}	c6250	76-11	Adobe Chief, SpeedSpy,TonicMajor	9
3Aug85-10Cby	1$\frac{1}{16}$	:48^{3}	1:13^{4}	1:47^{4}ft	*2¾	114	2^{1½}	2^{½}	1^{hd}	1^{3}	LaGrange D L^{8}	Ⓕ 6250	77-10	SmoothN'Gd,EnglshWzrd,Dwnsflng	8
26Jly85-1Cby	1$\frac{1}{16}$	:47^{4}	1:12^{4}	1:46 ft	*1	109^{5}	4^{2}	3^{1}	2^{hd}	1^{1½}	Bass S H^{7}	Ⓕ c5000	— —	SmoothN'Gd,MystclSng,SlvrStrshn	7
12Jly85-9Cby	1	:48^{4}	1:13	1:39 ft	7¾	107^{5}	3^{nk}	3^{nk}	3^{nk}	3^{¾}	Bass S H^{1}	Ⓕ 7500	— —	Snderell,SheWillTll,SmoothN'Good	8
11Jun85-3CD	1	:46^{3}	1:11^{3}	1:38^{2}ft	2½e	116	6^{6}	4^{5½}	4^{6½}	4^{8}	Montoya D^{5}	Ⓕ 7500	69-18	TwinHerts,JestersJoy,TrojnGoddss	9
15May85-5CD	6f	:21^{2}	:45^{1}	1:11^{4}ft	3¾e	116	7^{15}	7^{9¼}	7^{8¾}	6^{6¼}	Melancon G^{4}	Ⓕ 10000	80-14	Countess Suzie, PorchCat,IronGold	7
3May85-1CD	1	:47^{3}	1:14^{4}	1:41 ft	*8-5	116	7^{2¾}	4^{¾}	3^{3}	3^{3}	Fox W I Jr^{6}	Ⓕ c7500	61-14	She Will Tell, Joby, SmoothN'Good	8
29Mar85-11FG	1$\frac{1}{16}$	:47^{1}	1:13	1:47^{4}ft	*2	112	8^{10}	8^{11}	3^{4}	2^{hd}	Fox W I Jr^{4}	Ⓕ 8500	73-20	JestersJoy,SmoothN'Good,TiffyK.	10
8Mar85-7FG	6f	:22^{1}	:46^{2}	1:12^{2}ft	*7-5	116	10^{13}	8^{14}	6^{6¼}	4^{6¼}	RomeroRP^{4}	Ⓕ[S] 12500	77-19	ClrCrkCt,Mg'sBlossm,HnrAndGlry	10
15Feb85-8FG	6f	:22^{3}	:47^{1}	1:13^{1}ft	16	114	7^{9}	8^{13}	5^{6}	2^{hd}	Faul J H^{1}	Ⓕ[S] 15000	79-21	Dr.PrttyFst,SmothN'Gd,LdyL.AndL.	9

15Feb85—Steadied to avoid tiring horse

Aug 21 Cby 3f ft :36^{3} b

Goodnight My Love

KAENEL J L **115**
Own.—Shamie E

Ch. f. 3, by China Silk—Upcuma, by Crozier
Br.—Shamie E (Cal)
Tr.—Pappalardo John W **$10,000**
Lifetime 10 1 0 2 $8,250

1985 10 1 0 2 **$8,250**
1984 0 M 0 0

8Aug85-6Cby	1^{70}	:48^{1}	1:12^{3}	1:45^{2}ft	7	109^{5}	7^{13}	7^{12}	5^{7}	5^{5}	Bass S H^{3}	Ⓕ 20000	76-16	QutThVocs,JstBrlyAbl,StrdstMlody	7
1Aug85-5Cby	1	:47^{3}	1:14^{3}	1:41 ft	*9-5	109^{5}	8^{10}	4^{3}	1^{2½}	1^{5}	Bass S H^{7}	ⒻM16000	76-12	GoodnghtMyLv,ChthmHgh,KnSmk	8
18Jly85-4Cby	1^{70}	:47^{4}	1:12^{4}	1:44^{2}ft	11	113	9^{11}	6^{11}	4^{9½}	4^{10}	Hamilton M^{5}	ⒻMdn	— —	Opulence,VenturetteMiss,Bbu'sKey	9
30Jun85-7Cby	6f	:24	:47^{2}	1:13^{1}ft	8¼	115	6^{12}	6^{11}	6^{7¾}	4^{6½}	Hamilton M^{3}	ⒻMdn	— —	FeelsLikeLove,MeCry,DineWithDev	6
7Jun85-3Hol	1⅛	:48^{1}	1:12^{4}	1:50^{2}ft	19	109	7^{11}	7^{10}	7^{11}	7^{13¼}	Hawley S^{4}	Ⓕ 12500	84-06	Cecile,DuchessPetrone,MerryHdlinr	8
16May85-2Hol	1	:46	1:11	1:36^{4}ft	28	113	12^{17}	10^{19}	10^{19}	7^{18¾}	PedrozaMA^{1}	ⒻM28000	70-08	Don A Top, Grenalda, LuckySilver	12
11Apr85-3SA	1$\frac{1}{16}$	:46^{1}	1:11^{1}	1:45^{2}ft	7	114	10^{11}	8^{14}	8^{12}	3^{6}	Hawley S^{9}	ⒻM28000	68-18	TAtTn,RoylCurvs,GoodnghtMyLov	12
5Apr85-2SA	1	:46^{2}	1:11^{3}	1:38 ft	20	110^{5}	9^{6½}	8^{12}	8^{8}	6^{6}	DomngzRE^{7}	ⒻM45000	72-14	‡PussyCat,SenstionlDrm,KeepDting	9
22Mar85-3SA	1$\frac{1}{16}$	:46	1:11^{2}	1:45 ft	6	109^{5}	9^{17}	10^{12}	4^{7½}	3^{6}	DomngzRE^{2}	ⒻM28000	70-17	RcklssMss,DonATop,GdnghtMyLv	12
22Mar85—Very wide into stretch, bumped at 1/8															
22Feb85-3SA	6½f	:21^{3}	:44^{3}	1:18 ft	20	110^{5}	10^{19}	10^{24}	9^{16}	7^{5½}	DmngzRL^{5}	Ⓕ[S]M35000	74-18	Sntequos,SusnnRose,KpStorming	10

Jly 14 Cby 6f ft 1:15 b **Jly 8 Cby 5f ft 1:03 b**

Sonoita Mley

WARHOL V L **114**
Own.—Williamson R M

Ch. m. 6, by Yorkville—Tattling, by Commanding II
Br.—Short D (Cal)
Tr.—Crowe Marcel J **$10,000**
Lifetime 56 14 7 6 $52,996

1985 8 0 1 0 **$1,454**
1984 16 6 2 3 **$24,137**
Turf 5 1 0 0 **$3,985**

16Aug85-9Cby	5½f	:22^{3}	:46^{1}	1:05^{4}ft	6¾	114	1^{½}	2^{hd}	4^{3}	6^{6¾}	Warhol V L^{3}	Ⓕ 12500	84-09	Sotetta, La Liz, Porch Cat	8
13Jly85-8NP	6f	:22^{2}	:46^{1}	1:12^{1}gd	12	108^{5}	1^{3}	1^{2}	2^{nk}	6^{5¼}	Jumpsen N^{7}	Ⓕ 20000	83-22	LittlePrincess,EstrLit,Nlee'sFshion	7
30Jun85-7NP	6½f	:23	:46^{4}	1:18^{4}ft	4½	115	4^{3¼}	4^{3½}	6^{7}	6^{21}	Turcotte Y A^{7}	Ⓕ 16000	67-14	TirelssLdy,OwlwoodLn,FigonroLssi	6
30Jun85—Reared st.															
14Jun85-7NP	6f	:22^{4}	:46^{4}	1:12^{4}m	3¼	115	1^{2}	1^{4}	1^{nk}	5^{9½}	Levine C^{3}	Ⓕ 20000	75-25	Drwin'sDrlin,Nl'sFshon,OwlwoodLn	6
24May85-9NP	6f	:22^{4}	:46^{3}	1:13^{4}sy	5¼	115	3^{1}	3^{3}	5^{10}	6^{25¼}	Levine C^{6}	ⒻAw6800	55-26	BrightBouquet,Snowder,RinbowSkr	6
11May85-9StP	6f	:22^{1}	:45^{2}	1:10^{4}ft	11	114	1^{3}	1^{3}	1^{nk}	6^{4¼}	Levine C^{6}	ⒻLilac	89-14	Merrydown,RinbowSekr,HstyMort	10
1May85-9StP	6f	:22^{2}	:45^{3}	1:11^{1}ft	*3-2	107^{5}	1^{1}	1^{2}	2^{nk}	6^{5½}	Jumpsen N^{7}	ⒻAw6530	85-16	PlenumBee,RinbowSkr,SndHoppr	10
20Apr85-9StP	6f	:23	:47^{2}	1:15^{3}sy	*9-5	116	1^{3}	1^{5}	1^{3}	2^{hd}	TurcotteYA^{7}	ⒻAw6800	69-29	RinbowSeekr,SonoitMly,Nl'sFshion	7
3Nov84-8StP	6f	:22^{4}	:46	1:11^{4}ft	*2½	113^{5}	1^{1½}	1^{2¼}	1^{2¼}	1^{1½}	Mayo K^{4}	Ⓕ 16000	88-15	SonoitMley,PlenumBee,Nle'sFshion	9
21Oct84-8StP	6f	:22^{2}	:46	1:11^{3}ft	8¼	116	1^{1}	1^{2¼}	1^{4}	1^{3}	Ferris A S^{6}	Ⓕ 16000	89-12	SonoitMley,Geno'sAngle,PlenumBe	7

Aug 14 Cby 3f ft :38 b

Arctic Angel — Ch. f. 4, by Another Double—Miss Bonmire, by Mountain Fire
BASS S H 1155
Br.—Alexander Lucie D (Ky) 1985 12 2 4 1 $12,638
Tr.—Van Berg Jack C $10,000 1984 0 M 0 0
Own.—Lloyd Lucie Lifetime 12 2 4 1 $12,638

31Jly85-6Cby 6f :223 :462 1:113ft *8-5 1155 53 43½ 2½ 22¼ Bass S H6 Ⓕ 10000 88-14 SheWillTll,ArcticAngl,GimmiATip 10
18Jly85-7Cby 5½f :223 :47 1:063ft 2½ 1105 58 48 22½ 12 Bass S H2 Ⓕ 12500 — — Arctic Angel, Texoma, Trulinka 7
29Jun85-7Cby 5½f :232 :471 1:06 ft 8-5 115 54 53¼ 55½ 55½ HansenRD4 ⒻAw11000 — — FinalDancer,Adptble,ApricotCreme 5
18Jun85-9CD 6f :213 :461 1:123ft *2-3 1155 54 31½ 12 14 Bass S H4 ⒻM10000 82-16 Arctic Angel, Hai Sun,VirtualLady 11
4Jun85-2CD 6½f :232 :473 1:204gd 3 1175 32½ 34 23½ 23 Bass S H8 ⒻM10000 73-23 BoldndFlsh,ArctcAngl,BrdwyKtty 11
25May85-3CD 6f :22 :461 1:122ft 2 1175 33½ 24 23 22 Bass S H1 ⒻM10000 81-14 Dollmaker,ArcticAngel,WorkNMyrn 8
17May85-1CD 6f :212 :453 1:121gd 5 119 54½ 78¼ 811 812 Melancon L9 ⒻM15000 72-14 Livittothelimit,GreyAllure,RlFmin 11
8May85-2CD 6f :221 :462 1:114ft 3¼ 122 43½ 34½ 36 26 Melancon L5 ⒻM10000 80-16 Lon'sDlght,ArctcAngl,Nncy'sBlssng 7
14Apr85-2FG 5½f :23 :472 1:064ft 7 121 31½ 54¾ 45½ 35¼ Ardoin R1 ⒻMdn 79-21 LilliBeth,BestThoughts,ArcticAngl 11
22Mar85-1FG 6f :224 :471 1:124ft 6½ 115 73¼ 85¾1113 1117¼ Melancon G8 M15000 64-20 Cakewalk,LavishLady,OuiskiBayou 12
●Jly 13 Cby 4f ft :471 h

Irish Lora — Dk. b. or br. f. 3, by The Irish Lord—Nori O, by McTavish
SMITH M E 109
Br.—Steinmann H (Cal) 1985 12 1 0 1 $13,115
Tr.—Pappalardo John W $10,000 1984 0 M 0 0
Own.—Steinmann H Lifetime 12 1 0 1 $13,115

11Aug85-1Cby 6f :221 :452 1:121ft 15 115 42¼ 44 43½ 51¾ Kaenel J L3 Ⓕ 12500 85-12 Buckpasser'sGl,TruLdyRed,Trulink 9
11Jly85-3Hol 1 :453 1:101 1:362ft 19 116 610 616 617 618½ Estrada J Jr3 Ⓕ 25000 72-07 Don A Top,VitalScore,RockCanyon 6
19Jun85-6Hol 6f :221 :453 1:111ft 80 115 912 711 64¾ 53¾ Estrada J Jr11 Ⓕ 25000 87-05 ‡Wlker'sLdy,FireMissLedr,AnniLis 11
22May85-4Hol 6f :222 :454 1:104ft 37 118 96¼ 77½ 75¼ 77 Meza R Q4 Ⓕ 25000 86-08 TammyLu,FireMissLeder,AnnieLis 11
25Apr85-7Hol 1 :451 1:104 1:37 ft 24 115 88¾ 88¼ 812 817½ Sibille R2 Ⓕ 25000 70-09 Iva'sRich,Clearway,FireMissLeder 10
18Apr85-7SA 6½f :213 :45 1:164ft 60 118 76¼ 66½ 59 310 Estrada J Jr6 Ⓕ 32000 76-16 Proud Doll, Ritzy Chick, IrishLora 11
5Apr85-1SA 6f :214 :451 1:102ft 11 120 56½ 911 99¼ 88¼ Pincay L Jr11 Ⓕ 25000 78-14 QuitKid,ProudDoll,Perfction'sGift 12
5Apr85—Lugged out, wide final 3/8
28Mar85-3SA 6½f :22 :462 1:214sl 4¼ 117 63½ 52½ 3½ 12 HawleyS12 ⒻⓈM32000 61-31 IrishLora,KimStep,MentlBnkMgic 12
22Feb85-3SA 6½f :213 :443 1:18 ft 5e115 710 712 712 65 Hawley S8 ⒻⓈM35000 75-18 Sntequos,SusnnRose,KpStorming 10
6Feb85-4SA 1 1/16 :462 1:112 1:444ft 8 117 612 716 1026 1024 McHrguDG6 ⒻM32000 53-15 StksTWn,SnstnlDrm,MntlBnkMgc 11
6Feb85—Lugged out

Partner's Express — Dk. b. or br. f. 4, by Partner's Hope—Miss Snow Nose, by Nashua Chip
LAGRANGE D L 114
Br.—Axline W & C (Kan) 1985 10 0 1 1 $2,165
Tr.—Dickey George $10,000 1984 4 1 2 0 $1,583
Own.—Axline C Lifetime 14 1 3 1 $3,748

31Jly85-6Cby 6f :223 :462 1:113ft 40 114 96¾ 96¾ 74½ 812¼ Hoverson C2 Ⓕ 10000 78-14 SheWillTll,ArcticAngl,GimmiATip 10
21Jly85-3Cby 6f :221 :46 1:113ft 27 116 64¾ 64½ 77½ 710 Baze D7 Ⓕ 16000 — — DrlingDorothy,DiboloRinbow,St.Trs 7
12Jly85-7Cby 6½f :233 :464 1:18 ft 23 116 74¼ 77 67 59¾ Baze D3 Ⓕ 25000 — — JtullhMid,AxetheOdds,BettieBGood 8
2Jun85-5Aks 6f :224 :461 1:121ft 31 116 65 78 98½ 911 Frazier DL1 ⒻAw14400 65-27 Chocolate Kisses, Real Carri, Pool 9
19May85-10Ato 6f :231 :464 1:133ft 2½ 118 76 711 62¾ 65¾ JonsRV3 ⒻF Brown H 83-21 SchellyBo,SweetDr.,Stcey'sSidkick 8
13Apr85-5Fon 6f :223 :47 1:12 ft 14 116 42 42 42 45½ Shepherd DR1 Ⓕ 25000 86-10 Bright N Sunny, Real Carri, Lusive 7
6Apr85-7Fon 6f :223 :462 1:121ft 58 114 2hd 22 23 27 Frazier D L7 ⒻAw5300 84-16 GentleGil,Partner'sExpress,RelCrri 7
30Mar85-6Fon 6f :232 :48 1:134m 38 116 42 79½ 619 725¼ Beck D L6 Ⓕ 32000 58-21 Gentle Gil, Lil Happy, Eilsel 9
16Mar85-9Fon 6f :232 :472 1:121ft 27 115 63½ 76¼ 813 819 Frazier D L8 ⒻAw5618 72-16 Racing Jet, Bright NSunny,Tamyon 8
1Mar85-7Fon 4f :224 :47 ft 14 114 2 2½ 2½ 3hd Frazier D L8 ⒻAw5300 90-08 LilHppy,SilingJupon,Prtner'sExprss 8
Jly 30 Cby 3f ft :36 b Jly 11 Cby 3f ft :372 b Jly 6 Cby 4f ft :524 b Jun 30 Cby 4f ft :52 b

Class Counts — B. m. 5, by Turn And Count—Turner's Class, by Circle
HAMILTON M 118
Br.—Turner S A (Ky) 1985 10 1 1 1 $6,046
Tr.—Boggess Lee $10,000 1984 3 0 0 0
Own.—Bogges L & FalconFarmsLtd Lifetime 19 2 1 1 $13,696

16Aug85-9Cby 5½f :223 :461 1:054ft 14 118 86¼ 79 66 46¾ LaGrange DL2 Ⓕ 12500 84-09 Sotetta, La Liz, Porch Cat 8
4Aug85-6Cby 5½f :222 :461 1:053ft 23 116 52¼ 74¼ 67 56½ LaGrange DL6 Ⓕ 14000 85-10 DiboloRinbow,DrlingDorothy,Chtell 8
6Jly85-10Cby 1 1/16 :48 1:122 1:461ft 10 113 56½ 54½ 34 47 LaGrange DL6 Ⓕ 14000 — — Mrzi'sHollow,SwtOlShri,FinnwyLdy 6
28Jun85-4Cby 1 1/16 :501 1:151 1:474ft 4 115 1½ 2hd 42½ 44 LaGrange DL5 Ⓕ 12500 — — BnnerStone,CorrelKim,SweetOlShri 5
20Jun85-6FP 6f :223 :464 1:133ft *2-3 122 73¾ 53 4¾ 1nk Louviere G E6 Ⓕ 15000 75-23 ClssCounts,AfridtoEntr,DinWithWn 7
7Jun85-8FP 1 1/16 :472 1:13 1:464m 7¾ 117 41½ 41¼ 31½ 22 LouviereGE1 ⒻAw4900 75-20 Dicentra, Class Counts, High Three 9
2Jun85-8FP 6f :224 :462 1:112gd 10 117 52½ 64¼ 54½ 34 LouviereGE2 ⒻAw4200 82-17 LdyChlee,JstrsonsHony,ClssCounts 7
25May85-6FP 6f :224 :463 1:121ft 8 122 53½ 55½ 65¼ 55¼ LouviereGE9 ⒻAw4200 77-23 AlottWmpum,Betty'sMist,LittlBss 10
24Apr85-9TuP 6f :214 :44 1:083ft 8 114 52½ 65¼ 711 712½ LaGrngeDL5 ⒻAw6000 80-18 Cuervo, DronesFirefly,BlueSmokey 7
13Apr85-8TuP 6f :212 :454 1:094ft 15 114 1011 1010 95¼ 65 LaGrngeDL5 ⒻAw4000 82-14 WllBStnnng,DronsFrfly,FshonFrst 10
●Jly 24 Cby 5f sy 1:002 h

Read the Conditions

I can't overstate the importance of reading and understanding the "conditions" of a race. Start by circling the distance and the claiming price. Next, read the eligibility requirements and note any special conditions of the race — circling unique qualifications such as "non-winners of two races" or conditions that relate to specific dates, e.g. "non-winners of $4,000 since September, 30, 1985." Also note the weight allowances being offered. Then circle any entries that might be in the race.

7th Canterbury

6 FURLONGS. (1.09⅗) CLAIMING. Purse $6,500. Fillies and mares. 3-year-olds and upward. Weight, 3-year-olds, 115 lbs.; older, 120 lbs. Non-winners of a race since July 15 allowed 2 lbs. since June 15, 4 lbs. May 15, 6 lbs. Claiming price $10,000; if for $9,000 allowed 2 lbs. (Races when entered for $8,000 or less not considered.)

Coupled—Goodnight My Love and Irish Lora.

In this race, we're looking at fillies, 3-year-olds and up, going six furlongs for $10,000 down to $9,000 claiming.

HINT: Read the conditions as though you were the trainer of each horse. Your objective is to enter the horse in a race where a) the distance suits, b) the price or class level is a level where your horse can be competitive and c) the conditions give you an edge in terms of weight or competition. For example, if your horse was turned out for three months and has just returned to competition, you would look for a race which would favor horses who have not won since X date. In that your horse wasn't even racing during the period, he may have an edge versus those who were racing — but not winning — during that period.

Track Condition

If the race is to be run over a "fast" track, then circle the track condition for all past races that were run on an "off track." For the most part, you should ignore these races in your analysis. On the other hand, if the today's race were to be run over a "sloppy," "muddy" or "good" track, carefully note all past races run on an "off track." You would also note any horse who has a "mud mark" next to his name. (The race we are examining was run over a fast track.)

Frequently, you will be doing your homework the night before, and the weather may be a big question mark. If there is a chance that you might be faced with an "off track," use a different colored pen to make "off track notes." Horses who would move up in consideration on an "off track" are marked with a "M" next to their name. Also, underscore all running lines from races on an "off track" with the different color.

Class Notations

Claiming Price — First, determine whether each horse is moving up or down or competing at the same level or claiming price versus its most recent races. Arrows work well for this.

In this race, there are quite a few "drop-downs" (horses moving down in claiming price) including *Sonoita Mley* who has dropped from $20,000 down to $10,000 in just two races.

Next, note any horse who is "in jail," i.e. has been claimed in the past 30 days. These horses must run for a price no less than 25 percent higher than the price at which they were claimed for a period of 30 days. Put a "J" next to the arrow, indicating this mandatory rise in price.

Smooth and Good was claimed in her last race for $6,250 and consequently has to run for no less than $7,900. She's in today for $9,000. This mandatory rise in price coupled with all the "drop-downs" would indicate that this filly might be outclassed today. As such, put a question mark in the "company line" area.

Competition — Not all $10,000 races have the same level of competition. Sometimes the fields will be "soft," other times, very competitive. Study the top three finishers of past races and see who the horse has beaten or been beaten by. For example, you might find a horse who ran third, by 5 lengths, in his last race. The winner of that race, however, came back and won his next race running for $12,500. Obviously, the horse you are evaluating was outclassed in his last race. Irish Lora was beaten in her last race by *Buckpasser's Gal,* a very tough filly and a legitimate $12,500 — $16,000 filly. Circle horses in the "company line" which provide a basis for the horse's competitive level.

Field Size — Also note small fields. The final number of each running line tells the number of starters. As such, a horse that finishes third in a field of only six or seven may have only beaten the "dogs" in that field. Circle field size in past races with small fields.

Track Class — Note if a horse is coming from a better or lesser track. Sometimes a strong set of PP's was generated against weak competition or the reverse. Circle the track abbreviations and note any change in track class.

Past Odds Circle the odds of any horse that has repeatedly been a longshot. These horses obviously were outclassed when competing in these races. Also note "beaten favorites," (indicated by an asterisk preceding the odds) especially horses that make a habit out of disappointing their supporters.

Condition/Fitness Notations

Breaks in Training — Every horse requires time away from the races — "turn outs" and "fresheners." Draw a line under the date of each horse's last break in training and note the length of that period in the margin, especially layoffs over four months. Such a lengthy layoff usually indicates an injury. Also, pay attention to the year of past races. On more than one occasion I've found myself evaluating a horse who has been away from the track for a year or two.

Dates and Distance of Recent Races — Examine the dates of past races to determine patterns. Some horses run more frequently than others. Note any irregularities. Then check the distance to determine if there is any change versus his last couple of races or his "normal" distance. If there is a change, put a question mark next to the distance column.

Number of Starts — If there isn't any evidence of a break in training for a horse, examine the "numer of starts" box and put a question mark on any horse who appears to be "over-raced." This factor becomes more important towards the end of the summer.

Workouts — Note all workouts and circle any "bullet" works. Pay careful attention to the dates of these workouts to be sure you are looking at recent works. If a horse has no workouts or if they are unusually slow, put a question mark in that area.

Now let's look at this field after making our class notations ...

7th Canterbury

START — 6 FURLONGS — FINISH

6 FURLONGS. (1.09⅗) CLAIMING. Purse $6,500. Fillies and mares. 3-year-olds and upward. Weight, 3-year-olds, 115 lbs.; older, 120 lbs. Non-winners of a race since July 15 allowed 2 lbs.; since June 15, 4 lbs. May 15, 6 lbs. Claiming price $10,000; if for $9,000 allowed 2 lbs. (Races when entered for $8,000 or less not considered.)

Coupled—Goodnight My Love and Irish Lora.

Smooth N' Good

CRAIG K — **1075**
Own.—Huntington K

Dk. b. or br. f. 4, by Smooth Dancer—Alien Flower, by Good Turn
Br.—Cox & Jarvis (La)
Tr.—Huntington Dougie J **$9,000**
Lifetime 30 6 5 5 $32,564

1985	11	2	3	2	$12,216
1984	18	4	1	3	$19,448
Turf	1	0	0	1	$770

18Aug85-10Cby	1	:482	1:132	1:391ft	6¾	116	32	43½	55½	79¼	Melancon G6	c6250	76-11	Adobe Chief, SpeedSpy,TonicMajor	9
3Aug85-10Cby	1 1/16	:483	1:134	1:474ft	*2¾	114	21½	2½	1hd	13	LaGrange D L8	Ⓕ 6250	77-10	SmoothN'Gd,EnglshWzrd,Dwnsflng	8
16Jly85-1Cby	1 1/16	:474	1:124	1:46 ft	*1	1095	42	31	2hd	11½	Bass S H7	Ⓕ c5000	— —	SmoothN'Gd,MystclSng,SlvrStrshn	7
2Jly85-9Cby	1	:484	1:13	1:39 ft	7¾	1075	3nk	3nk	3nk	3¾	Bass S H1	Ⓕ 7500	— —	Snderell,SheWillTll,SmoothN'Good	8
11Jun85-3CD	1	:463	1:113	1:382ft	2½e	116	66	45½	46½	48	Montoya D5	Ⓕ 7500	69-18	TwinHerts,JestersJoy,TrojnGoddss	9
5May85-5CD	6f	:212	:451	1:114ft	3¾e	116	715	79¼	78¾	66¼	Melancon G4	Ⓕ 10000	80-14	Countess Suzie, PorchCat,IronGold	7
3May85-1CD	1	:473	1:144	1:41 ft	*8-5	116	72¾	4¾	33	33	Fox W I Jr6	Ⓕ c7500	61-14	She Will Tell, Joby, SmoothN'Good	8
9Mar85-11FG	1 1/16	:471	1:13	1:474ft	*2	112	810	811	34	2hd	Fox W I Jr4	Ⓕ 8500	73-20	JestersJoy,SmoothN'Good,TiffyK.	10
8Mar85-7FG	6f	:221	:462	1:122ft	*7-5	116	1013	814	66¼	46¼	RomeroRP4	ⒻS 12500	77-19	ClrCrkCt,Mg'sBlossm,HnrAndGlry	10
5Feb85-8FG	6f	:223	:471	1:131ft	16	114	79	813	56	2hd	Faul J H1	ⒻS 15000	79-21	Dr.PrttyFst,SmothN'Gd,LdyL.AndL.	9

15Feb85—Steadied to avoid tiring horse

Aug 21 Cby 3f ft :363 b

Goodnight My Love

KAENEL J L — **115**
Own.—Shamie E

Ch. f. 3, by China Silk—Upcuma, by Crozier
Br.—Shamie E (Cal)
Tr.—Pappalardo John W **$10,000**
Lifetime 10 1 0 2 $8,250

1985	10	1	0	2	$8,250
1984	0	M	0	0	

8Aug85-6Cby	170	:481	1:123	1:452ft	7	1095	713	712	57	55	Bass S H3	Ⓕ 20000	76-16	QutThVocs,JstBrlyAbl,StrdstMlody	7
1Aug85-5Cby	1	:473	1:143	1:41 ft	*9-5	1095	810	43	12½	15	Bass S H7	ⒻM16000	76-12	GoodnghtMyLv,ChthmHgh,KnSmk	8
8Jly85-4Cby	170	:474	1:124	1:442ft	11	113	911	611	49½	410	Hamilton M5	ⒻMdn	— —	Opulence,VenturetteMiss,Bbu'sKey	9
20Jun85-7Cby	6f	:24	:472	1:131ft	8¼	115	612	611	67¾	46½	Hamilton M3	ⒻMdn	— —	FeelsLikeLove,MeCry,DineWithDev	6
7Jun85-8Hol	1⅛	:481	1:124	1:502ft	19	109	711	710	711	713¼	Hawley S4	Ⓕ 12500	84-06	Cecile,DuchessPetrone,MerryHdlinr	8
6May85-2Hol	1	:46	1:11	1:364ft	28	113	1217	1019	1019	718¾	PedrozaMA1	ⒻM28000	70-08	Don A Top, Grenalda, LuckySilver	12
1Apr85-3SA	1 1/16	:461	1:111	1:452ft	7	114	1011	814	812	36	Hawley S9	ⒻM28000	68-18	TAtTn,RoylCurvs,GoodnghtMyLov	12
5Apr85-2SA	1	:462	1:113	1:38 ft	20	1105	96½	812	88	66	DomngzRE7	ⒻM45000	72-14	‡PussyCat,SenstionlDrm,KeepDting	9
2Mar85-3SA	1 1/16	:46	1:112	1:45 ft	6	1095	917	1012	47½	36	DomngzRE2	ⒻM28000	70-17	RcklssMss,DonATop,GdnghtMyLv	12
2Feb85-3SA	6½f	:213	:443	1:18 ft	20	1105	1019	1024	916	75½	DmngzRL5	ⒻSM35000	74-18	Sntequos,SusnnRose,KpStorming	10

22Mar85—Very wide into stretch, bumped at 1/8

Jly 14 Cby 6f ft 1:15 b **Jly 8 Cby 5f ft 1:03 b**

Sonoita Mley — Ch. m. 6, by Yorkville—Tattling, by Commanding II
WARHOL V L — 114 — Br.—Short D (Cal) — 1985 8 0 1 0 $1,454
Tr.—Crowe Marcel J — $10,000 — 1984 16 6 2 3 $24,137
Own.—Williamson R M — Lifetime 56 14 7 6 $52,996 — Turf 5 1 0 0 $3,985

16Aug85-9Cby 5½f :223 :461 1:054ft 6¾ 114 1½ 2hd 43 66¾ Warhol V L3 Ⓕ 12500 84-09 Sotetta, La Liz, Porch Cat 8
13Jly85-8NP 6f :222 :461 1:121gd 12 1085 13 12 2nk 65½ Jumpsen N7 Ⓕ 20000 83-22 LittlePrincess,EstrLit,Nlee'sFshion 7
30Jun85-7NP 6½f :23 :464 1:184ft 4½ 115 43½ 43½ 67 621 Turcotte Y A7 Ⓕ 16000 67-14 TirelssLdy,OwlwoodLn,FigonroLssi 6
30Jun85—Reared st.
14Jun85-7NP 6f :224 :464 1:124m 3¼ 115 12 14 1nk 59½ Levine C3 Ⓕ 20000 75-25 Drwin'sDrlin,Nl'sFshon,OwlwoodLn 6
24May85-9NP 6f :224 :463 1:134sy 5¼ 115 31 33 510 625¼ Levine C6 ⒻAw6800 55-26 BrightBouquet,Snowder,RinbowSkr 6
11May85-9StP 6f :221 :452 1:104ft 11 114 13 13 1nk 64¼ Levine C6 ⒻLilac 89-14 Merrydown,RinbowSekr,HstyMort 10
1May85-9StP 6f :222 :453 1:111ft *3-2 1075 11 12 2nk 65½ Jumpsen N7 ⒻAw6530 85-16 PlenumBee,RinbowSkr,SndHoppr 10
20Apr85-9StP 6f :23 :472 1:153sy *9-5 116 13 15 13 2hd TurcotteYA7 ⒻAw6800 69-29 RinbowSeekr,SonoitMly,Nl'sFshion 7
3Nov84-8StP 6f :224 :46 1:114ft *2½ 1135 11½ 12½ 12½ 11½ Mayo K4 Ⓕ 16000 88-15 SonoitMley,PlenumBee,Nle'sFshion 9
21Oct84-8StP 6f :222 :46 1:113ft 8¼ 116 11 12½ 14 13 Ferris A S6 Ⓕ 16000 89-12 SonoitMley,Geno'sAngle,PlenumBe 7
Aug 14 Cby 3f ft :38 b

Arctic Angel — Ch. f. 4, by Another Double—Miss Bonmire, by Mountain Fire
BASS S H — 1155 — Br.—Alexander Lucie D (Ky) — 1985 12 2 4 1 $12,638
Tr.—Van Berg Jack C — $10,000 — 1984 0 M 0 0
Own.—Lloyd Lucie — Lifetime 12 2 4 1 $12,638

31Jly85-6Cby 6f :223 :462 1:113ft *8-5 1155 53 43½ 2½ 22¼ Bass S H6 Ⓕ 10000 88-14 SheWillTll,ArcticAngl,GimmiATip 10
18Jly85-7Cby 5½f :223 :47 1:063ft 2½ 1105 58 48 22½ 12 Bass S H2 Ⓕ 12500 — — Arctic Angel, Texoma, Trulinka 7
29Jun85-7Cby 5½f :232 :471 1:06 ft 8-5 115 54 53¼ 55½ 55½ HansenRD4 ⒻAw11000 — — FinalDancer,Adptble,ApricotCreme 5
18Jun85-9CD 6f :213 :461 1:123ft *2-3 1155 54 31½ 12 14 Bass S H4 ⒻM10000 82-16 Arctic Angel, Hai Sun,VirtualLady 11
4Jun85-2CD 6½f :232 :473 1:204gd 3 1175 32½ 34 23½ 23 Bass S H8 ⒻM10000 73-23 BoldndFlsh,ArctcAngl,BrdwyKtty 11
25May85-3CD 6f :22 :461 1:122ft 2 1175 33½ 24 23 22 Bass S H1 ⒻM10000 81-14 Dollmaker,ArcticAngel,WorkNMyrn 8
17May85-1CD 6f :212 :453 1:121gd 5 119 54½ 78½ 811 812 Melancon L9 ⒻM15000 72-14 Livittothelimit,GreyAllure,RlFmin 11
8May85-2CD 6f :221 :462 1:114ft 3½ 122 43½ 34½ 36 26 Melancon L5 ⒻM10000 80-16 Lon'sDlght,ArctcAngl,Nncy'sBlssng 7
14Apr85-2FG 5½f :23 :472 1:064ft 7 121 31½ 54¾ 45½ 35¼ Ardoin R1 ⒻMdn 79-21 LilliBeth,BestThoughts,ArcticAngl 11
22Mar85-1FG 6f :224 :471 1:124ft 6½ 115 73¼ 85¾111311117¼ Melancon G8 M15000 64-20 Cakewalk,LavishLady,OuiskiBayou 12
●Jly 13 Cby 4f ft :471 h

Irish Lora — Dk. b. or br. f. 3, by The Irish Lord—Nori O, by McTavish
SMITH M E — 109 — Br.—Steinmann H (Cal) — 1985 12 1 0 1 $13,115
Tr.—Pappalardo John W — $10,000 — 1984 0 M 0 0
Own.—Steinmann H — Lifetime 12 1 0 1 $13,115

11Aug85-1Cby 6f :221 :452 1:121ft 15 115 42¼ 44 43½ 51¾ Kaenel J L3 Ⓕ 12500 85-12 Buckpasser'sGl,TruLdyRed,Trulink 9
11Jly85-3Hol 1 :453 1:101 1:362ft 19 116 610 616 617 618½ Estrada J Jr3 Ⓕ 25000 72-07 Don A Top,VitalScore,RockCanyon 6
19Jun85-6Hol 6f :221 :453 1:111ft 80 115 912 711 64¾ 53¾ Estrada J Jr11 Ⓕ 25000 87-05 ‡Wlker'sLdy,FireMissLedr,AnniLis 11
22May85-4Hol 6f :222 :454 1:104ft 37 118 96¼ 77½ 75¼ 77 Meza R Q4 Ⓕ 25000 86-08 TammyLu,FireMissLeder,AnnieLis 11
25Apr85-7Hol 1 :451 1:104 1:37 ft 24 115 88¾ 88¼ 812 817½ Sibille R2 Ⓕ 25000 70-09 Iva'sRich,Clearway,FireMissLeder 10
18Apr85-7SA 6½f :213 :45 1:164ft 60 118 76¼ 66½ 59 310 Estrada J Jr6 Ⓕ 32000 76-16 Proud Doll, Ritzy Chick, IrishLora 11
5Apr85-1SA 6f :214 :451 1:102ft 11 120 56½ 911 99¼ 88¼ Pincay L Jr11 Ⓕ 25000 78-14 QuitKid,ProudDoll,Perfction'sGift 12
5Apr85—Lugged out, wide final 3/8
28Mar85-3SA 6½f :22 :462 1:214sl 4½ 117 63½ 52½ 3½ 12 HawleyS12 ⒻⓈM32000 61-31 IrishLora,KimStep,MentlBnkMgic 12
22Feb85-3SA 6½f :213 :443 1:18 ft 5e 115 710 712 712 65 Hawley S8 ⒻⓈM35000 75-18 Snlequos,SusnnRose,KpStorming 10
6Feb85-4SA 1 1/16 :462 1:112 1:444ft 8 117 612 716 1026 1024 McHrguDG6 ⒻM32000 53-15 StksTWn,SnstnlDrm,MntlBnkMgc 11
6Feb85—Lugged out

Partner's Express — Dk. b. or br. f. 4, by Partner's Hope—Miss Snow Nose, by Nashua Chip
LAGRANGE D L — 114 — Br.—Axline W & C (Kan) — 1985 10 0 1 1 $2,165
Tr.—Dickey George — $10,000 — 1984 4 1 2 0 $1,583
Own.—Axline C — Lifetime 14 1 3 1 $3,748

31Jly85-6Cby 6f :223 :462 1:113ft 40 114 96¾ 96¾ 74½ 812¼ Hoverson C2 Ⓕ 10000 78-14 SheWillTll,ArcticAngl,GimmiATip 10
21Jly85-3Cby 6f :221 :46 1:113ft 27 116 64¾ 64½ 77½ 710 Baze D7 Ⓕ 16000 — — DrlingDorothy,DiboloRinbow,St.Trs 7
12Jly85-7Cby 6½f :233 :464 1:18 ft 23 116 74½ 77 67 59¾ Baze D3 Ⓕ 25000 — — JtullhMid,AxetheOdds,BettieBGood 8
2Jun85-5Aks 6f :224 :461 1:121ft 31 116 65 78 98½ 911 Frazier DL1 ⒻAw14400 65-27 Chocolate Kisses, Real Carri, Pool 9
19May85-10Ato 6f :231 :464 1:133ft 2½ 118 76 711 62¾ 65¾ JonsRV3 ⒻF Brown H 83-21 SchellyBo,SweetDr.,Stcey'sSidkick 8
13Apr85-5Fon 6f :223 :47 1:12 ft 14 116 42 42 42 45½ Shepherd DR1 Ⓕ 25000 86-10 Bright N Sunny, Real Carri, Lusive 7
6Apr85-7Fon 6f :223 :462 1:121ft 58 114 2hd 22 23 27 Frazier D L7 ⒻAw5300 84-16 GentleGil,Partner'sExpress,RelCrri 7
30Mar85-6Fon 6f :232 :48 1:134m 38 116 42 79½ 619 725¼ Beck D L6 Ⓕ 32000 58-21 Gentle Gil, Lil Happy, Eilsel 9
16Mar85-9Fon 6f :232 :472 1:121ft 27 115 63½ 76¼ 813 819 Frazier D L8 ⒻAw5618 72-16 Racing Jet, Bright NSunny,Tamyon 8
1Mar85-7Fon 4f :224 :47 ft 14 114 2 2½ 2½ 3hd Frazier D L8 ⒻAw5300 90-08 LilHppy,SilingJupon,Prtner'sExprss 8
Jly 30 Cby 3f ft :36 b — Jly 11 Cby 3f ft :372 b — Jly 6 Cby 4f ft :524 b — Jun 30 Cby 4f ft :52 b

Class Counts B. m. 5, by Turn And Count—Turner's Class, by Circle
HAMILTON M **118** Br.—Turner S A (Ky) 1985 10 1 1 1 $6,046
Tr.—Boggess Lee $10,000 1984 3 0 0 0
Own.—Bogges L & FalconFarmsLtd Lifetime 19 2 1 1 $13,696

16Aug85-9Cby	5½f	$:22^3$	$:46^1$	$1:05^4$ft	14	118	$8^{6\frac{1}{4}}$	7^9	6^6	$4^{6\frac{3}{4}}$	LaGrange DL^2	Ⓕ 12500	84-09	Sotetta, La Liz, Porch Cat	8
4Aug85-6Cby	5½f	$:22^2$	$:46^1$	$1:05^3$ft	23	116	$5^{2\frac{1}{4}}$	$7^{4\frac{1}{4}}$	6^7	$5^{6\frac{1}{2}}$	LaGrange DL^6	Ⓕ 14000	85-10	DiboloRinbow,DrlingDorothy,Chtell	8
6Jly85-10Cby	$1\frac{1}{16}$	:48	$1:12^2$	$1:46^1$ft	10	113	$5^{6\frac{1}{2}}$	$5^{4\frac{1}{2}}$	3^4	4^7	LaGrange DL^6	Ⓕ 14000	— —	Mrzi'sHollow,SwtOlShri,FinnwyLdy	6
28Jun85-4Cby	$1\frac{1}{16}$	$:50^1$	$1:15^1$	$1:47^4$ft	4	115	$1^{\frac{1}{2}}$	2^{hd}	$4^{2\frac{1}{2}}$	4^4	LaGrange DL^5	Ⓕ 12500	— —	BnnerStone,CorrelKim,SweetOlShn	5
20Jun85-6FP	6f	$:22^3$	$:46^4$	$1:13^3$ft	*2-3	122	$7^{3\frac{3}{4}}$	5^3	$4^{\frac{3}{4}}$	1^{nk}	Louviere G E^6	Ⓕ 15000	75-23	ClssCounts,AfridtoEntr,DinWithWn	7
7Jun85-8FP	$1\frac{1}{16}$	$:47^2$	1:13	$1:46^4$m	7¾	117	$4^{1\frac{1}{2}}$	$4^{1\frac{1}{4}}$	$3^{1\frac{1}{2}}$	2^2	$LouviereGE^1$	ⒻAw4900	75-20	Dicentra, Class Counts, High Three	9
2Jun85-8FP	6f	$:22^4$	$:46^2$	$1:11^2$gd	10	117	$5^{2\frac{1}{2}}$	$6^{4\frac{1}{4}}$	$5^{4\frac{1}{2}}$	3^4	$LouviereGE^2$	ⒻAw4200	82-17	LdyChlee,JstrsonsHony,ClssCounts	7
25May85-6FP	6f	$:22^4$	$:46^3$	$1:12^1$ft	8	122	$5^{3\frac{1}{2}}$	$5^{5\frac{1}{2}}$	$6^{5\frac{1}{4}}$	$5^{5\frac{1}{4}}$	$LouviereGE^9$	ⒻAw4200	77-23	AlottWmpum,Betty'sMist,LittlBss	10
24Apr85-9TuP	6f	$:21^4$	:44	$1:08^3$ft	8	114	$5^{2\frac{1}{2}}$	$6^{5\frac{1}{4}}$	7^{11}	$7^{12\frac{1}{2}}$	$LaGrngeDL^5$	ⒻAw6000	80-18	Cuervo, DronesFirefly,BlueSmokey	7
13Apr85-8TuP	6f	$:21^2$	$:45^4$	$1:09^4$ft	15	114	10^{11}	10^{10}	$9^{5\frac{1}{4}}$	6^5	$LaGrngeDL^5$	ⒻAw4000	82-14	WllBStnnng,DronsFrfly,FshonFrst	10

● Jly 24 Cby 5f sy $1:00^2$ h

Speed and Pace Notations

Running Styles — Examine each horse's running style and determine whether the horse is a "speed" or front-running type or a stretch-runner. Examine the running lines and fractional times to determine this style. Horses who have shown a lot of speed, mark with a large "S." Horse with some early speed, use a small "s." Horses who show early speed, but tire, mark "S/T." Closers or stretch runners are noted with an arrow, the length of which indicates how far back the horse lays back. Horses that show an even running style are marked with an "E."

In this field, there is a good balance of front-runners, horses that will be just off the pace and some that will be running late.

Pace and Running Time — Next, estimate what the pace will be for the first quarter and half mile. If there are at least two horses with good early speed, estimate the time for the first half mile — based on their most recent efforts. Then, assuming this pace, estimate the final running time. Put these estimates in the margin.

This estimate of pace and final running time will provide you with a rough scenario as to how the race will be run. It will also indicate what running style might be favored. For example, if there are four or five horses with a lot of early speed, they may kill each other off, setting it up for a closer to come on at the end. Conversely, if there is not a lot of speed in the race, a front runner may get an easy lead, control the pace and go wire-to-wire.

In this race, there are a number of horse that will press the pace during the early going, led by the speedball *Sonoita Mley.* Those horses who run "evenly" might also go for the lead. Given this, I guessed the pace to be brisk, no slower than :46 for the first half with a final time of 1:12.

Speed Ratings — Examine recent speed ratings and note horses who are improving race-to-race or who have, on occasion, posted high ratings at this distance. Then estimate each horse's "best possible" time for the distance, assuming that everything goes its way. If the horse's past races were at another track, then consult your Par Times chart (see Appendix). Also note unusually high or low track variants (refer back to "Speed" for more on this).

Weight and Jockey Changes

Note any significant changes in the weight a horse will carry versus his most recent races. Changes of more than five pounds should be noted with a "+" or "-" next to the weight. In this race, both *Irish Lora* (-6 lbs.) and *Smooth and Good* (-9 lbs.) are shedding weight versus their last race. Then note any rider changes versus the horse's last race.

If there is a change in rider, check to see if that rider has ridden the horse in the past and how well the combination did. If the rider change appears to be a plus, e.g. a change to a leading jockey at the meet, mark it accordingly. In this race, *Irish Lora* gets the services of leading rider Mike Smith for the first time. Mark this as a plus.

Other Notes

Lastly, note the following miscellaneous items when and where appropriate.

A. Equipment changes, such as "blinkers on"

B. First-time Lasix users

C. Unfavorable post positions in past races, e.g. the far outside in races at a mile

D. "Trouble" lines in past races

E. Breeding, especially for turf and maiden races.

F. Trainer, noting the leading trainers or a trainer who has a pattern of doing well in this type of race.

Now let's look at the PP's with all these preliminary notations in order to narrow down the field.

7th Canterbury

6 FURLONGS. (1.09⅗) CLAIMING. Purse $6,500. Fillies and mares. 3-year-olds and upward. Weight, 3-year-olds, 115 lbs.; older, 120 lbs. Non-winners of a race since July 15 allowed 2 lbs.; since June 15, 4 lbs. May 15, 6 lbs. Claiming price $10,000; if for $9,000 allowed 2 lbs. (Races when entered for $8,000 or less not considered.)

Coupled—Goodnight My Love and Irish Lora.

Smooth N' Good — -9
CRAIG K — 1075
Own.—Huntington K
Dk. b. or br. f. 4, by Smooth Dancer—Alien Flower, by Good Turn
Br.—Cox & Jarvis (La)
Tr.—Huntington Dougie — $9,000
Lifetime 30 6 5 5 $32,564
1985 11 2 3 2 $12,216
1984 18 4 1 3 $19,448
Turf 1 0 0 1 $770

8Aug85-10Cby 1 :48² 1:13² 1:39¹ft 6¾ 116 3² 43½ 55½ 79¼ Melancon G6 c6250 76-11 Adobe Chief, SpeedSpy,TonicMajor 9
3Aug85-10Cby 1 1/16 :48³ 1:13⁴ 1:47⁴ft *2¾ 114 21½ 2½ 1hd 1³ LaGrange D L8 Ⓕ 6250 77-10 SmoothN'Gd,EnglshWzrd,Dwnsflng 8
6Jly85-1Cby 1 1/16 :47⁴ 1:12⁴ 1:46 ft *1 1095 4² 3¹ 2hd 11½ Bass S H7 Ⓕ c5000 — — SmoothN'Gd,MystclSng,SlvrStrshn 7
2Jly85-9Cby 1 :48⁴ 1:13 1:39 ft 7¾ 1075 3nk 3nk 3nk 3¾ Bass S H1 Ⓕ 7500 — — Snderell,SheWillTll,SmoothN'Good 8
1Jun85-3CD 1 :46³ 1:11³ 1:38²ft 2½e 116 6⁶ 45½ 46½ 48 Montoya D5 Ⓕ 7500 69-18 TwinHerts,JestersJoy,TrojnGoddss 9
5May85-5CD 6f :21² :45¹ 1:11⁴ft 3¾e 116 7¹⁵ 79¼ 78¾ 66¼ Melancon G4 Ⓕ 10000 80-14 Countess Suzie, PorchCat,IronGold 7
3May85-1CD 1 :47³ 1:14⁴ 1:41 ft *8-5 116 72¾ 4¾ 3³ 3³ Fox W I Jr6 Ⓕ c7500 61-14 She Will Tell, Joby, SmoothN'Good 8
9Mar85-11FG 1 1/16 :47¹ 1:13 1:47⁴ft *2 112 8¹⁰ 8¹¹ 3⁴ 2hd Fox W I Jr4 Ⓕ 8500 73-20 JestersJoy,SmoothN'Good,TiffyK. 10
8Mar85-7FG 6f :22¹ :46² 1:12²ft *7-5 116 10¹³ 8¹⁴ 66¼ 46¼ RomeroRP4 ⒻⓈ 12500 77-19 ClrCrkCt,Mg'sBlossm,HnrAndGlry 10
5Feb85-8FG 6f :22³ :47¹ 1:13¹ft 16 114 7⁹ 8¹³ 5⁶ 2hd Faul J H1 ⒻⓈ 15000 79-21 Dr.PrttyFst,SmothN'Gd,LdyL.AndL. 9
15Feb85—Steadied to avoid tiring horse
Aug 21 Cby 3f ft :36³ b

Goodnight My Love — +6
KAENEL J L — 115
Own.—Shamie E
Ch. f. 3, by China Silk—Upcuma, by Crozier
Br.—Shamie E (Cal)
Tr.—Pappalardo John W — $10,000
Lifetime 10 1 0 2 $8,250
1985 10 1 0 2 $8,250
1984 0 M 0 0

8Aug85-6Cby 1 70 :48¹ 1:12³ 1:45²ft 7 1095 7¹³ 7¹² 5⁷ 5⁵ Bass S H3 Ⓕ 20000 76-16 QutThVocs,JstBrlyAbl,StrdstMlody 7
1Aug85-5Cby 1 :47³ 1:14³ 1:41 ft *9-5 1095 8¹⁰ 4³ 12½ 1⁵ Bass S H7 ⒻM16000 76-12 GoodnghtMyLv,ChthmHgh,KnSmk 8
8Jly85-4Cby 1 70 :47⁴ 1:12⁴ 1:44²ft 11 113 9¹¹ 6¹¹ 49½ 4¹⁰ Hamilton M5 ⒻMdn — — Opulence,VenturetteMiss,Bbu'sKey 9
0Jun85-7Cby 6f :24 :47² 1:13¹ft 8¼ 115 6¹² 6¹¹ 67¾ 46½ Hamilton M3 ⒻMdn — — FeelsLikeLove,MeCry,DineWithDev 6
7Jun85-8Hol 1⅛ :48¹ 1:12⁴ 1:50²ft 19 109 7¹¹ 7¹⁰ 7¹¹ 713¼ Hawley S4 Ⓕ 12500 84-06 Cecile,DuchessPetrone,MerryHdlinr 8
5May85-2Hol 1 :46 1:11 1:36⁴ft 28 113 12¹⁷ 10¹⁹ 10¹⁹ 718¾ PedrozaMA1 ⒻM28000 70-08 Don A Top, Grenalda, LuckySilver 12
1Apr85-3SA 1 1/16 :46¹ 1:11¹ 1:45²ft 7 114 10¹¹ 8¹⁴ 8¹² 3⁶ Hawley S9 ⒻM28000 68-18 TAtTn,RoylCurvs,GoodnghtMyLov 12
5Apr85-2SA 1 :46² 1:11³ 1:38 ft 20 1105 96½ 8¹² 8⁸ 6⁶ DomngzRE7 ⒻM45000 72-14 ‡PussyCat,SenstionlDrm,KeepDting 9
2Mar85-3SA 1 1/16 :46 1:11² 1:45 ft 6 1095 9¹⁷ 10¹² 47½ 3⁶ DomngzRE2 ⒻM28000 70-17 RcklssMss,DonATop,GdnghtMyLv 12
22Mar85—Very wide into stretch, bumped at 1/8
2Feb85-3SA 6½f :21³ :44³ 1:18 ft 20 1105 10¹⁹ 10²⁴ 9¹⁶ 75½ DmngzRL5 ⒻⓈM35000 74-18 Sntequos,SusnnRose,KpStorming 10
Jly 14 Cby 6f ft 1:15 b **Jly 8 Cby 5f ft 1:03 b**

Sonoita Mley S/T
WARHOL V L **114**
Own.—Williamson R M

Ch. m. 6, by Yorkville—Tattling, by Commanding II
Br.—Short D (Cal)
Tr.—Crowe Marcel J $10,000
Lifetime 56 14 7 6 $52,996

1985	8	0	1	0	$1
1984	16	6	2	3	$24
Turf	5	1	0	0	$3

30 days

16Aug85-9Cby	5½f	:22³	:46¹	1:05⁴ft	6¾	114	1½	2hd	4³	6⁶¾	Warhol V L³	Ⓕ 12500	84-09	Sotetta, La Liz, Porch Cat
13Jly85-8NP	6f	:22²	:46¹	1:12¹gd	12	108⁵	1³	1²	2nk	6⁵¼	Jumpsen N⁷	Ⓕ 20000	83-22	LittlePrincess,EstrLit,Nlee'sFshic
30Jun85-7NP	6½f	:23	:46⁴	1:18⁴ft	4½	115	4³¼	4³½	6⁷	6²¹	Turcotte Y A⁷	Ⓕ 16000	67-14	TirelssLdy,OwlwoodLn,FigonroLs
30Jun85—Reared st.														
14Jun85-7NP	6f	:22⁴	:46⁴	1:12⁴m	3½	115	1²	1⁴	1nk	5⁹½	Levine C³	Ⓕ 20000	75-25	Drwin'sDrlin,Nl'sFshon,OwlwoodL
24May85-9NP	6f	:22⁴	:46³	1:13⁴sy	5½	115	3¹	3³	5¹⁰	6²⁵¼	Levine C⁶	ⒻAw6800	55-26	BrightBouquet,Snowder,RinbowS
11May85-9StP	6f	:22¹	:45²	1:10⁴ft	11	114	1³	1³	1nk	6⁴¾	Levine C⁶	ⒻLilac	89-14	Merrydown,RinbowSekr,HstyMor
1May85-9StP	6f	:22²	:45³	1:11¹ft	*3-2	107⁵	1¹	1²	2nk	6⁵½	Jumpsen N⁷	ⒻAw6530	85-16	PlenumBee,RinbowSkr,SndHopp
20Apr85-9StP	6f	:23	:47²	1:15³sy	*9-5	116	1³	1⁵	1³	2hd	TurcotteYA⁷	ⒻAw6800	69-29	RinbowSeekr,SonoitMly,Nl'sFshi
3Nov84-8StP	6f	:22⁴	:46	1:11⁴ft	*2½	113⁵	1¹½	1²¼	1²¼	1¹½	Mayo K⁴	Ⓕ 16000	88-15	SonoitMley,PlenumBee,Nle'sFshi
21Oct84-8StP	6f	:22²	:46	1:11³ft	8¼	116	1¹	1²¼	1⁴	1³	Ferris A S⁶	Ⓕ 16000	89-12	SonoitMley,Geno'sAngle,Plenum

6 months ?

Aug 14 Cby 3f ft :38 b

lost ground

Arctic Angel S →
BASS S H **115⁵**
Own.—Lloyd Lucie

Ch. f. 4, by Another Double—Miss Bonmire, by Mountain Fire
Br.—Alexander Lucie D (Ky)
Tr.—Van Berg Jack C $10,000
Lifetime 12 2 4 1 $12,638

1985	12	2	4	1	$12
1984	0	M	0	0	

22 days ?

9 races in 14 wks.

31Jly85-6Cby	6f	:22³	:46²	1:11³ft	*8-5	115⁵	5³	4³½	2½	2²¼	Bass S H⁶	Ⓕ 10000	88-14	SheWillTll,ArcticAngl,GimmiATip
18Jly85-7Cby	5½f	:22³	:47	1:06³ft	2½	110⁵	5⁸	4⁸	2²½	1²	Bass S H²	Ⓕ 12500	— —	Arctic Angel, Texoma, Trulinka
29Jun85-7Cby	5½f	:23²	:47¹	1:06 ft	8-5	115	5⁴	5³½	5⁵½	5⁵½	HansenRD⁴	ⒻAw11000	— —	FinalDancer,Adptble,ApricotCren
18Jun85-9CD	6f	:21³	:46¹	1:12³ft	*2-3	115⁵	5⁴	3¹½	1²	1⁴	Bass S H⁴	ⒻM10000	82-16	Arctic Angel, Hai Sun,VirtualLad
4Jun85-2CD	6½f	:23²	:47³	1:20⁴gd	3	117⁵	3²½	3⁴	2³½	2³	Bass S H⁸	ⒻM10000	73-23	BoldndFlsh,ArctcAngl,BrdwyKtty
25May85-3CD	6f	:22	:46¹	1:12²ft	2	117⁵	3³½	2⁴	2³	2²	Bass S H¹	ⒻM10000	81-14	Dollmaker,ArcticAngel,WorkNMy
17May85-1CD	6f	:21²	:45³	1:12¹gd	5	119	5⁴½	7⁸½	8¹¹	8¹²	Melancon L⁹	ⒻM15000	72-14	Livittothelimit,GreyAllure,RlFmi
8May85-2CD	6f	:22¹	:46²	1:11⁴ft	3½	122	4³½	3⁴½	3⁶	2⁶	Melancon L⁵	ⒻM10000	80-16	Lon'sDlght,ArctcAngl,Nncy'sBlss
14Apr85-2FG	5½f	:23	:47²	1:06⁴ft	7	121	3¹½	5⁴¾	4⁵½	3⁵½	Ardoin R¹	ⒻMdn	79-21	LilliBeth,BestThoughts,ArcticAn
22Mar85-1FG	6f	:22⁴	:47¹	1:12⁴ft	6½	115	7³¼	8⁵¾	11¹³	11¹⁷¼	Melancon G⁸	M15000	64-20	Cakewalk,LavishLady,OuiskiBayc

● Jly 13 Cby 4f ft :47¹ h

Irish Lora −6
+ **SMITH M E** **109**
Own.—Steinmann H

Dk. b. or br. f. 3, by The Irish Lord—Nori O, by McTavish
Br.—Steinmann H (Cal)
Tr.—Pappalardo John W $10,000
Lifetime 12 1 0 1 $13,115

1985	12	1	0	1	$13
1984	0	M	0	0	

11Aug85-1Cby	6f	:22¹	:45²	1:12¹ft	15	115	4²½	4⁴	4³½	5¹¾	Kaenel J L³	Ⓕ 12500	85-12	Buckpasser'sGl,TruLdyRed,Trulin
11Jly85-8Hol	1	:45³	1:10¹	1:36²ft	19	116	6¹⁰	6¹⁶	6¹⁷	6¹⁸½	Estrada J Jr³	Ⓕ 25000	72-07	Don A Top,VitalScore,RockCany
19Jun85-6Hol	6f	:22¹	:45³	1:11¹ft	80	115	9¹²	7¹¹	6⁴¾	5³¾	Estrada J Jr¹¹	Ⓕ 25000	87-05	‡Wlker'sLdy,FireMissLedr,AnniL
22May85-4Hol	6f	:22²	:45⁴	1:10⁴ft	37	118	9⁶½	7⁷½	7⁵½	7⁷	Meza R Q⁴	Ⓕ 25000	86-08	TammyLu,FireMissLeder,AnnieL
25Apr85-7Hol	1	:45¹	1:10⁴	1:37 ft	24	115	8⁸¾	8⁸½	8¹²	8¹⁷½	Sibille R²	Ⓕ 25000	70-09	Iva'sRich,Clearway,FireMissLede
18Apr85-7SA	6½f	:21³	:45	1:16⁴ft	60	118	7⁶½	6⁶½	5⁹	3¹⁰	Estrada J Jr⁶	Ⓕ 32000	76-16	Proud Doll, Ritzy Chick, IrishLor
+ 5Apr85-1SA	6f	:21⁴	:45¹	1:10²ft	11	120	5⁶½	9¹¹	9⁹½	8⁸¼	Pincay L Jr¹¹	Ⓕ 25000	78-14	QuitKid,ProudDoll,Perfction'sGi
5Apr85—Lugged out, wide final 3/8														
28Mar85-3SA	6½f	:22	:46²	1:21⁴sl	4½	117	6³½	5²½	3½	1²	HawleyS¹²	ⒻⓈM32000	61-31	IrishLora,KimStep,MentlBnkMgi
22Feb85-3SA	6½f	:21³	:44³	1:18 ft	5e	115	7¹⁰	7¹²	7¹²	6⁵	Hawley S⁸	ⒻⓈM35000	75-18	Sntequos,SusnnRose,KpStormin
6Feb85-4SA	1$\frac{1}{16}$	:46²	1:11²	1:44⁴ft	8	117	6¹²	7¹⁶	10²⁶	10²⁴	McHrguDG⁶	ⒻM32000	53-15	StksTWn,SnstnlDrm,MntlBnkMg
6Feb85—Lugged out														

Partner's Express E
LAGRANGE D L **114**
Own.—Axline C

Dk. b. or br. f. 4, by Partner's Hope—Miss Snow Nose, by Nashua Chip
Br.—Axline W & C (Kan)
Tr.—Dickey George $10,000
Lifetime 14 1 3 1 $3,748

1985	10	0	1	1	$
1984	4	1	2	0	$

?

31Jly85-6Cby	6f	:22³	:46²	1:11³ft	40	114	9⁶¾	9⁶¾	7⁴½	8¹²½	Hoverson C²	Ⓕ 10000	78-14	SheWillTll,ArcticAngl,GimmiATi
21Jly85-3Cby	6f	:22¹	:46	1:11³ft	27	116	6⁴¾	6⁴½	7⁷½	7¹⁰	Baze D⁷	Ⓕ 16000	— —	DrlingDorothy,DiboloRinbow,St.
12Jly85-7Cby	6½f	:23³	:46⁴	1:18 ft	23	116	7⁴½	7⁷	6⁷	5⁹¾	Baze D³	Ⓕ 25000	— —	JtullhMid,AxetheOdds,BettieBG
2Jun85-5Aks	6f	:22⁴	:46¹	1:12¹ft	31	116	6⁵	7⁸	9⁸½	9¹¹	Frazier DL¹	ⒻAw14400	65-27	Chocolate Kisses, Real Carri, Po
19May85-10Ato	6f	:23¹	:46⁴	1:13³ft	2½	118	7⁶	7¹¹	6²¾	6⁵¾	JonsRV³	ⒻF Brown H	83-21	SchellyBo,SweetDr.,Stcey'sSidk
13Apr85-5Fon	6f	:22³	:47	1:12 ft	14	116	4²	4²	4²	4⁵½	Shepherd DR¹	Ⓕ 25000	86-10	Bright N Sunny, Real Carri, Lus
6Apr85-7Fon	6f	:22³	:46²	1:12¹ft	58	114	2hd	2²	2³	2⁷	Frazier D L⁷	ⒻAw5300	84-16	GentleGil,Partner'sExpress,RelC
30Mar85-6Fon	6f	:23²	:48	1:13⁴m	38	116	4²	7⁹½	6¹⁹	7²⁵½	Beck D L⁶	Ⓕ 32000	58-21	Gentle Gil, Lil Happy, Eilsel
16Mar85-9Fon	6f	:23²	:47²	1:12¹ft	27	115	6³½	7⁶½	8¹³	8¹⁹	Frazier D L⁸	ⒻAw5618	72-16	Racing Jet, Bright NSunny,Tam
1Mar85-7Fon	4f		:22⁴	:47 ft	14	114	2	2½	2½	3hd	Frazier D L⁸	ⒻAw5300	90-08	LilHppy,SilingJupon,Prtner'sExp

Jly 30 Cby 3f ft :36 b Jly 11 Cby 3f ft :37² b Jly 6 Cby 4f ft :52⁴ b Jun 30 Cby 4f ft :52 b

Class Counts
HAMILTON M **118**
Own.—Bogges L & FalconFarmsLtd

B. m. 5, by Turn And Count—Turner's Class, by Circle
Br.—Turner S A (Ky)
Tr.—Boggess Lee **$10,000**
Lifetime 19 2 1 1 $13,696

1985	10 1 1 1	$6,046
1984	3 0 0 0	

16Aug85-9Cby	$5\frac12$f	$:22^3$	$:46^1$	$1:05^4$ft	14	118	$8^{6\frac14}$	7^9	6^6	$4^{6\frac34}$	LaGrange DL^2	Ⓕ 12500	84-09	Sotetta, La Liz, Porch Cat	8
4Aug85-6Cby	$5\frac12$f	$:22^2$	$:46^1$	$1:05^3$ft	23	116	$5^{2\frac14}$	$7^{4\frac14}$	6^7	$5^{6\frac12}$	LaGrange DL^6	Ⓕ 14000	85-10	DiboloRinbow,DrlingDorothy,Chtell	8
6Jly85-10Cby	$1\frac1{16}$	:48	$1:12^2$	$1:46^1$ft	10	113	$5^{6\frac12}$	$5^{4\frac12}$	3^4	4^7	LaGrange DL^6	Ⓕ 14000	— —	Mrzi'sHollow,SwtOlShri,FinnwyLdy	6
28Jun85-4Cby	$1\frac1{16}$	$:50^1$	$1:15^1$	$1:47^4$ft	4	115	$1^{\frac12}$	2^{hd}	$4^{2\frac12}$	4^4	LaGrange DL^5	Ⓕ 12500	— —	BnnerStone,CorrelKim,SweetOlShi	5
20Jun85-6FP	6f	$:22^3$	$:46^4$	$1:13^3$ft	*2-3	122	$7^{3\frac34}$	5^3	$4^{\frac34}$	1^{nk}	Louviere G E^6	Ⓕ 15000	75-23	ClssCounts,AfridtoEntr,DinWithWn	7
7Jun85-8FP	$1\frac1{16}$	$:47^2$	1:13	$1:46^4$m	$7\frac34$	117	$4^{1\frac12}$	$4^{1\frac14}$	$3^{1\frac12}$	2^2	LouviereGE^1	ⒻAw4900	75-20	Dicentra, Class Counts, High Three	9
2Jun85-8FP	6f	$:22^4$	$:46^2$	$1:11^2$gd	10	117	$5^{2\frac12}$	$6^{4\frac14}$	$5^{4\frac12}$	3^4	LouviereGE^2	ⒻAw4200	82-17	LdyChlee,JstrsonsHony,ClssCounts	7
25May85-6FP	6f	$:22^4$	$:46^3$	$1:12^1$ft	8	122	$5^{3\frac12}$	$5^{5\frac12}$	$6^{5\frac14}$	$5^{5\frac14}$	LouviereGE^9	ⒻAw4200	77-23	AlottWmpum,Betty'sMist,LittlBss	10
24Apr85-9TuP	6f	$:21^4$	:44	$1:08^3$ft	8	114	$5^{2\frac12}$	$6^{5\frac14}$	7^{11}	$7^{12\frac12}$	LaGrngeDL^5	ⒻAw6000	80-18	Cuervo, DronesFirefly,BlueSmokey	7
13Apr85-8TuP	6f	$:21^2$	$:45^4$	$1:09^4$ft	15	114	10^{11}	10^{10}	$9^{5\frac14}$	6^5	LaGrngeDL^5	ⒻAw4000	82-14	WllBStnnng,DronsFrfly,FshonFrst	10

●Jly 24 Cby 5f sy $1:00^2$ h

Simple Eliminations

At this point, you can make some simple eliminations. Quickly examine the most recent races of the top two choices according to the DRF's or the local newspaper handicappers. Then evaluate the remaining entrants and eliminate those horses that are obviously outclassed, in poor form or running the wrong distance. There are usually two to four horses that can be eliminated without much analysis. Draw an oblique line through the names of these non-contenders. In this race, *Arctic Angel* is picked on top, with some support for *Smooth and Good, Irish Lora* and *Class Counts.*

At this point I would eliminate the following horses from further consideration ...

Goodnight My Love — This filly just broke her maiden. Moreover, she's entered at the wrong distance. She is a router, not a sprinter. However, she is part of an entry (with *Irish Lora*) and was probably entered by her trainer to make the race "fill," i.e. get the minimum number of entrants. If the races does fill, she'll probably be scratched. (In fact, that is exactly what happened.)

Sonoita Mley — This filly was out of action for six months from November 1984 through April 1985. Prior to that, she had been running well in the $16,000 range and had good earnings for 1984 before the turn out. The length of the turn out coupled with a sharp drop in price and bad form since April indicates she suffered an injury back in November. She hasn't shown a thing as her connections continue to drop her down in price. Current form is bad. She's only beaten a total of four horses in her last five races. Moreover, she's "short," i.e. she need a taxi to carry her speed beyond a half mile. All she is capable of doing in this race is ensuring a fast pace. And since there is enough speed in the race, she has no chance to "steal" the race by getting a big, uncontested lead.

Partner's Express — "Express" is a real misnomer here. This filly has shown little. She was able to get on the board when running at Fonner Park (Fon) — but that track is not in this league. In her last race, she ran against a comparable field, went off at 40-1 and ran like it. Definitely outclassed again today.

Running Lines & Charts

By going through the above process, you will progressively narrow down the field to a manageable number of contenders — hopefully, five or less. The final step in marking the PP's involves analyzing the running lines of past races.

Pay particular attention to each horse's last two or three races. Underline good efforts. Current form is the best indicator of what to expect today. Races run two or three months ago may only be "fond memories. Then look for and note unusual races. For example, a horse may be near the lead after the first quarter mile, then drop back to the rear after a half mile then come on again at the finish. A running line such as this might indicate that the horse may have encountered traffic problems in the far turn. Check the Results Chart for that race to see if the horse encountered trouble in the race. In fact, you should check the most recent charts on all your top choices. The charts will provide you with considerably more data then the running lines — including the conditions, additional fractional times, equipment, the start, and — importantly — the comments section.

When studying the running lines, look for strong "moves" a horse may have made during a recent race. These are indicated by significant gains in terms of lengths-behind-the-leader from call to call, especially between the first and second call. Horses that can improve their position by four + lengths in the turn should be noted. Also note horses making a late move in the stretch and, conversely, horses that lose ground in the stretch — especially winners of their last race that "just hung on." These horses might be tailing off in terms of form. Lastly, mark horses that have been engaged in "wars" in their most recent race or two. Horses who are pressed or forced to run all out, head-to-head throughout most of a race may come up short in their next effort if not freshened.

Selecting the Probable Winner

In this race, we are down to four possibles. After evaluating their running lines, I would eliminate *Class Counts* because of dull current form/speed. She might have been competitive at Fairmount Park (FP), but not here.

Class Counts E — 118 — B. m. 5, by Turn And Count—Turner's Class, by Circle
HAMILTON M — Br.—Turner S A (Ky) — 1985 10 1 1 1 $6,046
Tr.—Boggess Lee — $10,000 — 1984 3 0 0 0
Own.—Bogges L & FalconFarmsLtd — Lifetime 19 2 1 1 $13,696

16Aug85-9Cby	5½f	:22³	:46¹	1:05⁴ft	14	118	8⁶¼	7⁹	6⁶	4⁶¾	LaGrange DL²	Ⓕ 12500	84-09	Sotetta, La Liz, Porch Cat		8
4Aug85-6Cby	5½f	:22²	:46¹	1:05³ft	23	116	5²¼	7⁴¼	6⁷	5⁶½	LaGrange DL⁶	Ⓕ 14000	85-10	DiboloRinbow,DrlingDorothy,Chtell		8
6Jly85-10Cby	1 1/16	:48	1:12²	1:46¹ft	10	113	5⁶½	5⁴½	3⁴	4⁷	LaGrange DL⁶	Ⓕ 14000	— —	Mrzi'sHollow,SwtOlShri,FinnwyLdy		6
28Jun85-4Cby	1 1/16	:50¹	1:15¹	1:47⁴ft	4	115	1½	2hd	4²½	4⁴	LaGrange DL⁵	Ⓕ 12500	— —	BnnerStone,CorrelKim,SweetOlShri		5
20Jun85-6FP	6f	:22³	:46⁴	1:13³ft	*2-3	122	7³¾	5³	4¾	1nk	Louviere G E⁶	Ⓕ 15000	75-23	ClssCounts,AfridtoEntr,DinWithWn		7
7Jun85-8FP	1 1/16	:47²	1:13	1:48⁴m	7¾	117	4¹½	4¹¼	3¹½	2²	LouviereGE¹	ⒻAw4900	75-20	Dicentra, Class Counts, High Three		9
2Jun85-8FP	6f	:22⁴	:46²	1:11²gd	10	117	5²½	6⁴¼	5⁴½	3⁴	LouviereGE²	ⒻAw4200	82-17	LdyChlee,JstrsonsHony,ClssCounts		7
25May85-6FP	6f	:22⁴	:46³	1:12¹ft	8	122	5³½	5⁵½	6⁵¼	5⁵¼	LouviereGE⁹	ⒻAw4200	77-23	AlottWmpum,Betty'sMist,LittlBss		10
24Apr85-9TuP	6f	:21⁴	:44	1:08³ft	8	114	5²½	6⁵¼	7¹¹	7¹²½	LaGrngeDL⁵	ⒻAw6000	80-18	Cuervo, DronesFirefly,BlueSmokey		7
13Apr85-8TuP	6f	:21²	:45⁴	1:09⁴ft	15	114	10¹¹	10¹⁰	9⁵¼	6⁵	LaGrngeDL⁵	ⒻAw4000	82-14	WllBStnnng,DronsFrfly,FshonFrst		10

● Jly 24 Cby 5f sy 1:00² h

The favorite — *Arctic Angel* — won two races ago. But that race was only 5 1/2 furlongs and was run rather slowly (:47 for the half and a final time of 1:063). In her last race, she dropped a notch in price, went up to six furlongs and finished second. Note that she was second in the stretch by a half, yet finished second by two and a half — tiring and losing ground in the stretch. This filly is trending downwards on her "form curve" after compressing so many races into such a short period. She has been absent from competition for 22 days (without a workout). I think this filly needs a longer break or "freshener" before she'll win again at this level.

Arctic Angel
BASS S H 1155
Own.—Lloyd Lucie

Ch. f. 4, by Another Double—Miss Bonmire, by Mountain Fire
Br.—Alexander Lucie D (Ky) 1985 12 2 4 1 $12,638
Tr.—Van Berg Jack C $10,000 1984 0 M 0 0
Lifetime 12 2 4 1 $12,638

31Jly85-6Cby	6f	:223	:462	1:113ft	*8-5	1155	53	43½	2½	22¼	Bass S H6	Ⓕ 10000	88-14	SheWillTll,ArcticAngl,GimmiATip	10
18Jly85-7Cby	5½f	:223	:47	1:063ft	2½	1105	58	48	22½	12	Bass S H2	Ⓕ 12500	— —	Arctic Angel, Texoma, Trulinka	7
29Jun85-7Cby	5½f	:232	:471	1:06 ft	8-5	115	54	53¼	55½	55½	HansenRD4	ⒻAw11000	— —	FinalDancer,Adptble,ApricotCreme	5
18Jun85-9CD	6f	:213	:461	1:123ft	*2-3	1155	54	31½	12	14	Bass S H4	ⒻM10000	82-16	Arctic Angel, Hai Sun,VirtualLady	11
4Jun85-2CD	6½f	:232	:473	1:204gd	3	1175	32½	34	23½	23	Bass S H8	ⒻM10000	73-23	BoldndFlsh,ArctcAngl,BrdwyKtty	11
25May85-3CD	6f	:22	:461	1:122ft	2	1175	33½	24	23	22	Bass S H1	ⒻM10000	81-14	Dollmaker,ArcticAngel,WorkNMyrn	8
17May85-1CD	6f	:212	:453	1:121gd	5	119	54½	78¼	811	812	Melancon L9	ⒻM15000	72-14	Livittothelimit,GreyAllure,RIFmin	11
8May85-2CD	6f	:221	:462	1:114ft	3¼	122	43½	34½	36	26	Melancon L5	ⒻM10000	80-16	Lon'sDlght,ArctcAngl,Nncy'sBlssng	7
14Apr85-2FG	5½f	:23	:472	1:064ft	7	121	31½	54¾	45½	35¼	Ardoin R1	ⒻMdn	79-21	LilliBeth,BestThoughts,ArcticAngl	11
22Mar85-1FG	6f	:224	:471	1:124ft	6½	115	73¼	85¾	1113	1117¼	Melancon G8	M15000	64-20	Cakewalk,LavishLady,OuiskiBayou	12

●Jly 13 Cby 4f ft :471 h

Smooth N' Good has good current form, albeit at middle distance sprints. She has the ability to come from off the pace and was able to do so at today's distance of six furlongs (15Feb85). Lastly, she is in light (107 lbs.) On the negative side, she's taking a sharp rise in price/class, has an apprentice rider who has only won one race in her brief career, and falls a little short in terms of speed. 1:12 might not be in her grasp — but still a possibility coming from off the pace if the choice falters.

Smooth N' Good
CRAIG K 1075
Own.—Huntington K

Dk. b. or br. f. 4, by Smooth Dancer—Alien Flower, by Good Turn
Br.—Cox & Jarvis (La) 1985 11 2 3 2 $12,216
Tr.—Huntington Dougie $9,000 1984 18 4 1 3 $19,448
Lifetime 30 6 5 5 $32,564 Turf 1 0 0 1 $770

18Aug85-10Cby	1	:482	1:132	1:391ft	6¾	116	32	43½	55½	79¼	Melancon G6	c6250	76-11	Adobe Chief, SpeedSpy,TonicMajor	9
3Aug85-10Cby	1 1/16	:483	1:134	1:474ft	*2¾	114	21½	2½	1hd	13	LaGrange D L8	Ⓕ 6250	77-10	SmoothN'Gd,EnglshWzrd,Dwnsflng	8
26Jly85-1Cby	1 1/16	:474	1:124	1:46 ft	*1	1095	42	31	2hd	11½	Bass S H7	Ⓕ c5000	— —	SmoothN'Gd,MystclSng,SlvrStrshn	7
12Jly85-9Cby	1	:484	1:13	1:39 ft	7¾	1075	3nk	3nk	3nk	3¾	Bass S H1	Ⓕ 7500	— —	Snderell,SheWillTll,SmoothN'Good	8
11Jun85-3CD	1	:463	1:113	1:382ft	2½e	116	66	45½	46½	48	Montoya D5	Ⓕ 7500	69-18	TwinHerts,JestersJoy,TrojnGoddss	9
15May85-5CD	6f	:212	:451	1:114ft	3¾e	116	715	79¼	78¾	66¼	Melancon G4	Ⓕ 10000	80-14	Countess Suzie, PorchCat,IronGold	7
3May85-1CD	1	:473	1:144	1:41 ft	*8-5	116	72¾	4¾	33	33	Fox W I Jr6	Ⓕ c7500	61-14	She Will Tell, Joby, SmoothN'Good	8
29Mar85-11FG	1 1/16	:471	1:13	1:474ft	*2	112	810	811	34	2hd	Fox W I Jr4	Ⓕ 8500	73-20	JestersJoy,SmoothN'Good,TiffyK.	10
8Mar85-7FG	6f	:221	:462	1:122ft	*7-5	116	1013	814	66¼	46¼	RomeroRP4	ⒻS 12500	77-19	ClrCrkCt,Mg'sBlossm,HnrAndGlry	10
15Feb85-8FG	6f	:223	:471	1:131ft	16	114	79	813	56	2hd	Faul J H1	ⒻS 15000	79-21	Dr.PrttyFst,SmothN'Gd,LdyL.AndL.	9

15Feb85—Steadied to avoid tiring horse
Aug 21 Cby 3f ft :363 b

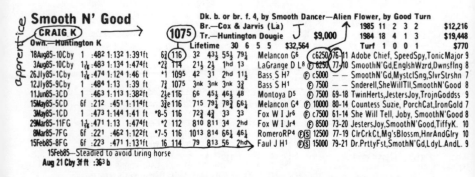

That leaves us with *Irish Lora.* On the plus side, the fast pace will not be a problem. She has good speed and can come from just off the pace or be on the lead. In terms of class, she is dropping down after having been second, beaten by only one and three quarters lengths by a tough filly (*Buckpasser's Gal*). And in that race, she made a decent move in the stretch. Prior to that she was running at Santa Anita and Hollywood — two high class strips. Her last race was the first over the track, and horses generally need "a trip over the track" before scoring. The trainer must feel she is ready because he entered two horses to make the race "go." And lastly, she gets a new rider today — Mike Smith — leading jockey at the meeting.

Irish Lora S → −6 **109** **Dk. b. or br. f. 3, by The Irish Lord—Nori O, by McTavish**
SMITH M E **Br.—Steinmann H (Cal)** **1985 12 1 0 1 $13,115**
Own.—Steinmann H **Tr.—Pappalardo John W** **$10,000** **1984 0 M 0 0**
Lifetime 12 1 0 1 $13,115

11Aug85-1Cby	6f	$:22^1$	$:45^2$	$1:12^1$ft	15	115	$4^{2\frac14}$	4^4	$4^{3\frac12}$	$5^{1\frac34}$	Kaenel J L[3]	Ⓕ 12500	85-12	Buckpasser'sGl,TruLdyRed,Trulink	9
11Jly85-3Hol	1	$:45^3$	$1:10^1$	$1:36^2$ft	19	116	6^{10}	6^{16}	6^{17}	$6^{18\frac12}$	Estrada J Jr[3]	Ⓕ 25000	72-07	Don A Top,VitalScore,RockCanyon	6
19Jun85-6Hol	6f	$:22^1$	$:45^3$	$1:11^1$ft	80	115	9^{12}	7^{11}	$6^{4\frac34}$	$5^{3\frac34}$	Estrada J Jr[11]	Ⓕ 25000	87-05	‡Wlker'sLdy,FireMissLedr,AnniLis	11
22May85-4Hol	6f	$:22^2$	$:45^4$	$1:10^4$ft	37	118	$9^{6\frac14}$	$7^{7\frac12}$	$7^{5\frac14}$	7^7	Meza R Q[4]	Ⓕ 25000	86-08	TammyLu,FireMissLeder,AnnieLis	11
25Apr85-7Hol	1	$:45^1$	$1:10^4$	1:37 ft	24	115	$8^{8\frac34}$	$8^{8\frac14}$	8^{12}	$8^{17\frac12}$	Sibille R[2]	Ⓕ 25000	70-09	Iva'sRich,Clearway,FireMissLeder	10
18Apr85-7SA	6½f	$:21^3$	:45	$1:16^4$ft	60	118	$7^{6\frac14}$	$6^{6\frac12}$	5^9	3^{10}	Estrada J Jr[6]	Ⓕ 32000	76-16	Proud Doll, Ritzy Chick, IrishLora	11
5Apr85-1SA	6f	$:21^4$	$:45^1$	$1:10^2$ft	11	120	$5^{6\frac12}$	9^{11}	$9^{9\frac14}$	$8^{8\frac14}$	Pincay L Jr[11]	Ⓕ 25000	78-14	QuitKid,ProudDoll,Perfction'sGift	12
5Apr85—Lugged out, wide final 3/8															
28Mar85-3SA	6½f	:22	$:46^2$	$1:21^4$sl	4¼	117	$6^{3\frac12}$	$5^{2\frac12}$	$3^{\frac12}$	1^2	HawleyS[12]	ⒻⓈM32000	61-31	IrishLora,KimStep,MentlBnkMgic	12
22Feb85-3SA	6½f	$:21^3$	$:44^3$	1:18 ft	5e	115	7^{10}	7^{12}	7^{12}	6^5	Hawley S[8]	ⒻⓈM35000	75-18	Sntequos,SusnnRose,KpStorming	10
6Feb85-4SA	1 1/16	$:46^2$	$1:11^2$	$1:44^4$ft	8	117	6^{12}	7^{16}	10^{26}	10^{24}	McHrguDG[6]	ⒻM32000	53-15	StksTWn,SnstnlDrm,MntlBnkMgc	11
6Feb85—Lugged out															

Irish Lora got my nod and went to post at odds of 5-2, a nifty price in a small field. Obviously, I wouldn't have dragged you through this whole exercise if Irish Lora didn't romp. Actually, every horse in the race ran "true to form."

SEVENTH RACE Canterbury AUGUST 23, 1985 — **6 FURLONGS. (1.09⅗) CLAIMING. Purse $6,500. Fillies and mares. 3–year–olds and upward. Weight, 3–year–olds, 115 lbs.; older, 120 lbs. Non–winners of a race since July 15 allowed 2 lbs.; since June 15, 4 lbs. May 15, 6 lbs. Claiming price $10,000; if for $9,000 allowed 2 lbs. (Races when entered for $8,000 or less not considered.)**

Value of race $6,500; value to winner $3,900; second $1,300; third $715; fourth $390; fifth $195. Mutuel pool $106,074.

Last Raced	Horse	Eqt.	A.	Wt	PP	St	¼	½	Str	Fin	Jockey	Cl'g Pr	Odds $1
11Aug85 ^{1}Cby^5	Irish Lora	b	3	109	4	2	$3^{2\frac12}$	$3^{3\frac12}$	$1^{1\frac12}$	$1^{1\frac12}$	Smith M E	10000	2.70
18Aug85 ^{10}Cby^7	Smooth N' Good	b	4	108	1	6	6	4^1	3^1	$2^{1\frac12}$	Craig K[5]	9000	8.10
31Jly85 ^{6}Cby^2	Arctic Angel	b	4	115	3	5	$4^{\frac12}$	5^{hd}	$5^{1\frac12}$	$3^{1\frac12}$	Bass S H[5]	10000	1.00
16Aug85 ^{9}Cby^6	Sonoita Mley		6	114	2	3	$1^{3\frac12}$	$1^{\frac12}$	2^{hd}	$4^{\frac12}$	Warhol V L	10000	4.60
16Aug85 ^{9}Cby^4	Class Counts		5	118	6	1	5^{hd}	6	6	5^3	Hamilton M	10000	7.20
31Jly85 ^{6}Cby^8	Partner's Express		4	114	5	4	2^{hd}	2^{hd}	4^1	6	LaGrange D L	10000	19.30

OFF AT 7:01. Start good. Won driving. Time, :22⅕, :45⅘, :58⅘, 1:12⅕ Track fast.

$2 Mutuel Prices:			
4–IRISH LORA	7.40	3.80	2.60
1–SMOOTH N' GOOD		7.20	3.60
3–ARCTIC ANGEL			2.40

Summary

The approach I've outlined for marking the Past Performances should help you convert the myriad of mice-type numbers and abbreviations to a manageable number of notes. Once you have made these notes, draw back and look at the race as a whole. Develop a mental picture of the race and how it will be run. Will speed prevail? Is the pace likely to be suicidal? Will post position influence the outcome? Will a change in riders or a shift in weights affect the outcome? Answers to these and other questions will come out of your notes. The next step is to concentrate on those horses that emerge as "possible contenders."

This is the "homework" we all must do. It's a lot of fun and an absolutely essential part of the process.

STEP TWO

GOING TO THE RACES

XV. Going to the Races

The following morning, several unknowns will vanish — the weather, track condition and the scratches. You can get the former by looking out the window and the latter by listening to my daily radio show at 8:10 a.m. (10:10 a.m. on weekends) on KSTP AM 1500. (In the event your radio is in the pawn shop or you miss the show, there is a "Scratchline" you can call to get both the day's scratches and track condition. I feel obligated to warn you that these taped messages will be delivered without the wit and insight that effervesces throughout my show.)

While waiting for the micro-wave to heat up your frozen french toast, read the Racing page in the morning paper. Study the Results Charts of the previous day's races and note any trends, e.g. did the winners go wire-to-wire or did many of them come from off the pace? What jockeys or trainers had a good day? What post positions appeared to be more favorable during the early going? In short, study these charts to determine any possible trends or track biases from the preceding day. If there has been no change in the weather or track condition, you might look for these biases to continue.

The first clue as to whether or not you did your homework well will be if any of your "possibles" appear among the selections made by the newspaper's handicappers. Don't panic if none of the local geniuses picked your choice. You may have found the "sleeper" of the month. Then again, you may need to visit your ophthalmologist.

Before you head out to the track, you should make your final "on paper" selections based on your morning inputs. Then rate these selections in terms of your relative confidence in each. Lastly, establish a rough budget for the day and allocate these funds to each race you believe is "playable." (More on these two tasks under "Betting Shrewdly.")

Proper Gear

You've got to have the right gear to go the races. Tacky sports jackets and funny hats are always good for the guys — and the gals look great in big floppy straw hats. Once properly attired, make sure you have all your "stuff 'n things." In addition to the *Daily Racing Form,* you should arm yourself with some "optional equipment" that will both improve your chances and increase your enjoyment of the game.

Binoculars — A good set of binoculars is essential for the truly degenerate horseplayer. My personal preference are the lightweight, 10 power, pocket-sized models manufactured by good optical companies such as Leica and Nikon. Although a tad expensive, these glasses are powerful, bright and easy to carry. (A good place to shop for binoculars is in the direct mail sections of photography magazines such as *Modern* or *Popular Photography.* You can save up to 50 percent over retail by going this route.)

Notepad — I use a leather program holder I've had for years. It has a variety of small pockets and slots for holding mutuel tickets, notepad, pens, etc. These program holders/notebooks are available at the track giftshop or you can fashion your own out of a passport holder or a "pocket secretary."

Official Track Program — On sale at the track, The daily program is probably the most under utilized handicapping tool available. For six bits you get important information not available from other sources. Aside from the obvious — horses' name. betting number, post position — the program provides equipment changes (e.g. "blinkers on"), medication (e.g. first-time Lasix users), rider weights and, most importantly — the morning line. The morning line is established by a professional "pricemaker" and reflects his best estimate of what the final odds on each horse will be. ("How to Read the Program" is contained in the Appendix.)

I do a lot of marking in the program, particularly when looking at the horses in the paddock. I save all my old programs, because they are often good for quick reference when trying to find an old chart or to determine equipment changes and the like.

Tip Sheets & Public Handicappers

When Canterbury Downs opened last year, tip sheets were like belly buttons — everyone had one. But as the season progressed, most of these sheets died a natural and deserved death.

One method of appraising "Tip Sheets" and public handicappers is to keep in mind the principle of "Price = Value." Tip Sheets at the track cost $2.00, local newspapers cost 25¢ and my radio show on KSTP-AM is free. On second thought ...

Seriously, these "opinions" must be considered, not in terms of making your selections, but for other reasons. The most important of which is the influence public selectors have on the betting public and the odds. Public selectors also flag certain horses that you might have overlooked in your analysis. Sometimes a horse that is buried deep in the "Also Eligibles" gets into a race because of scratches. So you should recheck any horse that gets support from the public handicappers to avoid such oversights.

You must remember, however, that public selectors, because of publishing and distribution requisites, make their selections the day before, prior to scratches and changes in the track condition. As such, you should check to see on what basis they make their selections. Are they for a "fast" or "off" track.

A final caution ... Beware of how certain tip sheets are marketed. The vendors will claim "seven winners yesterday," which is very deceptive because they count a "winner" to be any of their top three (and sometimes four) choices that wins.

Touts

Touts are those individuals who claim to have "insider" information and share that information with their "clients" also known as "marks." Touts come from all sectors, but the majority have some peripheral connection to the track such as an exercise rider or a jockey's agent (small-time or unemployed). And their scam is a pretty good one. It doesn't take a Harvard MBA to narrow a race down to three or four horses. The tout does that and then "gives" each client a different horse. After the race he will snuggle up to the the "winner" as he stands in line to cash his ticket. He will, of course, use some intimidating tactic, e.g. "I wish I had the money to play that one ... I know you were smart enough to step out and go heavy, right?" All of this is done to ensure he gets a good "commission." And for those clients holding the losing tickets, he has a litany of excuses — the best of which is "They (owner/ trainer/jockey) stiffed the horse this time so they can get a huge price the next time out. Mark him down, we'll score big next time."

Equally dangerous are what I call "amateur touts." These are well-meaning individuals who have a mistaken opinion of their handicapping skills and are anxious to share — if not impose their opinions —on any willing victim. Frequently they are elevator operators, men's room attendants or bartenders at the track. Before plunging on their advice, ponder this — if they were as good as they profess, wouldn't they consider an occupational change?

Computer Aids

In our world of micro chips and micro-waves, there is a pervasive expectation by many to reduce all matters — large and small — to simplistic, yet precise systems. We all want results at the push of a button — quickly and accurately. Handicapping has and will continue to elude such a simple reduction. Handicapping is more of an art than a science. There must be 2,458 hardware and software handicapping gadgets being marketed today. The growth of personal computers has created a new breed of handicapper — the "equine conehead." Frankly, these devices and "programs" aren't worth much — especially that hand-held gizmo.

The computer has been harnessed for generating and maintaining large data bases, percentages, speed figures and the like. William L. Quirin, Ph.D. has been a pioneer in this regard. These data are available from sources such as Woodside Associates, P.O. Box 798. Millerton, NY 12546. Generating and maintaining these data — on a national basis — is an enormous task. Consequently, you are better advised to subscribe to such services rather than trying to develop and maintain your own files.

Properly equipped, you will enter the racetrack with your *Daily Racing Form,* binoculars, the official program, several pens, notepad, copious notes from my radio show and a big, fat rabbit's foot.

Arrive Early

Arriving early makes infinite sense. You avoid traffic, you get settled in a good spot to view the proceedings — and you will have time to review everything in context — with the program, the weather, track condition, rider/equipment changes and the like. Also, you will have an opportunity to view the video replays of the previous day's races. (Not to mention the added incentive of being present for the daily Fans' Forum hosted by yours truly in the winner's circle.)

Now that you've done your homework, are properly equipped and are in place at the track — you have successfully completed the first of three steps necessary to be a winner. The next step is "Paddock Handicapping" ...

XVI. Paddock Handicapping

We squeeze the melons, kick the tires and feel the fabric before we buy things. Doesn't it make sense to look at the horse you're "buying" before risking the mortgage money? And believe me, you don't need a degree in veterinary medicine to spot a sharp versus a dull horse in the paddock. So go to the paddock and inspect your "paper" choice before betting. Horses arrive in the paddock about 20 to 25 minutes before post time. They are then saddled and walked around the paddock rink — in clear view of the fans — before going to post.

What to Look For

Many handicappers do their homework and then go directly to the mutuel machines — never once looking at the horse they are about to bet. I've asked these "paper players" why they never go to the paddock, and their response is usually ... "I can't tell one horse from another. I don't know what to look for." These players are at a big disadvantage because there are definite signals you can pick up on by watching the horses in the paddock — and it's a lot easier than you might think.

With a little practice, you will be able to differentiate between the "fit, ready and anxious" runner versus the "sore, bored or unhappy" horse. Tom Ainslie and Bonnie Ledbetter have written a fascinating book, *The Body Language of Horses,* which is unquestionably the best book on the subject, and I recommend it highly. In fact, it is required reading. But for those of you who can only afford to buy one book this month, let me provide you with some guidelines for "checking out the goods."

First, go to the paddock, not to select a horse but to assure yourself that the horse you have selected on paper is fit and healthy. The paddock check is just one more "test" your choice must pass before you step up to the mutuel window. Your visit to the paddock may also answer questions you have regarding the basic soundness of certain horses — especially "drop-downs" i.e. claimers who are taking a sharp drop in price.

A healthy, eager and happy horse communicates his well-being by both his appearance and his behavior in the saddling area ...

1) **Appearance** — A healthy horse will have a shiny almost glowing coat. His color will be bright, and frequently his hindquarters will be dappled with color highlights. A healthy coat comes from a good diet, proper care and grooming. I like to see a horse that is clean and pampered, indicating that the groom fusses over his charge. Sometimes you'll see a horse's mane and tail braided. Granted, cute little bows and ribbons aren't going to make a horse run faster — but they indicate that the horse is receiving special care and a little TLC. All of these are good indicators.

Another sign of fitness is weight. Horses that have been racing for an extended period — without a break in training —

frequently lose a lot of weight, and their ribs will be clearly visible. On the other hand, horses coming back after a long layoff might be overweight and still have a "hay belly" with no ribs visible. A fit horse, however, will be "tucked up" in the flanks, and the back ribs will be just barely visible.

2) **Bright-Eyed —** Another sign of health and well-being is when your horse is "bright-eyed." Horses with problems have filmy or dull eyes. An alert horse will be looking around, checking out everything in the paddock. A dull horse will usually look down and express a general disinterest in the whole proceeding.

3) **Sweating —** A very visible sign of discomfort or nervousness is when a horse breaks out in a heavy sweat before a race. Heavy sweating or "washing-out" is easily spotted as the horse will almost lather up in the chest and neck area. And frequently the horse might lather up between its rear legs (kidney sweat). This is symptomatic of extreme nervousness and is something to watch for, particularly when evaluating lightly-raced, inexperienced youngsters. "Washing out" may also be a sign that the horse is sore and reluctant to go onto the track. Horses are a lot smarter than most people think. They know the routine, and when they are led into the paddock, they know they will be racing shortly thereafter. Both the nervous and reluctant horse can "wash-out" in the paddock, leaving them drained both physically and emotionally for the job at hand. Unless it is an unusually hot and humid day and all the horses are sweating, I recommend that you pass on such horses.

4) **Leg Bandages —** Many players will automatically eliminate any horse that runs with leg wraps or bandages, especially front wraps. This is a mistake because bandages do not necessarily mean the horse is unsound. The majority of horses today run with bandages of one type or another. For the most part, you can disregard bandages on the hind legs. These are generally "run-downs" or protective wraps for a horse who "runs down" or burns his heels when they hit the racing surface. Short bandages on the front legs are usually rundowns, too. Front wraps that extend up to just below the knee are a different story. These

are generally support bandages for an ailing tendon or ligament. Another type of bandage you'll see on some horses entering the paddock are "cold waters." These are cloth bandages soaked in ice water to keep down inflammation and also to numb sore legs. Many horses that have bad ankles or other leg problems will be stood in buckets of ice for several hours before a race. And when they are brought from the barn to the paddock, "cold waters" are used to maintain this "iced" condition.

One last consideration ... some trainers will put bandages on a horse for no reason other than to discourage other horsemen from claiming their horse. It's a popular ploy when a trainer is running a horse below his value to steal a purse or cash a bet. And it makes the player's job a little tougher. That's why we have to watch how the horse moves for signs of problems.

For the recreational horseplayer, I suggest that you totally ignore the question of bandages and make your evaluation on the basis of overall appearance, demeanor and motion.

5) **Good Carriage & Demeanor —** A healthy, happy and eager horse will demonstrate these qualities by his carriage and demeanor. Some positive signs are when a horse's ears are pricked up and pointed forward — responsive to the various paddock sounds. This horse is alert. On the other hand, watch for horses who have their ears pinned back. These guys are angry or irritated. A proud horse will arch his neck slightly with his head angled down when he moves. His tail will be arched slightly. On the other hand, a sour, irritated horse will droop his head and swat his tail horizontally, in a slapping fashion. When standing still, a ready horse might paw at the ground with a foreleg, while a bored horse will shift his weight from one side to another. And a hurting horse will try to keep weight off a sore leg. He will either balance on three legs, slightly bending the sore leg, or else he might lift the affected leg slightly.

6) **Walking —** A sound horse will walk with a smooth and even stride — his head held high and straight. A sore horse, on the other hand, will hang his head and bob it from side to side

in an effort to balance himself when taking weight off of a bum wheel. His stride will be uneven, and sometimes he may even stumble slightly — especially if he's been "iced" and his legs are numb. These horses may "paddle" when they walk or swing their legs out instead of striding straight forward. In short, a sore horse will look awkward when he walks.

While you're at the paddock, you might get some clues from watching the people as well as the horses. Watch the groom, and how he or she handles and relates to the horse. If the horse is right and they are "trying" that day you can tell it by the way they treat the horse. Check out the owners and trainers. If they're wearing suits, they probably think they're going to have their picture taken. And if the trainer has just gotten a haircut ... the horse is a dead cinch to win.

The Post Parade

You can gain further insights by observing the horses during the post parade in front of the grandstand and during the warm-ups. When you can't get to the paddock, this will be your only "inspection" opportunity.

Check the horses in the same fashion you would in the paddock in terms of appearance and demeanor. Watch for washiness or other signs of uneasiness. Some horses don't react negatively until they step onto the track. And a calm horse in the paddock might change quickly when paraded onto the track in front of a noisy crowd. Look for horses who are "on their toes." They prance and sometimes dance sideways. These horses are ready.

Immediately before a race, the jockeys gallop their mounts in order to warm them up. Sore horses usually require a longer warm-up to get the circulation stimulated in the affected areas. You'll see these horses galloping back and forth on the backstretch, while the other horses are walking to the gate.

Throughout this entire "inspection" process, make notes in your program on all the horses. These notes will be helpful in the future to determine if there are any changes in terms of appearance or demeanor. Also, you will know which horses show negative signs in the paddock but still run well. You may have eliminated a horse today, but if your notes are good, you will be able to accept his bad paddock presence in the future.

Summary

Horses do communicate — albeit in a non-verbal fashion. And you will be able to understand their "body language" with a little practice. One way to learn this skill quickly is to go to the track one day without looking at the *Daily Racing Form.* Don't do any analysis, and don't look at the tote board. Just buy a program and spend the whole day in the paddock, making notes and then selections based strictly on each horse's appearance and demeanor. You may be quite surprised at the results.

Okay, you've now done your homework and have determined that your horse was accompanied by a groom and not a paramedic in the paddock. Before charging off to the windows, you have one more task — evaluating the odds and "value" of your wager...

STEP THREE

BETTING SHREWDLY

XVII. Betting the Winners

The final factor in the equation for success at the racetrack is knowing how to bet. As Hamlet said ..." To bet or not to bet. That is the question." Perhaps Shakespeare should have added reference to "when" and "how much." Because it's the answers to these questions that will determine whether you leave the track in a long, black limo or a big, red bus.

You may not believe this, but selecting winners is easy — betting properly is tough. For some unknown reason, normally financially responsible individuals — let loose in a racetrack — develop some bad personality traits — not the least of which are greed, impatience and recklessness. Once horseplayers pass through the turnstiles, they frequently abandon the financial principles that guide their personal and business lives. And these same good citizens can be heard muttering, as they leave the track in defeat ..." I knew I shouldn't have ..." Examples of such irrational behavior include:

1) Changing your bet at the last minute — switching to another horse because: a) you heard someone tout the horse (one you gave no chance); b) a tip sheet selected the horse, and they picked the last winner, or 3) the guy in front of you in line bet a ton of money on the horse.

2) Betting the horse who was the longest price on the board, without even knowing the horse's name.

3) Betting too much on a short-priced horse (e.g. three to five shot) because you needed a big absolute return. (The old saying is, "If you have the $5, whadaya need the $3 for?")

4) Betting only the exacta in the last race, using longshots hoping to get even.

5) Betting a horse because of its name e.g. "Irish Lassie" or "Bill's Girl" with the belief that someone from above was sending you a message — and you would be doomed for an eternity if the horse wins and you didn't bet it.

6) Asking your spouse or your four-year-old which horse they like.

I could go on but it's too painful to recall all my past sins. Believe me, there isn't a horseplayer on the planet who hasn't committed each and every one of these totally irrational acts — deeply regretting it later.

The message here is simple ... we must exercise some self-discipline if we want to leave the track with our IRA intact. I have to admit that being a little irrational is okay every once in a while. After all, we go to the races to have fun. It's not my intention to strip you of hunch-playing or the occasional "goofy bet." Rather, I want to help you to minimize this kind of activity and prevent it from taking over your mind and your wallet.

Common Sense Approach

The first aspect of betting winners at the track is money management — exercising a little common sense and self-discipline. Stated simply ... Bet with your head, not over it. Let me suggest some good rules to follow in this regard ...

1) **Daily Budget/Bankroll** — Determine in advance how much "fun money" you will be comfortable putting at risk, i.e. blowing. If you were to lose it all and are still agonizing over it after you've left the parking lot, it was too much.

2) **Separate Wallet** — Keep your "bankroll" separate from other cash you've brought along for parking, food and refreshments. I usually put a rubber band around my bankroll (and at the end of some days, a small paper clip has sufficed.)

3) **Records** — Keep track of how much you bet and win/lose, race by race and daily. I do it in my program and then transfer the daily total to a notebook later. These records are important, especially at tax time.

4) **Saving Tickets** — The eleventh commandment reads: "Thou shalt never throw away thy mutuel tickets." Aside from ecological considerations, there are a couple of good reasons for this practice. To begin with, there are frequently "inquiries" or claims of foul lodged after the running of a race which, if upheld, may convert a losing ticket into a winner. Last year at Canterbury Downs, over $300,000 worth of winning tickets were never cashed — and I'll bet that 99.9 percent of these were tossed away unwittingly. I've also had the experience of rechecking tickets the next day against the charts and have found an occasional uncashed winner in the pile.

Secondly, if you win an "IRS" exacta or the "Pick Six," the feds will know about it. You have to fill out a 1099 form for any payoff of 300-1, and they withhold 30 percent of payoffs greater than 500-1. If you want to get any of that money back, you must have evidence of losses to offset your winnings. And don't wait until you hit the big IRS payoff to start your collection. The IRS examines these losing tickets and is generally suspect of those with heel prints on them.

5) **Beg, Borrow, Steal & Cash Machines —** If you blow your daily bankroll, don't cash a check or tap into a cash machine or borrow from your spouse. On these bad days when you find yourself in a hole, don't dig faster. Horseplayers have slumps just like everyone else. Don't try to bet yourself out of it. You're better off sitting back and rechecking your homework to see if you mis-figured or overlooked a horse. And if your homework checks out, grab a beer, go down to rail and holler at all the jockeys for putting you on the porch of the poor house.

When & How Much to Bet

The second aspect of betting winners involves recognizing the value of each play and knowing when and how much to bet. **This is probably the single most important factor in determining your success at the races.** The following guidelines are very important, and if you follow them, you might recapture the price of this fine book and make a few bucks in the process.

1) **Don't Dance Every Dance —** This is probably single most violated principle at the racetrack. Players just can't pass up a race. They have to bet on all nine or ten races a day. And by so doing, they are almost assured of losing. As a public handicapper, I must give an "opinion" on all nine races, every day of the season. On my better days, I might have five or six winners. But over the entire 83 day season last year, my top choices won 31% of the time or an average of about three winners a day. And this was a high percentage compared to other handicappers — both locally and nationally. Many races are "unplayable" for a variety of reasons. You should watch these races, rather than play them. Some friends of mine justify playing these "unplayable" races by just making small bets. I counter that these four or five so-called small bets add up over the day, and these bucks would be better risked on a race where you have a solid play. So pick your spots.

2) **Vary Your Bets —** Although I'm not in favor of making small bets on bad races, I do subscribe to the principle of varying the amount of your bet in direct proportion to your confidence level in each selection and the odds being offered or value of the play. First, identify the four or five races that are playable, then assign a confidence level to each race, e.g. one to five stars. Then put down the odds you feel that horse should go off at — in effect, you make your own "morning line." When the race comes up and the odds are right, make the bet. Now, in the event that the odds are much lower than you'd like, you should either cut back your bet, look for a better value or, preferably, pass the race. Conversely, if the odds are longer, bet more. As they say, "Bet a lot, to win a lot. Bet a little, to win a little." Unfortunately, most people do the reverse. They bet more on a horse because the odds are lower and they want a higher absolute return. And when their horse is going off at long odds, they cut back their bet (fearing that everyone else knows something they've overlooked). Don't be cautious when the public offers you an "overlay" at a fat price, step up and step out.

The principle here is that you shouldn't let the odds affect your confidence in your selection. Race horses do not: a) subscribe to the *Daily Racing Form,* b) buy tip sheets, c) listen to men's room attendants, d) listen to my morning radio show (except in my barn), and they don't e) study the tote board. As such, they are not going to run any differently if the odds are high or low. Public opinion and the odds should only influence your betting — not your selections.

On those marvelous days when your choices are romping home one after another, and your bankroll is bulging, you might step up your bets a little. Conversely, when you're not hitting on all cylinders, it might be good to cut back a notch or two. A final thought ... once you are ahead, stay there. Play with the profits and stash your original bankroll. Don't give it back.

3) **Limit Exotic Wagers —** I recommend that you limit your bets on the "exotic" wagers (i.e. Daily Doubles, Exactas and Pick Six) to no more than 20 to 25 percent of your total daily bankroll.

It's tough enough to pick a winner much less other outcomes. Moreover, the track and state's "takeout" on the exotic wagers is 35 percent higher than on the straight win, place or show wagers (23 percent versus 17 percent).

Last year, there was a near epidemic of the dreaded disease "exacta-itis," which was accompanied by an attendant syndrome "picksixism" — both afflictions have been known to be contagious and sometimes fatal to your financial well-being.

4) **Don't Fight the Percentages** — All horseplayers get "urges" to buck the crowd, go against the grain — in short, to fight trends and percentages. There are hundreds of "principles" in the game of handicapping. Most of these "rules" are well-founded and supported by historical data. Granted there are always exceptions to these "rules," but you shouldn't make a habit out of trying to catch these exceptions.

One example of this is betting on low percentage plays, e.g. a filly running against colts. I'm not saying "never bet" against the odds — rather, I'm saying do it on occasion and only when you feel that other factors significantly offset the general rule.

Summary

Common sense, confidence in your selections, recognizing real "value" and a little self-discipline are the keys to betting winners at the pony palace. It's a tough game to make a lot of money at. However, it's incredibly easy to lose big if you're not prudent. In the following chapters, we'll take a look at "value," overlays, longshots, exotics and other special plays.

XVIII. Knowing the Odds

In order to determine what is and what isn't a smart bet, you must know the odds. The odds in the program and on the tote board are the odds to win — expressed in terms of profit per dollar wagered. For example, if a horse goes off at odds of 3-1 and wins, he would pay $8.00 and change for each two dollars wagered (three times $2.00 equals $6.00 plus your original bet of $2.00 equals $8.00). (A complete table of odds, probable payoffs and winning probabilities is included in the Appendix.)

Although the tote board doesn't post odds for place and show bets, these can be estimated through a simple arithmetic exercise. (A step-by-step explanation of these calculations is contained in the Appendix.)

The Morning Line

The morning line is established by the track's line-maker in the morning, after scratches have been made. This line is that individual's best estimate of what odds each horse will go off at when the gate opens. It does not necessarily reflect his opinion as to which is the best horse or the best bet. Rather it is his estimate of how the public will wager. The official morning line appears in the official track program. You will find other lines or"graded handicaps" in both the *Daily Racing Form* and in local newspapers. You must remember that these are unofficial lines and may vary significantly from the official track line.

The utility of the morning line is in direct proportion to the line-maker's ability. At Canterbury Downs, Dan Teta made the line in 1985, and it was a very accurate line. Other tracks have line-makers who couldn't make an accurate line for a "walk-over."

Monitoring the Tote Board

When the tote board opens before each race, the opening odds reflect the official morning line. You should monitor the action on the tote board and record the odds three times in your program. First, note what is called the "first flash." That is the first change after the morning line. This reflects "advance wagering" by fans who bet in advance. The "first flash" becomes more relevant in the later races when people advance bet and then head home or people who are tired of standing in line and make a number of bets at one time. For the most part this is "dumb money" and should be subtracted from the total pools to determine where the "smart money" is going. Next, record the odds ten minutes before post time and again, two minutes before post time. Note the flow of money, especially in races where "barn money" might be a factor. ("How To Read The Tote Board" is contained in the Appendix.)

Longshots & Overlays

There is nothing more thrilling than cashing a fat bet on a 20-1 longshot. And a part of this thrill is that these occasions occur about once every 3.7 years! Playing longshots, per se, is lethal to your financial well-being. You must remember that horses aren't born 20-1 shots, they earn this distinction through repeatedly dismal efforts. Most 20-1 shots are better suited for transporting portly Shriners in the Aquatennial Parade than for racing.

There are "diamonds in the rough," however, and these are referred to as "overlays." Simply stated, an overlay is any horse that goes to post at odds significantly higher than its value. Overlays surface when other horses in the field are over-played by the public, e.g. 5-2 or 2-1 shots bet down to even money or less. These over-bet favorites or "underlays" frequently arise when a horse is picked heavily by the public selectors and tip sheets. And sometimes they are produced by a "universal tip" that sweeps through the grandstand before the race. They are also created on weekends, when the occasional players venture forth and bet on the leading or "hot" jockey or trainer.

The key to betting overlays is your ability to recognize the value of the play coupled with knowing the percentages. I generally establish my own morning line or probable odds for my selections. If the actual odds are lower than this target, I may pass the race or look for a better value. If the odds are higher, then I will go strongly on the play. If you are new to the game, then use the morning line as your starting point. If a horse is listed at 3-1 in the program and is going off at 9-1, that horse is an overlay worth considering. Again, using the morning line is only recommended when the track's line-maker has a good track record.

The advantage of spotting and playing overlays becomes quite clear when you look at the percentages. A legitimate 3-1 shot will win one out of five starts. So if you were to bet $2 on ten consecutive 3-1 shots, you would invest $20, win two bets paying from $8.00 to $8.80 each or $16.00 to $17.60 total, leaving you minus $2.40 to $4.00. However, if you play ten 3-1 shots overlayed at 9-1, you will still win twice, but you'll collect $40.00+ and end up plus $20.00.

You have to be sensible when it comes to determining what constitutes an overlay. A horse that's 20-1 in the morning line and is going off at 30-1 is not an overlay. Overlays must have a legitimate chance and not just be under-bet. Overlays are most attractive when you don't like the favorite in a race, especially if the public is betting the "chalk" (favorite) heavily.

Overlays also pop up in exacta races and later in the day, when the public pays too much attention to the gimmick bets and ignores good values in the straight pools. And as the day progresses, players who are stuck will either press or double up on the favorites or take flyers on longshots in an effort to regroup. By so doing, they create some nice overlays in the medium price (3-1 to 6-1) range.

Hidden "Action"

One thing in racing will never change — owners and trainers are known to make a bet or two. When they have a horse that is "ready" they do their best to keep the fact a secret to keep the price up. Just as some horsemen "darken" the form on their horses, they go to equal lengths to mask their betting support. The most common practices are to bet in the final minute or to bet their horse only in the exotic pools. There isn't much you can do about last minute bets, but you can spot horses that are getting a disproportionate amount of action in the exacta and daily double pools. Note the probable payoffs which are flashed on the TV monitors to spot these horses. These situations are most common in maiden races or when there is a "shipper" or mystery horse in the field.

Summary

Overlays are God's gift to the experienced and knowledgeable handicapper. They keep our rent paid and our refrigerators filled. Longshots attract a sizable following of optimists — all trying to capture lightning in a bottle. As such, longshots are also gifts for the pros, because they fatten up the payoff on legitimate horses. The trick is being able to distinguish between the two — and recognizing the value of the bet is the key.

XIX. Win, Place or Show?

There are three basic wagers you can make on any given race — win, place or show. When you bet a horse to win, you collect only if your horse finishes first. When you bet a horse to place, you collect if your horse finishes either first or second. When you bet a horse to show, you collect if your horse finishes first, second or third. Why not bet to show, you ask? Well, the payoffs are commensurate with the risks you take.

Bet to Win

Most successful horseplayers I know bet to win almost exclusively. There are times and circumstances where place or show bets are okay, but I believe that you will be better off in the long run to bet your selections to win only.

Place & Show Betting

I have to be honest ... I don't like to bet to lose. Granted, show bets are safer and you cash a lot of tickets, but to me, it's like being pecked to death by a dull-beaked duck. When playing favorites, you risk $2.00 to win as little as 20-80 cents This means that you have to cash about four out of five tickets to break even. And if you were to cash seven out of nine show bets playing heavy favorites, you would end up with a whopping profit of about $1.60 for the day. That's not enough to pay for your *Daily Racing Form.*

Hedges — Place and show bets, however, can be used as a "hedge" or insurance policy for your win bets in the event your horse gets nosed out at the wire. For years, people would "insure" their bets by betting a horse "across the board" which means $2 win, $2 place and $2 show. Before the new computer mutuel windows, there was even a special "Combination" sellers window that combined these three bets on a single ticket.

Several years ago, I analyzed the payoffs on several hundred races and determined that "across the board" wagers were a bad bet. Further analysis revealed the following formula, which, if followed, will generate a significantly higher return than an "across the board" bet. Using $2 as a base unit, you can "insure" your win bet according to the following table ...

	Pritch's Wagering Formula		
Odds to Win	**Amount to Win**	**Amount to Place**	**Amount to Show**
1-5 to 4-5	No Bet	No Bet	No Bet
Even to 9-5	$ 6	$ 0	$ 0
2-1 to 7-2	$ 2	$ 4	$ 0
4-1 and over	$ 2	$ 0	$ 4

Overlays — On occasion, you might find an overlay in either the place or show pools. This usually occurs when the public overlooks the favorites in these pools. When this happens, you will get payoffs such as — $3.60 to win, $3.20 to place and $3.00

to show. Getting place and show prices such as these on a 4-5 shot is tantamount to stealing. And it happened quite a few times last season. So keep your eyes peeled for such overlays.

Estimating Place and Show Prices

The tote board provides only the odds to win. Place and show odds can't be posted because they hinge on which horses finish first, second and third and share these secondary pools. The tote board does, however, provide the amount of money bet on each horse in the place and show pools. And with these data, you can determine minimum payoffs for any horse in the race. A chart demonstrating the process is included in the Appendix.

Betting Entries

An entry is when two or more horses are entered in a race by either the same trainer or owner. These horses are coupled as an entry for betting purposes and will be listed in the program as number 1 and 1A, 2 and 2B etc.

Betting entries is an attractive proposition for many players — after all, you are getting two horses for the price of one. Heck of a bargain. Given some of the tactical reasons a trainer will run an entry discussed previously in "Other Factors," this thinking doesn't always hold up. It does apply, however, in several circumstances.

I look for entries with different ownership. Since each owner is in the game for a profit, the trainer has to put their horses where they belong. Entries are also worth considering when the conditions of the race are unique — particularly in allowance or handicap races.

When you find an entry composed of two horses — both of which have a legitimate chance — these can be excellent betting opportunities in the place and show pools. If the entry runs 1-2 in a race, the place price is frequently equal and sometimes greater than the win price. And the same applies to the show pool if both horses finish in the money, i.e 1-2, 1-3 or 2-3.

In October of 1985, I was in Chicago and spotted an entry of two claimers that had competed at Canterbury Downs the preceding summer. The horses were *Mr. Pistil* and *Cowboy Shoes*. *Mr. Pistil* had won two sprints at Canterbury in an impressive fashion. Both of these victories coming after he had been given Lasix for the first time. *Cowboy Shoes* had run for $10,000 and met with a tough trip. *Mr. Pistil* was a a speedy, front-runner, and *Cowboy Shoes* was a stretch-running sort. Both horses were entered in a $10-$9,000 claiming race at Hawthorne.

1st Hawthorne

6 FURLONGS. (1.08⅘) CLAIMING. Purse $7,700. 3-year-olds and upward. Weight, 3-year-olds, 118 lbs.; older, 122 lbs. Non-winners of two races since August 30 allowed 3 lbs.; a race, 6 lbs.; two races in 1985, 8 lbs.; a race, 10 lbs. Claiming price $10,000; if for $9,000 allowed 3 lbs.

Coupled—Cowboy Shoes and Mr. Pistil.

Mr. Pistil — Dk. b. or br. c. 4, by Pocket Flower—Lanyons Lick, by Lanyon

Own.—Truscott J — **119** — Br.—Truscott John (Neb) — Tr.—Glass Orin J Jr — $9,000

1985 8 3 0 1 $10,624
1984 5 2 0 1 $4,136

Lifetime 13 5 0 2 $14,760

5Oct85-4Cby	6f	:22^1	:45^3	1:11^{1}ft	*6-5	115	$1^{1/2}$	$1^{1\,1/2}$	1^3	1^3	Kutz D^3	8000	92-15	Mr. Pistil, Mt. Tabor Rd., BigRalph	9
26Sep85-4Cby	6f	:22	:45	1:11 ft	13	115	$1^{1/2}$	$1^{1/2}$	$1^{1\,1/2}$	$1^{3\,1/2}$	Kutz D^6	6250	93-13	Mr.Pistil,Dnil'sPrcious,FvordMood	10
25Aug85-6Aks	6f	:22	:44^3	1:09^{3}ft	16	114	1^2	1^{hd}	2^1	$4^{3\,1/4}$	McGurn C^{10}	6000	86-10	J. Conway, FortdeGold,BrazenEgo	12
17Aug85-4Aks	6f	:22^1	:45^3	1:11^{4}m	11	116	1^2	1^2	2^2	$10^{10\,1/2}$	McGurn C^{10}	6500	67-25	Namletak,BeBckShortly,OsgeBully	10
4Aug85-6Aks	6f	:23	:46^2	1:12 ft	12	116	$2^{1/2}$	$2^{1/2}$	$5^{3\,1/2}$	$6^{5\,3/4}$	Walker B J Jr^6	8500	71-27	DevilHimself,BeBackShortly,Leckie	9
26Jly85-9Aks	6f	:22^2	:45	1:11 ft	6¾	116	1^{hd}	2^3	2^2	$3^{6\,1/2}$	Compton P^1	8500	75-24	IndinPrince,DevilHimself,Mr.Pistil	10
14Jly85-4Aks	6f	:22^3	:45^2	1:11 ft	20	117	$1^{1/2}$	$1^{1/2}$	1^1	1^3	Compton P^3	[S] 5000	82-20	Mr. Pistil, Par's Pal,Beau'sWinner	12
29Jun85-1Aks	6f	:22^2	:46	1:12 ft	33	117	$2^{1/2}$	$2^{1/2}$	5^2	$8^{8\,1/4}$	Compton P^4	[S] 6500	69-20	SmoothBow,GlssCrft,Admirl'sDrm	10
11Nov84-3LnN	6f	:24	:48	1:15 ft	2¾	117	1^{hd}	$2^{1/2}$	$1^{1/2}$	$1^{2\,1/2}$	Compton P^6	Aw3605	77-25	Mr.Pistil,IffenAPlesure,Prevl'sTss	10
31Oct84-1LnN	6f	:24^2	:48^4	1:15^{2}m	3½	118	1^3	$1^{1\,1/2}$	1^2	1^7	Compton P^{10}	[S]Mdn	75-34	Mr.Pistil,DmximJunior,FrmrHrryB.	10

Cowboy Shoes — B. g. 6, by Great Sun—Nijmi, by Sailor

Own.—G & M Stables Inc — **111** — Br.—Fitzgerald Ruth&JacksonJean (Ky) — Tr.—Glass Orin J Jr — $9,000

1985 6 1 0 0 $5,520
1984 10 2 0 2 $22,670
Turf 2 0 0 0 $306

Lifetime 47 11 6 7 $105,804

27Sep85-5Cby	6f	:23	:46^1	1:11^{4}ft	*2¼	115	$4^{2\,1/2}$	$6^{5\,1/2}$	5^5	4^5	Pettinger D R^1	10000	84-14	HeedThePledge,HomeInBreez,Dtsy	6
24Aug85-10Aks	6f	:22^2	:45	1:10 ft	6½	113	3^2	4^3	3^2	1^{hd}	Walker B J Jr^6	8000	87-15	Cowboy Shoes, Ilatan, Never Fail	11
17Aug85-6Aks	6f	:22^2	:45^2	1:12 m	4	116	5^7	5^8	6^{10}	$6^{3\,1/2}$	Walker B J Jr^8	11000	73-25	Radial, Carnival Light, No Pomp	9
13Jun85-7Aks	6f	:23^1	:46^2	1:11^{2}ft	3¼	116	$5^{2\,1/2}$	4^3	$4^{6\,1/2}$	$4^{9\,1/2}$	McGurn C^2	25000	70-28	OrngeSqush,Lyin'Brss,SirSouthside	6
13Jun85—Bore in air															
2Jun85-7Aks	6f	:22^3	:45^2	1:11^{2}ft	5	112	$3^{1\,1/2}$	$3^{1\,1/2}$	4^5	4^6	McGurn C^6	30000	74-27	Inebriator, Roses Turn, L'Naterne	6
22Feb85-9Fon	4f		:22^4	:46^{1}ft	9	119	6	$7^{5\,3/4}$	$5^{8\,1/2}$	$7^{8\,3/4}$	Shepherd D R^4	Aw5618	85-10	JkeThePrince,Kiplinger,HoldthBns	7
27Nov84-7Key	1^{70}	:46^2	1:11^2	1:42^{3}ft	11	116	1^{hd}	$1^{1/2}$	2^{hd}	$4^{4\,1/4}$	Gomez M A^1	18000	83-19	OffbetHeir,DoublExplosion,InnrRm	9
9Nov84-7Med	1$\frac{1}{16}$	:47^3	1:11^4	1:45^{2}ft	8	116	$2^{1/2}$	$2^{1\,1/2}$	$3^{4\,1/2}$	4^{10}	Kaenel J L^4	20000	72-20	Three Of Clubs,Kastanie,RevenToo	8
22Oct84-5Med	6f	:23^1	:47	1:13 sy	12	116	8^{17}	7^{13}	6^{11}	$6^{6\,3/4}$	Morgan M R^4	25000	70-24	JustAnyTime,MasterQuick,Propgnd	8
30Sep84-8Key	1$\frac{1}{16}$	:47^2	1:11^1	1:44^{1}ft	12	117	8^{12}	8^{15}	8^{16}	$8^{19\,3/4}$	Morgan M R^7	Aw16000	63-21	ChocoltDncr,LordDL'Orn,ClssicStd	8

●Sep 25 Cby 3f sl :36 h (d)

The entry went off at an incredibly generous 4-1. *Mr. Pistil* won the race easily, and *Cowboy Shoes* got second. The entry paid $11.00 to place. I flew home "first class" that night.

FIRST RACE
Hawthorne
OCTOBER 19, 1985

6 FURLONGS. (1.08$\frac{1}{5}$) CLAIMING. Purse $7,700. 3-year-olds and upward. Weight, 3-year-olds, 118 lbs.; older, 122 lbs. Non-winners of two races since August 30 allowed 3 lbs.; a race, 6 lbs.; two races in 1985, 8 lbs.; a race, 10 lbs. Claiming price $10,000; if for $9,000 allowed 3 lbs. 18TH DAY. WEATHER CLOUDY. TEMPERATURE 58 DEGREES.

Value of race $7,700; value to winner $4,620; second $1,540; third $847; fourth $462; fifth $231. Mutuel pool $67,721.

Last Raced	Horse	Eqt.	A.	Wt	PP	St	¼	½	Str	Fin	Jockey	Cl'g Pr	Odds $1
5Oct85 ^{4}Cby^{1}	Mr. Pistil		4	119	8	1	4^{1}	$4^{1\frac{1}{2}}$	1^{hd}	$1^{2\frac{3}{4}}$	Cordova D W	9000	a-4.10
27Sep85 ^{5}Cby^{4}	Cowboy Shoes	b	6	113	5	6	7^{hd}	7^{4}	4^{4}	2^{hd}	Walker B J Jr	9000	a-4.10
12Oct85 ^{5}Haw^{2}	Angel Light		5	116	6	7	8^{6}	6^{2}	$3^{\frac{1}{2}}$	3^{hd}	King E L Jr	10000	2.30
30Sep85 ^{9}Haw^{5}	Tyrantson	b	4	119	3	4	2^{1}	1^{hd}	$2^{2\frac{1}{2}}$	$4^{8\frac{3}{4}}$	Richard D	10000	2.40
11Sep85 ^{8}Cls^{5}	Kiplinger	b	5	112	1	2	$1^{\frac{1}{2}}$	$2^{3\frac{1}{2}}$	5^{2}	$5^{\frac{1}{2}}$	Meier R	10000	12.70
27Sep85 ^{8}FP^{1}	Queen's Royal Boy		5	119	9	5	$5^{1\frac{1}{2}}$	$5^{\frac{1}{2}}$	6^{1}	$6^{\frac{3}{4}}$	Fires E	9000	6.80
26May85 ^{10}Aks^{7}	Test Pilot		8	114	7	9	9	9	$8^{\frac{1}{2}}$	$7^{\frac{3}{4}}$	Gavidia W	10000	40.70
9Oct85 ^{8}FP^{3}	Nightline Oak	b	5	116	4	3	$3^{1\frac{1}{2}}$	3^{hd}	7^{1}	$8^{1\frac{1}{4}}$	Lindsay R	10000	6.20
5Oct85 ^{4}Haw^{4}	Competent	b	4	116	2	8	6^{hd}	$8^{1\frac{1}{2}}$	9	9	Bullard B A	10000	16.30

a-Coupled: Mr. Pistil and Cowboy Shoes.

OFF AT 1:30. Start good. Won ridden out. Time, :22$\frac{1}{5}$, :45$\frac{4}{5}$, :58$\frac{2}{5}$, 1:10$\frac{3}{5}$ Track good.

Official Program Numbers↘

$2 Mutuel Prices:

1-MR. PISTIL (a-entry)	10.20	11.00	5.00
1-COWBOY SHOES (a-entry)	10.20	11.00	5.00
7-ANGEL LIGHT			2.80

Dk. b. or br. c, by Pocket Flower—Lanyons Lick, by Lanyon. Trainer Glass Orin J Jr. Bred by Truscott John (Neb).

MR. PISTIL circled rivals on turn, took command inside eighth pole and drew out under steady handling. COWBOY SHOES, outrun early, settled in stride in upper stretch but unable to menace stablemate. ANGEL LIGHT rallied well between horses. TYRANTSON took the lead outside KIPLINGER late turn, faltered final furlong. KIPLINGER flashed speed for a half mile, tired. QUEEN'S ROYAL BOY raced evenly outside. Horses. TEST PILOT showed little. NIGHTLINE OAK tired from early efforts while three wide. COMPETENT was through early.

Summary

I recommend that the serious player concentrate his bankroll on straight win bets versus place and show bets. If you are conservative or if you get "those looks" from your spouse every time you head for the window, then insure your win bets according the formula outlined in the preceding.

Entries frequently offer good values, particularly in the secondary pools. And show bets are fun for the "first-timers" at the track. Although show betting gives you a lot of "winners" — it doesn't do much in terms of getting you and VISA on even footing.

XX. Exotic Wagers

In addition to the traditional win, place and show wagers, most tracks offer a number of other wagering options. These so-called "exotic" or "gimmick" wagers include the daily double, exactas (or perfectas), quinellas, trifectas (or Triples), Pick Six, Pick Eight and even Pick Nine. At Canterbury Downs, we are offered a daily double on the first and second races, four to five exactas daily and the Pick Six on the third through the eighth races. These plays are fun and frequently quite rewarding.

Exotic wagers are popular with the average racegoer because they hold the promise of large payoffs on minimum bets. Recently, a man at Bay Meadows won the Pick Six and received $1.2 million on a two dollar bet. Another lucky gent collected $1.9 million at Santa Anita with a winning Pick Nine wager. The possibility of high returns, however, is accompanied by both high risk and a higher takeout by the track.

There are, however, a number of good plays in the exotic area. Unfortunately, many fans don't do their arithmetic when playing these bets and end up frustrated because they cash tickets, but lose money. Even though probable payoffs are displayed for both exactas and daily doubles, you have to calculate the profit potential on the exotics by dividing the expected return by the total amount invested when buying more than one combination. What happens all too frequently, especially with exactas, is the player invests $16.00 to $24.00, wins and only gets $19.80 in return. Let's examine each of the gimmick bets in more detail ...

Daily Double

The original exotic wager is the daily double, where you are required to select the winners of the first two races, prior to the first race. Last year at Canterbury Downs, the highest daily double payoff was $1,172.00 and the lowest was $7.80 — creating an average daily double payoff of $87.00. The median payoff was probably in the $35-$45 range, however. It's a fun bet and can be played a number of different ways — the most popular of which are "wheeling" and "crisscrossing."

The Wheel — This method is used when you are very confident about a single horse in one of the two races. You take that particular horse and "wheel" or combine him with all (or most) of the horses in the the other race. There's "front-wheeling" which means you are using a single horse in the first race, and "back-wheeling" when you use a single horse in the second race. If you are wheeling a favorite, it is your hope that a longshot wins in the other race — producing a high payoff.

Wheeling the Favorite — Let's say you wheel the favorite, horse "A" in the first race. Horse "A" (the favorite at 2-1) wins the first race. In the second race, you have the following payoffs based on a nine horse field and consequently, a $18.00 investment:

Horse	Morning Line	DD Payoff
#1	7-2	$20
#2	4-1	$28
#3	15-1	$202
#4	12-1	$74
#5	6-5	$14
#6	30-1	$346
#7	12-1	$86
#8	15-1	$102
#9	12-1	$98

Although this board offers some nice returns, you must consider the following probability table for the top choices versus the outsiders in the second race (A complete probability table is contained in the Appendix) :

Horse	Odds	% Probability of Winning
#5	6-5	40.3%
#1	7-2	18.6%
#2	4-1	16.1%
#4	12-1	6.2%
#7	12-1	6.2%
#9	12-1	6.2%
#3	15-1	4.0%
#6	30-1	1.4%
		24.0%

Without going into a lot of math, it is very probable that a winning double in this scenario would pay in the range of $14.00 to $28.00. From this return, you would subtract your $18.00 investment and basically end up even. Consequently, I don't recommend wheeling favorites because everyone does it, and hence the risk is rarely commensurate with the return. It is an acceptable play, however, in certain cases. The first situation is when you don't like the favorite in the second race, particularly when the horse is listed at odds of less than 2-1 in the program. The second situation is when all the possible payoffs represent a profit of at least 50 percent. This occurs when there are no clear-cut choices in one race or when there are large fields in both races.

Wheeling an Overlay — In this case, you would wheel Horse "B" at 4-1 in the first race against the same ten horses in the second race. This would produce the following possibilities ...

Horse	Morning Line	DD Payoff
#1	7-2	$60
#2	4-1	$88
#3	15-1	$302
#4	12-1	$174
#5	6-5	$34
#6	30-1	$446
#7	12-1	$166
#8	15-1	$202
#9	12-1	$198

You don't have to be a rocket scientist to see that this approach offers a more rewarding scenario than wheeling the "lock," but is has greater risks as well. Nevertheless, I prefer this type of play if the overlay has a legitimate chance. A variant of this approach, which reduces the amount of money at risk, is to do a "partial wheel," i.e. wheel the overlay with half the field in the second — usually the shortest-priced horses. Then if the overlay wins the first race, you can hedge against the horses you left out. (More on "hedging" later.)

Crisscrossing — This technique involves selecting two or three horses in each race and crisscrossing them to produce all the possible combinations. For example, you might take horses "A" and "B" in the first race and crisscross them with horses "A", "B" and "C" in the second. This would produce six different combos: A-A, A-B, A-C, B-A, B-B and B-C and would cost $12.00.

I employ this approach when confronted with wide open races, where all of the possible payoffs are reasonable. It's not a good play if there are strong favorites in either race. Crisscrossing the top choices is one of the worst bets at the track. You must consider the payoffs as they relate to your total investment. Spending $12.00 to win $20.00 is like betting a 3-5 shot. It's not a good play.

"Hedging" Your Doubles — You frequently can "hedge" or insure your daily double after the first race if you've done a partial wheel or a criss-cross. Let's say that your horse wins the first race and you are "live" in the second race with three horses.

In the event the winner of the first race was the favorite or close to it, you might consider buying win tickets on two to three other horses (not covered in your doubles) in the second, varying the amount on each to get the same return. On the other hand, if the winner of the first race was an outsider, then you may be able to buy all the remaining horses in the second race and guarantee a profit.

Hedging is recommended when an overlay wins the first race. But remember, everything you spend in "insurance" reduces your net profit if you win the double. It's a conservative approach but definitely should be considered when the winner of the first pays a big price and you have at least three horses hooked to that winner in the second half of the double.

Exactas

Exactas are the most common and popular of the gimmick bets. To win, you must select the first and second place finishers — in exact order — in a given race. Like the daily double, there are a number of ways to play the exacta, the most popular of which are "wheeling" and "boxing."

Exacta Wheel — This technique is similar to the daily double wheel where you "key" on a single horse and combine or "wheel" that horse with the balance of the field. You can wheel a horse either on top (i.e. to finish first) or on the bottom (i.e. to finish second). In a ten horse field, wheeling one horse would produce nine combinations and cost $18.00.

Exacta Boxes — Boxing is the technique where you combine two, three, four or more horses to cover every possible combination of two of those horses finishing 1-2. A three-horse exacta box, for example, using horses "A", "B" and "C" would generate six different combinations (A-B, A-C, B-A, B-C, C-A and C-B) and cost $12.00.

Some Guidelines For Playing Exactas

As in all wagers, we must be sensitive to the return-on-investment or ROI of exacta plays. The prospect of collecting $100.00+ payoffs sometimes makes players over-invest in this wager and subsequently reduce their ROI to an unacceptable level. To help you avoid this pitfall, you might consider the following:

Wheeling Favorites — Avoid wheeling a favorite unless all possible payoffs generate a profit greater than would be realized by betting the same amount to win on the key horse. You can "heavy up" on certain combinations to produce this result. For example you might wheel all horses for $2 each, then separately buy additional combinations on the shorter-priced horses. To demonstrate this principle, let's assume that horse "A" is your key horse and is going off at 5-2 in the win pool. And when you look at the probable exacta payoffs, you see the following:

Combo	Payoff	Combo	Payoff
A-B	$28.20	A-G	$128.00
A-C	47.80	A-H	65.80
A-D	74.40	A-I	32.40
A-E	22.40	A-J	18.20
A-F	38.80		

To wheel horse "A" would cost $18.00, and if the horse wins you will automatically win the exacta because you have the winner with every other horse in the race. Now examine the profit potential (return less cost of the wager) and you stand to make from 20¢ to $110.00 and a simple average of the payoffs is $50.76 less the $18.00 bet or a net profit of $32.76. But in reality, it is more likely that one of the top three choices will run second. Statistically speaking, one of these horses will finish second 67 percent of the time. Therefore, let's weigh the payoffs for those three horses — B, E and J — 67 percent and the remaining payoffs at 33 percent. This will produce a projected weighted-average payoff of $37.47 or a net profit of only $19.47.

Now let's compare this probable average profit of $19.47 for the exacta to what you would get by betting your key horse to win only. Taking the $18.00 you would have invested in the exacta and betting it to win at 5-2 odds, you would get a payoff of $63.00 for a net profit of $45.00 — more than twice what you are likely to get from wheeling the same horse in the exacta. Granted, the longshot will come in occasionally — but, over time, you are frequently better off betting the favorite to win than wheeling him in the exacta. It all depends on the ROI.

Wheeling Overlays and Longshots — This is a much better play and can reward you with monster payoffs going into the thousands. If you like a horse that is going off at a price, then wheel the horse. Frequently the favorites are wheeled top and bottom, automatically depressing the price for your combination. When that occurs, heavy up with the shorter-priced combinations.

If I really like a horse that is going off at let's say 5-1 or longer, I do the following: a) wheel the horse on top, b) wheel the horse on the bottom, and then c) bet an amount equal to what the two wheels cost to "show" on the horse. If the horse wins or runs second you will cash both your exacta and your show bet — realizing a nifty score. If the horse runs third, the show price will usually be at least $4.00, and you will recover all of your original bet and breakeven or even make a small profit. Using this approach, you lose only if the horse runs off the board. It's a good play and a good use of a hedge (show) bet because you can collect on the hedge bet in addition to the winning bet.

Exacta Boxes — Boxing horses is both convenient and conservative. And like all "convenience items" it comes with a premium — a reduced ROI. The most common mistake exacta players make is to box the top three favorites. A three horse box costs $12, and when it "wins," the payoffs are usually $20.00 to $30.00 and sometimes less — making the play a less than even money bet. Now getting a $20.00 return on a $2 bet is a heck of a deal, but you're spending $12.00 to make $8.00. Every time you make a three-horse box you are buying at least five losing tickets.

Exacta boxes do make sense under the following circumstances:

1) You don't like the favorite and expect that horse to be off the board, and

2) You are including at least one horse who is going off at odds of 5-1 or greater.

One final thought regarding exacta boxes ... Many "boxers" get knocked out.

Preferred Exacta Plays — I generally play "mini-wheels" when making exactas. I take my key horse and make two or three combinations with that horse on top. And I generally vary the amount of each combination after evaluating the return. For example, I will put the key horse, horse "A" with "D" for $4.00, with horse "F" for $6.00 and horse "H" for $8.00 for a total of $18.00. And on some occasions, I might reverse my top horse with one of the three or bet the key horse to place, "just in case ..." Also, I'll wheel a longshot or do a three horse box with some good priced horses, especially when I question the legitimacy of the favorite.

A final warning ... "Exacta-itis" is a very consuming and addictive disease at the track. Some people go nuts and make more combinations than you'll find on a Chinese menu. They have fun, wave their winning ticket in your face and cash tickets — but they don't make any money.

I love to watch players with "exacta-itis" after a race. You'll see them pouring through their stack of exacta tickets searching to see if they've won. They usually have made so many combinations, they don't know which horses to root for.

Parlays

A "parlay" bet is when you re-invest the total proceeds won in one race into another race(s). It is not a wager the track offers — rather it is a betting technique some players employ. I like parlays in two circumstances ...

1) "Chalk" Parlays — This when you are faced with a race card loaded with stick-outs or short-priced favorites (the "chalk"). I can't bet 4-5 shots, but I might do a three-race win parlay on these horses. Let's say that you pick up the program and find three races where your top picks are all short-priced favorites (7-5 or less).

Race Number	Favorite's Odds	Payoffs
2	6-5	$4.40
4	Even	$4.00
8	4-5	$3.80
		$12.20

If you were to bet $2.00 to win on each of these races separately (a total of $6.00) and all three won — you would collect $12.20 and realize a profit of $6.20. Not very exciting. However, if you were to bet the total $6.00 on the first horse and then parlay the total proceeds into the next two races, you would realize a profit of over $40.00. Obviously, there is a greater risk, but if you are intent on betting these three races, why not go for it?

2) **Place & Show Parlays —** Given the same circumstances as above, you might consider either a place or show parlay on these favorites. It's less risky, but still fun. I prefer place parlays, using three or four races (more than four is asking a lot. Remember, pigs get fat, and hogs get slaughtered).

I also like place parlays when I am playing overlays to win in any or all of these races. This way I can collect on both bets, if the overlay wins and the parlay horse runs second (... what was I saying about pigs and hogs ...?)

Summary

Playing the exotic wagers is fun and can provide you with payoffs large enough for the downstroke on that bass boat you've been coveting. But like all wagers, you must be sensitive to the relative value of each play. The over-riding principle is to evaluate the possible payoffs in terms of both probability and profitability.

In this examination, you will be able to differentiate between high and low ROI options. Further, you should compare the "probable" return on the exacta versus what a straight "win" bet would produce.

Parlays are an interesting way to stretch your budget and have some action in otherwise "unplayable" races. Parlays are also a good "group activity." If you are with a group of friends at the track, everyone can toss a few bucks into the "parlay kitty" and then pick a horse. (Group parlays are one of the few "show" bets I recommend.)

My favorite "gimmick" bet, however, is the Pick Six ...

XXI. Pick Six

A major attraction at Canterbury Downs during its inaugural season was the "Pick Six" — a two dollar wager requiring the player to select the winners of six consecutive races, the third through the eighth races. The pools were huge and people were winning thousands of dollars every week, including payoffs of over $129,000, $75,000 and $63,000.

I had seen the Pick Six at other tracks where the participation was low, and the return was far below the commensurate risk — making it a sucker bet. My attitude towards the Pick Six changed dramatically when this bet was introduced at Canterbury Downs. Unlike other markets, Minnesotans embraced the play and pumped money into the daily pool with both fists. Soon it became apparent that the large carry-over pools — coupled with less than full fields — offered a good play for the experienced handicapper. The challenge was to figure out how to play it.

I developed an approach to playing the Pick Six which worked. I personally won the Pick Six five times in 1985 — including payoffs of $25,132 and $13,724. And I did so without spending a lot of cash. In fact, my five winning tickets cost me an average of $48.00 each. There were rumors abounding that outside betting syndicates were arriving in town to "buy" the Pick Six with six-figure investments. These rumors were without foundation, and the track's statistics support this. The average (median) cost of all the winning tickets was $12.00 according to Canterbury Downs officials. Another interesting stat — and one worth noting — is that there were an incredible number of single $2 winning tickets. This is significant for two reasons: 1) it made "buying" the pool a precarious play for betting syndicates because, irrespective of how many longshots came in, there was a strong probability that the pool would be shared by several winners. People playing license plates and the like make it very risky for the big players to plunge. Another interesting statistic from 1985 was the level of participation. On carry-over days, over 85 percent of those attending would buy one or more tickets. This high level of participation increased the "random" chances of winning for the small player. All of the above has made the Pick Six a legitimate wager for the average racegoer — and a risky play for high rollers trying to "buy" the pool.

Pick Six Strategy

Preliminary Steps — You are best advised to play the Pick Six on those days when there is a "carry-over" or going-in pool of over $100,000. This size pot will attract at least an additional $250,000 based on last year's patterns. Once the pot is built up, my approach to playing the Pick Six includes the following preliminary steps ...

1. Identify the "Key Horses" — these are the so-called "cinch" or short-priced horses the average player will "key" (i.e. use as a single selection in a given race).
2. Determine those races which are wide open — those with large, well balanced fields and no particular stand-out.

3. Identify outside or "mystery" horses that could upset at a price.

4. Watch the first two races closely to determine if there are any biases to the track. Determine whether speed will carry or not.

Basic Principles — In each of the following Pick Six techniques, there are certain common rules ...

1. You must have at least two "key" horses or singletons on your ticket.

2. It is less costly to add fourth, fifth and sixth horses in one race than to add a second horse to a singleton.

3. Make more than one ticket, and you'll increase your chances of having multiple "pick five" consolation winners than if you put all your combos one a single ticket.

4. Play to win big and that requires that at least two of the six winners pay over $16.00 — and usually one that pays over $20.00. Don't make tickets using all logical choices. Such "favorites" tickets did win, but the payoffs were paltry e.g. $445, $885 and $1,250.

5. Create "insurable" or "hedge-able" tickets when it comes down to the last race. Generally this requires that you have two, or preferably three, horses in the eighth race. And these should be the top choices or favorites in that race. (More on this aspect later).

6. Make separate "saver" tickets, rather than adding horses to your primary or main ticket(s).

7. And lastly, don't invest more than 20 percent of your daily bankroll on the Pick Six. Get a group together and share tickets.

Recommended Approach

Let's discuss the above principles and then create a prototype ticket ...

1. **Key Horses —** You must find two and sometimes three races where you will go with a single horse. The "key" horses are best taken in the higher class races, allowance and high-ticket, older claimers. The "figure" horses are least likely to be upset in these types of races. It's also better to select your key horses from races with smaller fields. This is smart for two reasons. First, and obviously, there are fewer horses to beat and smaller fields generally have fewer traffic problems etc. The second reason is that most players like to blanket or take "all" the horses in smaller fields when making bigger tickets. As a consequence, they have less coverage in those races with larger fields — races which are more likely to produce an "upset" winner.

2. **False Favorites —** More Pick Six tickets were shredded last year when odds-on horses disappointed. If you can spot these beatable favorites, you will be one of the few to "be alive" after these upsets. I call these races the "Great Eliminators," because so many players drop by the wayside after a prohibitive favorite bites the dust. Most horseplayers spend too much time trying to dope out the tough races and "assume" that their key horses will run to form. This is a critical mistake because if the chalk runs out, those who are still in the fight are in a small group — eligible for a a big payoff. Cheap claimers and maiden races head the list in this category. Cheap horses are generally inconsistent and seem to take turns beating each other. And maiden races frequently produce upsets by horses who have a dramatic change in form or by little known first-time starters. Another upset candidate is the odds-on claimer taking a sharp drop in price. Frequently these "favorites" are running on three legs. When faced with such races, I will take the favorite and one or two other horses — and these horses need not be the second choice or co-favorites. Look for upset horses — horses that have a real chance if everything goes their way. Look for horses who have won at a price in the past.

When looking at these races, I look for ways the favorite might lose — bad post position, unfavorable pace, track condition, etc. Then, assuming I find a scenario in which the favorite ends up in the toilet, I look to see how such a scenario might be to the advantage of another horse(s); for example, if the favorite is a front-running speedster who likes to be on the lead — and only wins when he gets the lead. If there are at least two other horses who can challenge the favorite during the early going, he may falter and fade in the stretch. And usually he will take the other speedsters who pushed him down the tube with him. Now we have eliminated the choice and two other horses. Next, examine the balance of the field and identify which horses would benefit from a suicidal early pace — the stretch-running types. Then take two or three of these and use them in place of or in addition to the favorite.

3. **Blanket the Field** — Some races come up so well-balanced that finding a key horse or a solid play is almost impossible. In these races, I look to eliminate two to four horses that couldn't win with a half mile headstart. Then I "blanket," or cover the balance of the field, hoping that a long-priced horse comes in.

Using the above tactics you might end up with a ticket that looks like the following ...

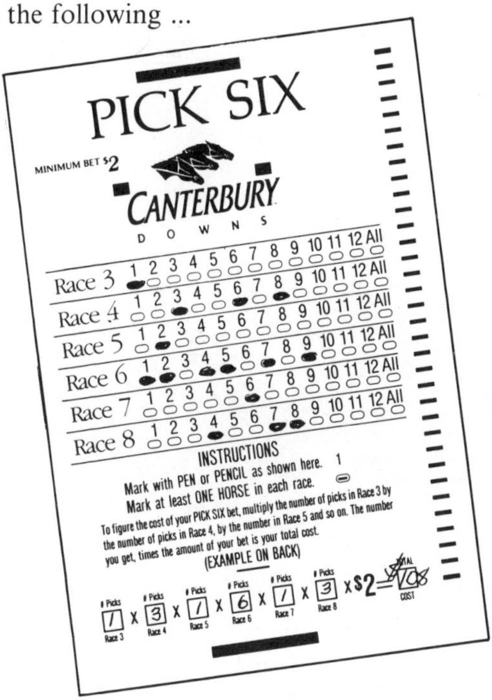

PICK SIX

MINIMUM BET $2

CANTERBURY DOWNS

Race 3 1 2 3 4 5 6 7 8 9 10 11 12 All
Race 4 1 2 3 4 5 6 7 8 9 10 11 12 All
Race 5 1 2 3 4 5 6 7 8 9 10 11 12 All
Race 6 1 2 3 4 5 6 7 8 9 10 11 12 All
Race 7 1 2 3 4 5 6 7 8 9 10 11 12 All
Race 8 1 2 3 4 5 6 7 8 9 10 11 12 All

INSTRUCTIONS

Mark with PEN or PENCIL as shown here.

Mark at least ONE HORSE in each race.

To figure the cost of your PICK SIX bet, multiply the number of picks in Race 3 by the number of picks in Race 4, by the number in Race 5 and so on. The number you get, times the amount of your bet is your total cost.

(EXAMPLE ON BACK)

Picks 1 (Race 3) X # Picks 3 (Race 4) X # Picks 1 (Race 5) X # Picks 6 (Race 6) X # Picks 1 (Race 7) X # Picks 3 (Race 8) X $2 = $108 TOTAL COST

Race 3	#1	Key horse
Race 4	#3, 6, 8	Favorite plus two outsiders
Race 5	#2	Key horse
Race 6	#1,2,4,5,7,9	Blanket
Race 7	#6	Key horse
Race 8	#4,7,8	Top three selections

Total Cost $108.00

Hedging — Let's assume that you have five winners in the first five races. Going into the the final race, you are "alive" with three horses in an eight horse field. Now what? Rather than sweat, make unkeepable vows to God and drink copious amounts of alcohol — HEDGE. This is a terrific spot to be in — you are already a winner. Here's how to do it ...

1. Record the win odds for the five horses not covered in your Pick Six ticket. Since you have taken the top three choices in the race, the other horses will go off at odds such as:

Horse	Odds
1	8-1
2	12-1
3	22-1
5	7-1
6	6-1

2. Estimate what the Pick Six might pay if you win. This will depend largely on a) the size of the pool and b) the estimated number of winners. The latter will be influenced by the odds of the horses that won the first five races. Let's say your ticket will be worth from $7,500 to $10,000. Use the lower figure.

3. Take a percentage of your estimated winnings — approximately 10-20% — and use this amount to insure or hedge your ticket. To hedge, you simply bet all the remaining horses to win, varying the amount in proportion to the odds. With a hedge budget of $1,000, you would allocate those dollars as follows ...

Horse	Odds	Hedge Bet
1	8-1	$200
2	12-1	$150
3	22-1	$100
4	Pick Six	0
5	7-1	$250
6	6-1	$300
7	Pick Six	0
8	Pick Six	0
TOTAL HEDGE		$1,000

Now that you have made these insurance bets, you are guaranteed a profit, irrespective of the outcome. You have a total investment at this point of $1,108 — your original bet plus the hedges. The chart below shows the outcome in terms of net profit when you hedge and when you don't.

Winning Horse	Your Payoff	Net Profit/(Loss) Hedged	No Hedge
1	$1,800	+$692	($108)
2	$1,800	+$692	($108)
3	$2,300	+$1,192	($108)
4	$7,500	+$6,392	+$7,500
5	$2,000	+$892	($108)
6	$2,100	+$992	($108)
7	$7,500	+$6,392	+$7,500
8	$7,500	+$6,392	+$7,500

Obviously, you can increase your hedge bets and play around with all kinds of combinations. But the principle is clear. Anything can happen in a horse race. And you should take out insurance when there is no downside risk.

(I know ... I know. You're saying, "Where does that idiot Pritchard think I can come up with $1,000." If you find yourself in the situation discussed above, you can always find other people to "buy in" on the ticket or finance the insurance bet for a percentage. If you don't mind a little usury, track me down.)

Choice Plus Outsider Approach

Another (and less expensive) approach involves taking a single "key" horse in two races. Then take your top choice plus a legitimate outsider in the other four races. The second horse or outsider should be 5-1 or higher in the morning line. This ticket will cost $32.00. Alternatively, take three singletons, two doubles and one triple. This ticket will cost $48.00.

Summary

You should play the Pick Six only on those days when there is a carry-over pool and you can "key" at least two races. If the card is too tough, save your money or make a single two dollar ticket. Lastly, the amount you or your group invests in the Pick Six should be in proportion to the size of the pool. Good luck.

XXII. Recap

To be successful and have a lot of fun at the track, we should follow the three steps outlined in the preceeding ...

I. Do Your Homework

II. Look at the Horses

III. Bet Shrewdly

Homework & Selecting Winners — The *Daily Racing Form* is absolutely essential for determining probable outcomes. The Past Performances provide us with a comprehensive history of the entrants. To qualify horses, we look at the factors of Distance, Class level and Track Condition. Once qualified, we then determine each horse's "best possible effort" by analyzing the factors of Pace, Post Position, Weight, Jockey and Trainer. And then we narrow the remaining horses down to our selection based on current form by looking at the factors of Speed and Condition.

Paddock Handicapping — Many things in life look great "on paper," but are disappointing in the flesh — and thoroughbreds are no exception. Racehorses are athletes, subject to dramatic changes in form and condition from week to week. Because of this, you are well advised to inspect the horses in the paddock before you bet to be sure that you get what you pay for.

Betting Shrewdly — I'll say it again — "Selecting winners is easy, betting properly is tough." The key to having some financial success at the track lies in your ability to recognize the "value" of your bet. This requires that you know the odds and the percentages of each wager. You must know when and when not to bet. And you must consider the amount of the bet as well.

One of the marvelous aspects of the game is that you can never learn it all. It doesn't take long to get a handle on the basics. After that, it's practice, practice, practice. The more you play, the more you learn. Despite my catty comments in the foreword, there are a number of terrific books on racing and handicapping. Put some of them on your Christmas list — they'll make even a Minnesota winter more bearable.

Good luck, and I'll see you in the winner's circle.

"They put the blinkers on the chalk, but he's short, probably be up the track and off the board..."

XXIII. Glossary of Racing Terms

Added Money - Purse money supplemented by the track to stakes posted by owners and breeders.

Allowance horse - A horse which competes primarily in allowance, stakes or handicap races. These horses are of higher quality/value than claiming-type horses.

Allowance race - A non-claiming race for better quality horses in which published conditions stipulate weight allowances according to previous earnings and/or number or type of victories.

Also Eligibles - Horses entered in a race that will run only if one of the designated starters is scratched.

Also Rans - Horses that finish out-of-the-money.

Apprentice - A jockey is considered an apprentice rider for twelve months following his/her fourth win.

Apprentice Allowance - Weight concession granted to horses ridden by apprentice riders. These allowances range from five to ten pounds.

Backside - The stable area.

Backstretch - The far straightaway of the track; the stable area.

Back up - When horses fatigue and slow down, usually in the stretch.

Bad Actor - An unruly or difficult horse to handle.

Bear In - Run towards the inside rail rather than straight.

Bear Out - Run towards the outer rail rather than straight.

Bleeder - A horse that suffers from respiratory stress and bleeds after intense exertion, e.g. a race.

Blinkers - Eye cups attach to a hood which partially restricts a horse's peripheral vision.

Bloodlines - Pedigree.

Blow Out - A short workout shortly before a race.

Bolt - To abruptly alter course and head off in a different direction.

Breed - To mate horses; type of horse.

Breeze - Running with the rider exercising some restraint, usually during a morning workout.

Breeder - Owner of a mare when she has her foal.

Broodmare - A female horse used for breeding.

Bucked Shins - An inflammation of the shins from over-exertion - a common problem of 2YO's when they begin to train hard or race.

Bug Boy - Apprentice rider.

Bull Ring - Tracks that are less than a mile in circumference, e.g. 1/2 or 5/8 of a mile.

Caulks (or "calks") - A type of racing plate (horseshoe) frequently used when the racing surface is muddy. Caulks have cleats which improve the horse's footing on an "off-track" or on the grass.

Chalk - The betting favorite.

Claimers - Horses which run primarily in claiming races.

Claim - To purchase a horse which is entered in a race for a specific claiming or purchase price. Claims must be placed with the Clerk of Claims no later than ten minutes before the post time of the race in which the horse is entered. Purchaser must take possession of the horse immediately after the race, irrespective of its condition or finish in the race. Any earnings a horse might make in that race go to the previous owner.

Claiming races - A race where horses entered can be purchased or "claimed" for a designated price by any licensed owner or trainer residing at that track. The most common type of race, constituting approximately 70 percent of all races run.

Climbing - When a horse runs in an upward fashion - head up and shortened strides - usually when fatigued.

Clocker - Track or DRF employee who times the workouts in the mornings.

Closer - A horse who runs from off the pace; a stretch-runner.

Colors - Distinctively patterned and colored jacket and cap worn by the jockey, identifying the horse's owner.

Colt - An unaltered male horse which has not reached his fifth birthdate.

Condition - Equine form or fitness; to train a horse.

Conditions book - Publication in which the track announces purses, terms of eligibility and weight formulas of future races.

Conditions - Terms of a race, including purse size, eligibility for entry, distance and weight allowances.

Connections - A horse's trainer, owner, groom, etal.

Conformation - A horse's basic physicality and appearance.

Daily Double - A wager whereby the better must select the winners of two consecutive races, usually the first and second races, prior to the first race.

Dam - A female parent of a horse.

Declare - To scratch out of a race.

Drop-down - A horse dropping down in price (in a claiming race).

Early Foot - Good early speed.

Entry - Two or more horses owned or trained by the same interests, entered in the same race and coupled in the wagering.

Exacta - A wager whereby the better must select the first and second place horses - in exact order - in a single race.

Exotic Bets - Bets such as the daily double, exactas and the Pick Six.

Exercise riders - Stable employees who gallop horses during morning workouts.

False Pace - An unusually slow early pace.

Farrier - Horseshoer.

Field - All entrants in a race; two or more outside horses coupled in the wagering when starting more than twelve horses in a race.

Filly - A female horse which has not reached her fifth birthdate.

Flash - A change in the odds on the tote board.

Foal - A horse born prior to January 1 of any year, after which date such horse is considered a yearling.

Footing - The condition of the track's running surface.

Furlong - 1/8 of a mile.

Gelding - Altered male horse.

Gimmick Bets - Exotic wagers such as the daily double and exactas.

Groom - Stable employee who cares for specific horses and accompanies those horses to and from the paddock when racing.

Halter - Hand held rope or strap by which horses are led; to claim a horse.

Handicap - A race contested by better quality horses in which the Racing Secretary or Track Handicapper assigns weights designed to equalize the winning chances of entrants; to study horses' records in an effort to determine the probable winner of a race.

Handily - A workout where the rider is asking for speed, rolling his knuckles on the horse's neck in a pumping fashion; a race won with little urging at the end.
Handle - Total sum bet on a race or in a day or other period of time.

Horse - Technically, any unaltered male horse, aged five or older; what will leave you a fortune if your father doesn't.

Hooked - When a horse is pressured by another horse running along side of it.

Hotwalker - A stable employee (or electrical device) that walks horses to cool them out after a race or a workout.

In the Money - Finishing first, second or third.

Inquiry - When either the stewards, rider or trainer makes a claim of foul against another rider in a race.

Jail - A 30-day period following a claim when the claimed horse must run for a price at least 25 percent higher than the price at which it was claimed.

Jockey - A racerider.

Jockey Agent - Individual who helps riders obtain mounts in return for 20 percent or more of the jockey's earnings.

Journeyman - A full-fledged jockey after he passes his apprentice period.

Lug In - To bear in.

Maiden - A horse that has not yet won a race.

Mare - A female horse aged five or older.

Morning Glory - Horses who run well in morning workouts, but not in races.

Morning Line - The track's line-maker's best estimate of the probable post time odds for each horse.

Odds On - Odds that are less than even money.

Off-the-Board - Failure to finish in the money, i.e. first, second or third.

Off the Pace - Running behind the early leaders.

Off-Track - A running surface that is rated anything other than fast.

Overlay - An under-bet horse; a good value.

Paddock - At the track, the saddling area. On the farm, a fenced pasture, generally restricted to specific types of horses, e.g. mares or stallions.

Parlay - A wagering technique whereby the better re-invests the proceeds from a bet on one race into another race or races.

Pool - Total amount of money wagered in a race, by category.

Pull Up - In a race, when a jockey pulls up and stops a horse short off the finish; after a race, the manner or condition a horse comes out of a race physically.

Racing Secretary - Track official who prescribes the conditions for races, and frequently serves as track handicapper, assigning weights to entrants in Handicap races. Serves as liaison between horsemen and track management, assigns stalls and supervises the claiming procedures.

Route - A distance race of a 1 1/8 miles or longer.

Router - A horse who generally runs in distance races.

Scratch - To withdraw a horse from a race after it's been entered.

Shadow Roll - A cloth or sheepskin roll placed on the muzzle of a horse to block his vision of the ground. Used to prevent a horse from jumping over shadows on the track or to lower their head to extend their stride.

Shedrow - The barn area at the track.

Shipper - A horse that arrives at a track from another track, usually after the meeting has begun; any horse that travels from one track to another.

Short - When a horse tires at the end of a race, usually after a layoff.

Short-priced - Low odds or paying a small mutuel price.

Silks - Colors, generally made of nylon, worn by jockeys.

Sire - Father of a horse.

Stakes race - A race in which the purse consists of nomination, entrance and starting fees plus money added by the track itself.

Stallion - An unaltered male horse; male horse used exclusively for breeding purposes.

Starter Race - Races for horses who have started for a specific claiming price. Usually run over a distance.

Stick-out - An obvious choice in a race.

Thoroughbreds - A breed of horses originated by the breeding of Arabian stallions with English mares, used principally for flat and steeplechase racing, the breeding of which is generally registered by the Jockey Club.

Tight - Fit or ready horse.

Training track (Trt) - Separate track where workouts are held and horses are schooled in the starting gate.

Washy -When a horse is sweating profusely, usually due to nervousness.

Weanling - A horse which is less than one year old and has been separated from its mother.

Wheel - To make either an exacta or daily double using a single "key" horse with the balance of the field or the second race.

Workouts - Serious training gallops whereby the rider asks the horse for speed. Usually run over short distances and recorded/reported by the track clockers.

Yearling - A horse which is actually one-year-old, or is deemed to be one-year-old on the first of January following the date of its birth.

XXIV. Appendix and Reference Guide

A. Key to *Daily Racing Form* Symbols & Abbreviations

FOREIGN-BRED HORSES

An asterisk (*) preceding the name of the horse indicates foreign-bred. (No notation is made for horses bred in Canada and Cuba.)

MUD MARKS

✱—Fair mud runner X—Good mud runner
⊗—Superior mud runner

COLOR

B—Bay Blk—Black Br—Brown Ch—Chestnut Gr—Gray
Ro—Roan Wh—White Dk b or br—Dark bay or brown

SEX

c—colt h—horse g—gelding rig—ridgling f—filly m—mare

PEDIGREE

Each horse's pedigree lists, in the order named, color, sex, age, sire, dam and grandsire (sire of dam).

BREEDER

Abbreviation following breeder's name indicates the state, Canadian province, place of origin or foreign country in which the horse was foaled.

TODAY'S WEIGHT

With the exception of assigned-weight handicap races, weights are computed according to the conditions of the race. Weight includes the rider and his equipment; saddle, lead pads, etc., and takes into account the apprentice allowance of pounds claimed. It does not include a jockey's overweight, which is announced by track officials prior to the race. The number of pounds claimed as an apprentice allowance is shown by a superior (small) figure to the right of the weight.

TODAY'S CLAIMING PRICE

If a horse is entered to be claimed, the price for which he may be claimed appears in bold face type to the right of the trainer's name.

RECORD OF STARTS AND EARNINGS

The horse's racing record for his most recent two years of competition appears to the extreme right of the name of the breeder and is referred to as his "money lines." This lists the year, number of starts, wins, seconds, thirds and earnings. The letter "M" in the win column of the upper line indicates the horse is a maiden. If the letter "M" is in the lower line only, it indicates the horse was a maiden at the end of that year.

TURF COURSE RECORD

The horse's turf course record shows his lifetime starts, wins, seconds, thirds and earnings on the grass and appears directly below his money lines.

LIFETIME RECORD

The horse's lifetime record shows his career races, wins, seconds, thirds and total earnings. The statistics, updated with each start, include all his races — on dirt, grass and over jumps — and are located under the trainer's name.

DISTANCE

a—preceding distance (a6f) denotes "about" distance (about 6 furlongs in this instance).

FOREIGN TRACKS

◆—before track abbreviation indicates it is located in a foreign country.

RACES OTHER THAN ON MAIN DIRT TRACK

⊡—following distance denotes inner dirt course.
Ⓣ—following distance indicates turf (grass) course race.
🅃—following distance indicates inner turf course.
[S]—following distance indicates steeplechase race.
[H]—following distance indicates hurdle race.

TRACK CONDITIONS

ft—fast fr—frozen gd—good sl—slow sy—sloppy
m—muddy hy—heavy
Turf courses, including steeplechase and hurdles:
hd—hard fm—firm gd—good yl—yielding sf—soft

SYMBOLS ACCOMPANYING CLOSING ODDS

* (preceding)—favorite e (following)—entry
f (following)—mutuel field

APPRENTICE OR RIDER WEIGHT ALLOWANCES

Allowance indicated by superior figure following weight—117^5.

ABBREVIATIONS USED IN POINTS OF CALL

no—nose hd—head nk—neck

DEAD-HEATS, DISQUALIFICATIONS

ꜜ—following the finish call indicates this horse was part of a dead-heat (an explanatory line appears under that past performance line).

†—following the finish call indicates this horse was disqualified. The official placing appears under the past performance line. An explanatory line also appears under the past performance of each horse whose official finish position was changed due to the disqualification.

‡—before the name of any of the first three finishers indicates the horse was disqualified from that position.

POST POSITION

Horse's post position appears after jockey's name—Smith T^3.

FILLY OR FILLY-MARE RACES

Ⓕ—preceding the race classification indicates races exclusively for fillies or fillies and mares.

RESTRICTED RACES

🅂—preceding the race classification denotes state-bred races restricted to horses bred in a certain state (or a given geographic area) which qualify under state breeding programs.

🅁—preceding the race classification indicates races that have certain eligibility restrictions other than sex or age.

RACE CLASSIFICATIONS

10000—Claiming race (eligible to be claimed for $10,000). Note: The letter c preceding claiming price (c10000) indicates horse was claimed.

M10000—Maiden claiming race (non-winners—eligible to be claimed).

10000H—Claiming handicap (eligible to be claimed).

o10000—Optional claiming race (entered NOT to be claimed).
10000o—Optional claiming race (eligible to be claimed).
Mdn—Maiden race (non-winners).
AlwM—Maiden allowance race (for non-winners with special weight allowances).
Aw10000—Allowance race with purse value.
HcpO—Overnight handicap race.
SplW—Special weight race.
Wfa—Weight-for-age race.
Mtch—Match race.
A10000—Starter allowance race (horses who have started for a claiming price shown, or less, as stipulated in the conditions).
H10000—Starter handicap (same restrictions as above).
S10000—Starter special weight (restricted as above). Note: Where no amount is specified in the conditions of the "starters" race dashes are substituted, as shown below:
A——— H——— S———
50000S—Claiming stakes (eligible to be claimed).

STAKES RACES

In stakes races, with the exception of claiming stakes, the name or abbreviation of name is shown in the class of race column. The letter "H" after name indicates the race was a handicap stakes. The same procedure is used for the rich invitational races for which there are no nomination or starting fees. The letters "Inv" following the abbreviation indicate the race was by invitation only.

SPEED RATINGS

This is a comparison of the horse's final time with the track record established prior to the opening of the racing season at that track. The track record is given a rating of 100. One point is deducted for each fifth of a second by which a horse fails to equal the track record (one length is approximately equal to one-fifth of a second). Thus, in a race in which the winner equals the track record (a Speed Rating of 100), another horse who is beaten 12 lengths (or an estimated two and two-fifths seconds) receives a Speed Rating of 88 (100 minus 12). If a horse breaks the track record he receives an additional point for each one-fifth second by which he lowers the record (if the track record is 1:10 and he is timed in 1:09⅗, his Speed Rating is 102). In computing beaten-off distances for Speed Ratings, fractions of one-half length or more are figured as one full length (one point). No Speed Ratings are given for steeplechase or hurdle events, for races of less than three furlongs, or for races for which the horse's speed rating is less than 25.
When Daily Racing Form prints its own time, in addition to the official track time, the Speed Rating is based on the official track time.
Note: Speed Ratings for new distances are computed and assigned when adequate time standards are established.

TRACK VARIANTS

This takes into consideration all of the races run on a particular day and could reflect either the quality of the competition, how many points below par the track happened to be, or both. The speed Rating of each winner is added together, then an average is taken based on the number of races run. This average is deducted from the track par of 100 and the difference is the Track Variant (example: average Speed Rating of winners involved is 86, par is 100, the Track Variant is 14). When there is

a change in the track condition during the course of a program the following procedure is employed in compiling the Variant: races run on dirt tracks classified as fast, frozen or good, and those listed as hard, firm or good on the turf, are used in striking one average. Strips classified as slow, sloppy, muddy or heavy on the dirt, or yielding and soft on the turf, are grouped for another average. If all the races on a program are run in either one or the other of these general classifications only one average is used. The lower the Variant the faster the track or the better the overall quality of the competition.
Note: A separate Track Variant is computed for races run on the turf (grass), straight course races, and for races run around turns at distances of less than 5 furlongs.

TROUBLE LINES

When a horse experiences trouble in a race, this information is reported, with the date of the incident, in a capsule description directly below the past performance line for that race.

WORKOUTS

Each horse's most recent workouts appear directly under the past performances. For example, Jly 20 Hol 3f ft :38b indicates the horse worked on July 20 at Hollywood Park. The distance of the work was 3 furlongs over a fast track and the horse was timed in 38 seconds, breezing. A "bullet" ● appearing before the date of a workout indicates that the workout was the best of the day for that distance at that track.

Abbreviations used in workouts

b—breezing d—driving e—easily g—worked from the gate h—handily bo—bore out Ⓣ—turf course Tr—trial race tr.t following track abbreviation indicates horse worked on training track.

B. Points of Call in the *Daily Racing Form*

	Points of Call				Fractional Times Given At These Points of Call		
Distance of Race	1st Call	2nd Call	3rd Call	4th Call			
2 Furlongs	Start	--	Stretch	Finish	--	--	Finish
5/16 Mile	Start	--	Stretch	Finish	--	--	Finish
3 Furlongs	Start	--	Stretch	Finish	1/4	--	Finish
3 1/2 Furlongs	Start	1/4	Stretch	Finish	1/4	3/8	Finish
4 Furlongs	Start	1/4	Stretch	Finish	1/4	--	Finish
4 1/2 Furlongs	Start	1/4	Stretch	Finish	1/4	1/2	Finish
5 Furlongs	3/16	3/8	Stretch	Finish	1/4	1/2	Finish
5 1/2 Furlongs	1/4	3/8	Stretch	Finish	1/4	1/2	Finish
6 Furlongs	1/4	1/2	Stretch	Finish	1/4	1/2	Finish
6 1/2 Furlongs	1/4	1/2	Stretch	Finish	1/4	1/2	Finish
7 Furlongs	1/4	1/2	Stretch	Finish	1/4	1/2	Finish
1 Mile	1/2	3/4	Stretch	Finish	1/2	3/4	Finish
1 Mile, 70 yards	1/2	3/4	Stretch	Finish	1/2	3/4	Finish
1 1/16 Miles	1/2	3/4	Stretch	Finish	1/2	3/4	Finish
1 1/8 Miles	1/2	3/4	Stretch	Finish	1/2	3/4	Finish
1 3/16 Miles	1/2	3/4	Stretch	Finish	1/2	3/4	Finish
1 1/4 Miles	1/2	1 mile	Stretch	Finish	1/2	1 mile	Finish
1 5/16 Miles	1/2	1 mile	Stretch	Finish	1/2	1 mile	Finish
1 3/8 Miles	1/2	1 mile	Stretch	Finish	1/2	1 mile	Finish
1 1/2 Miles	1/2	1 1/4	Stretch	Finish	1/2	1 1/4	Finish
1 5/8 Miles	1/2	1 3/8	Stretch	Finish	1/2	1 1/4	Finish
1 3/4 Miles	1/2	1 1/2	Stretch	Finish	1/2	1 1/2	Finish
1 7/8 Miles	1/2	1 5/8	Stretch	Finish	1/2	1 1/2	Finish
2 Miles	1/2	1 3/4	Stretch	Finish	1/2	1 3/4	Finish
2 1/16 Miles	1/2	1 3/4	Stretch	Finish	1/2	1 3/4	Finish
2 1/8 Miles	1/2	1 3/4	Stretch	Finish	1/2	1 3/4	Finish
2 1/4 Miles and Longer	1/2	2 miles	Stretch	Finish	1/2	2 miles	Finish

NOTE: The second call in most races is made 1/4 mile from the finish; the stretch call is made 1/8 mile from the finish. Thus, in races at 5 furlongs (5/8 mile), the stretch call is made after 1/2 mile (4 furlongs) has been run. The fractional time is given for the leading horse at that point.

C. Track Abbreviations & Purse Value Index (PVI)

Major North American Tracks

AC	(Agua) Caliente, Mexico	(3)
Aks	Ak-Sar-Ben, Neb.	(12)
Alb	Albequerque, N. Mex.	(6)
AP	Arlington Park, Ill.	(14)
Aqu	Aqueduct, N.Y.	(31)
AsD*	Assiniboia Downs, Canada	(4)
Atl	Atlantic City, N.J.	(8)
Ato*	Atokad Park, Neb.	(1)
Bel	Belmont, N.Y.	(31)
Bil*	Billings, Mont.	(2)
BM	Bay Meadows, Calif.	(12)
Bal	Balmoral, Ill.	(5)
BRD	Blue Ribbon Downs, Okla.	(2)
Cby	Canterbury Downs, Minn.	(9)
CD	Churchill Downs, Ky.	(12)
Cls*	Columbus, Neb.	(4)
Crc	Calder Race Course, Fla.	(12)
CT*	Charles Town, W. Va.	(3)
DeD*	Delta Downs, La.	(3)
Del	Delaware Park, Del.	(5)
Det	Detroit Race Course, Mich.	(6)
Dmr	Del Mar, Calif.	(22)
ElP	Ellis Park, Ky.	(4)
EP*	Exhibition Park, Canada	(6)
EvD	Evangeline Downs, La.	(3)
FE*	Fort Erie, Canada	(4)
FG	Fair Grounds, La.	(9)
FL	Finger Lakes, N.Y.	(5)
Fno	Fresno, Calif.	(4)
Fon*	Fonner Park, Neb.	(4)
FP	Fairmount Park, Ill.	(4)
GG	Golden Gate Fields, Calif.	(12)
GP	Gulfstream Park, Fla.	(15)
GS	Garden State Park, N.J.	(19)
Haw	Hawthorne, Ill.	(10)
Hia	Hialeah, Fla.	(12)
Hol	Hollywood Park, Calif.	(30)
JnD*	Jefferson Downs, La.	(4)
Kee	Keeneland, Ky.	(20)
LA*	Los Alamitos, Calif.	(10)
LaD	Louisiana Downs, La.	(12)
Lat	Latonia, Ky.	(6)
Lga	Longacres, Wash.	(8)
LnN*	Lincoln State Fair, Neb.	(3)
LrL	Laurel Race Course, Md.	(11)
Med	Meadowlands, N.J.	(15)
Mth	Monmouth Park, N.J.	(14)
NP*	Northlands Park, Canada	(5)
OP	Oaklawn Park, Ark.	(14)
Pen	Penn National, Pa	(4)
Pha	Philadelphia Park, Pa.	(11)
Pim	Pimlico, Md.	(10)
Pla	Playfair, Wash.	(2)
Pln	Pleasanton, Calif.	(10)
PM	Portland Meadows, Ore.	(2)
Pom*	Pomona, Calif.	(15)
PP	Pikes Peak Meadows, Colo.	NA
RD	River Downs, Ohio	(6)
Rkm	Rockingham Park, N.H.	(5)
Rui*	Ruidosa Downs, N. Mex.	(4)
SA	Santa Anita, Calif.	(29)
Sac	Sacramento, Calif.	(6)
Sar	Saratoga, N.Y.	(33)
SFe*	Santa Fe, N. Mex.	(4)
Spt	Sportsman's Park, Ill.	(13)
StP*	Stampede Park, Canada	(4)
Suf	Suffolk Downs, Mass.	(5)
Sun	Sunland Park, N. Mex.	(2)
Tam	Tampa Bay Downs, Fla.	(3)
Tdn	Thistledown, Ohio	(6)
Tim*	Timonium, Md.	(5)
TuP	Turf Paradise, Ariz.	(4)
Wat	Waterford Park, W. Va.	(2)
WO	Woodbine, Canada	(15)
YM	Yakima Meadows, Wash.	(1)

* Tracks less than a mile in circumference

** The Purse Value Index (PVI) is the average net purse per race rounded to the nearest thousand for the 1985 season. These figures include both overnight and stakes purses.

D. How to Read the Daily Program

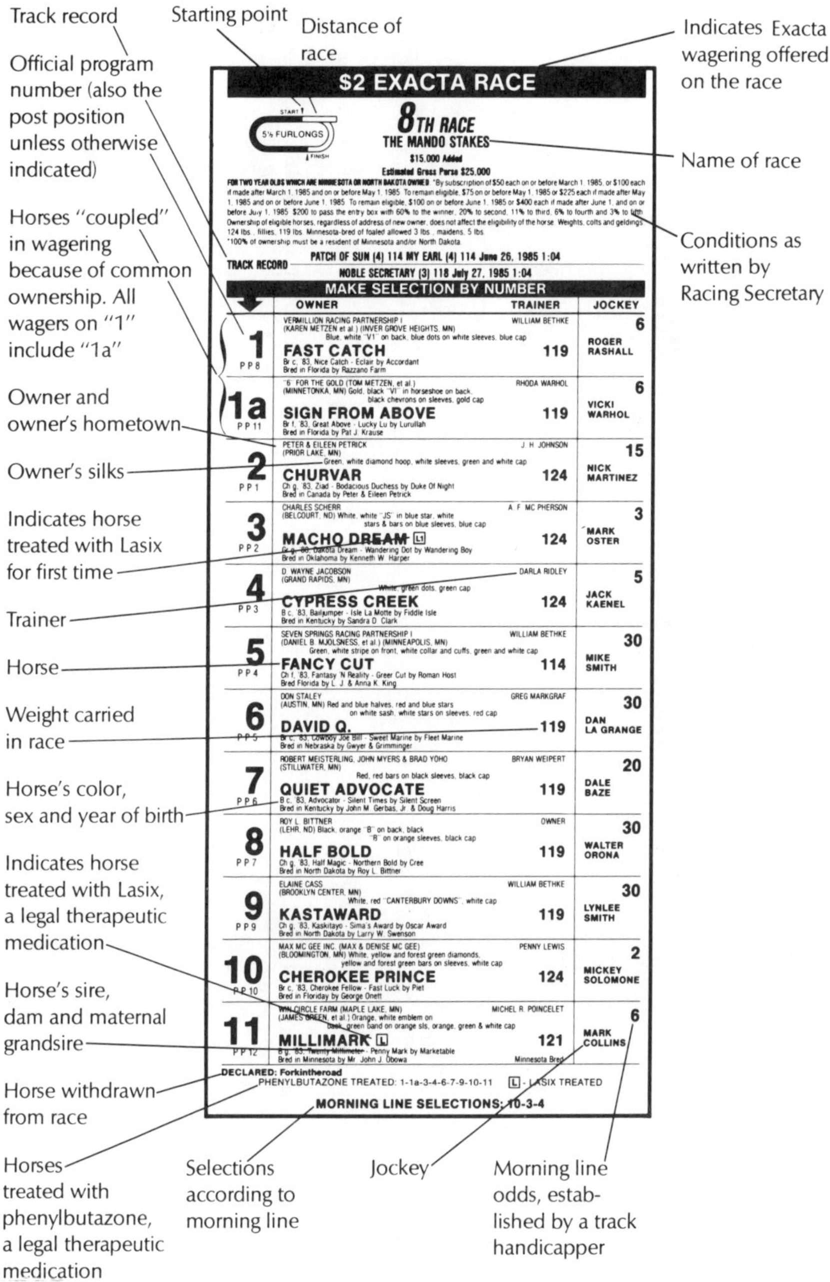

$2 EXACTA RACE

START — 5½ FURLONGS — FINISH

8TH RACE
THE MANDO STAKES
$15,000 Added
Estimated Gross Purse $25,000

FOR TWO YEAR OLDS WHICH ARE MINNESOTA OR NORTH DAKOTA OWNED. *By subscription of $50 each on or before March 1, 1985, or $100 each if made after March 1, 1985 and on or before May 1, 1985. To remain eligible, $75 on or before May 1, 1985 or $225 each if made after May 1, 1985 and on or before June 1, 1985. To remain eligible, $100 on or before June 1, 1985 or $400 each if made after June 1, and on or before July 1, 1985. $200 to pass the entry box with 60% to the winner, 20% to second, 11% to third, 6% to fourth and 3% to fifth. Ownership of eligible horses, regardless of address of new owner, does not affect the eligibility of the horse. Weights, colts and geldings 124 lbs., fillies, 119 lbs. Minnesota-bred of foaled allowed 3 lbs., maidens, 5 lbs.
*100% of ownership must be a resident of Minnesota and/or North Dakota.

TRACK RECORD — **PATCH OF SUN (4) 114 MY EARL (4) 114 June 26, 1985 1:04**
NOBLE SECRETARY (3) 118 July 27, 1985 1:04

MAKE SELECTION BY NUMBER

	OWNER	TRAINER	JOCKEY
1 PP8	VERMILLION RACING PARTNERSHIP I (KAREN METZEN et al.) (INVER GROVE HEIGHTS, MN) Blue, white "V1" on back, blue dots on white sleeves, blue cap **FAST CATCH** **119** Br c, '83, Nice Catch - Eclair by Accordant Bred in Florida by Razzano Farm	WILLIAM BETHKE	**6** **ROGER RASHALL**
1a PP11	"6" FOR THE GOLD (TOM METZEN, et al.) (MINNETONKA, MN) Gold, black "VI" in horseshoe on back, black chevrons on sleeves, gold cap **SIGN FROM ABOVE** **119** Br f, '83, Great Above - Lucky Lu by Lurullah Bred in Florida by Pat J. Krause	RHODA WARHOL	**6** **VICKI WARHOL**
2 PP1	PETER & EILEEN PETRICK (PRIOR LAKE, MN) Green, white diamond hoop, white sleeves, green and white cap **CHURVAR** **124** Ch g, '83, Ziad - Bodacious Duchess by Duke Of Night Bred in Canada by Peter & Eileen Petrick	J. H. JOHNSON	**15** **NICK MARTINEZ**
3 PP2	CHARLES SCHERR (BELCOURT, ND) White, white "JS" in blue star, white stars & bars on blue sleeves, blue cap **MACHO DREAM** [L1] **124** Gr g, '80, Dakota Dream - Wandering Dot by Wandering Boy Bred in Oklahoma by Kenneth W. Harper	A. F. MC PHERSON	**3** **MARK OSTER**
4 PP3	D. WAYNE JACOBSON (GRAND RAPIDS, MN) White, green dots, green cap **CYPRESS CREEK** **124** B c, '83, Bailjumper - Isle La Motte by Fiddle Isle Bred in Kentucky by Sandra D. Clark	DARLA RIDLEY	**5** **JACK KAENEL**
5 PP4	SEVEN SPRINGS RACING PARTNERSHIP I (DANIEL B. MJOLSNESS, et al.) (MINNEAPOLIS, MN) Green, white stripe on front, white collar and cuffs, green and white cap **FANCY CUT** **114** Ch f, '83, Fantasy 'N Reality - Greer Cut by Roman Host Bred Florida by L. J. & Anna K. King	WILLIAM BETHKE	**30** **MIKE SMITH**
6 PP5	DON STALEY (AUSTIN, MN) Red and blue halves, red and blue stars on white sash, white stars on sleeves, red cap **DAVID Q.** **119** Br c, '83, Cowboy Joe Bill - Sweet Marine by Fleet Marine Bred in Nebraska by Gwyer & Grimminger	GREG MARKGRAF	**30** **DAN LA GRANGE**
7 PP6	ROBERT MEISTERLING, JOHN MYERS & BRAD YOHO (STILLWATER, MN) Red, red bars on black sleeves, black cap **QUIET ADVOCATE** **119** B c, '83, Advocator - Silent Times by Silent Screen Bred in Kentucky by John M. Gerbas, Jr. & Doug Harris	BRYAN WEIPERT	**20** **DALE BAZE**
8 PP7	ROY L. BITTNER (LEHR, ND) Black, orange "B" on back, black "B" on orange sleeves, black cap **HALF BOLD** **119** Ch g, '83, Half Magic - Northern Bold by Cree Bred in North Dakota by Roy L. Bittner	OWNER	**30** **WALTER ORONA**
9 PP9	ELAINE CASS (BROOKLYN CENTER, MN) White, red "CANTERBURY DOWNS", white cap **KASTAWARD** **119** Ch g, '83, Kaskitayo - Sima's Award by Oscar Award Bred in North Dakota by Larry W. Swenson	WILLIAM BETHKE	**30** **LYNLEE SMITH**
10 PP10	MAX MC GEE INC. (MAX & DENISE MC GEE) (BLOOMINGTON, MN) White, yellow and forest green diamonds, yellow and forest green bars on sleeves, white cap **CHEROKEE PRINCE** **124** Br c, '83, Cherokee Fellow - Fast Luck by Piet Bred in Floriday by George Onett	PENNY LEWIS	**2** **MICKEY SOLOMONE**
11 PP12	WIN CIRCLE FARM (MAPLE LAKE, MN) (JAMES GREEN, et al.) Orange, white emblem on back, green band on orange sls, orange, green & white cap **MILLIMARK** [L] **121** B g, '83, Twenty Millimeter - Penny Mark by Marketable Bred in Minnesota by Mr. John J. Obowa — Minnesota Bred	MICHEL R. POINCELET	**6** **MARK COLLINS**

DECLARED: Forkintheroad
PHENYLBUTAZONE TREATED: 1-1a-3-4-6-7-9-10-11 [L] - LASIX TREATED
MORNING LINE SELECTIONS: 10-3-4

Medication listings created for sample.

E. How to Read the Tote Board

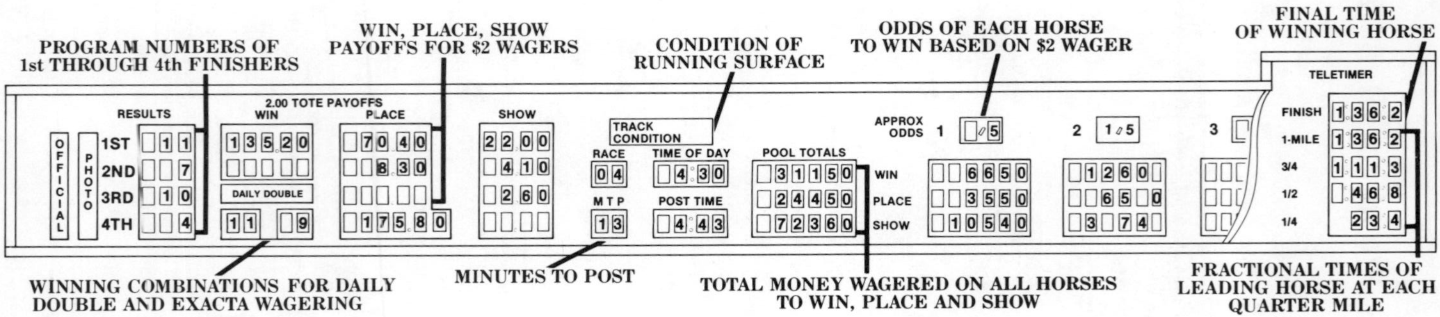

F. Odds, Payoffs & Probabilities

The following chart details what the approximate return will be on a $2.00 win bet on a horse that goes off at the odds listed. You must remember that the odds are expressed in terms of profit-per-dollar wagered. Following the payoff is the percent probability of winning for a horse going off at such odds.

Odds	Payoff	% Winning	Odds	Payoff	% Winning
1-9	$2.20	71.3	5-2	$7.00	23.0
1-5	2.40	71.3	3-1	8.00	20.9
2-5	2.80	71.3	7-2	9.00	18.6
1-2	3.00	71.3	4-1	10.00	16.1
3-5	3.20	55.3	9-2	11.00	15.5
4-5	3.60	51.3	5-1	12.00	12.3
1-1	4.00	47.0	6-1	14.00	11.0
6-5	4.40	40.3	7 1	16.00	9.9
7-5	4.80	37.9	8-1	18.00	8.2
3-2	5.00	37.9	9-1	20.00	8.2
8-5	5.20	35.5	10-1	22.00	6.0
9-5	5.60	30.9	12-1	26.00	6.0
2-1	6.00	28.9	15-1	32.00	4.0
			20-1 and over	42.00	1.4

G. Computing Place & Show Payoffs

The tote board provides you with the total pools, i.e. dollars wagered on each horse to win, place and show. The odds displayed on the board, however, are only the odds to win. Place and show odds cannot be displayed because they are contingent on which horses share in the pools.

You can estimate the minimum payoffs for place and show bets by using the following formula. When doing this, you assume that the these pools will be shared by thoses horses with the greatest amount of money bet on in each pool. (Obviously, if any other horse, especially a longshot, finishes second or third, the payoffs will be proportionately higher).

The "tote board" below shows the dollar amounts bet on each horse in a seven horse field, and the totals for each pool.

	Total	**1**	**2**	**3**	**4**	**5**	**6**	**7**
Win	-	-	-	-	-	-	-	-
Place	$20000	4800	3400	1400	1700	5200	1000	2500
Show	$16000	3700	1800	1100	1500	4900	800	2200

Place Price

To determine what the minimum payoff for horse # 4 to place, We would follow these steps:

1) Deduct 20% from the total place pool (to account for the state and track "takeout"): $20,000 less 20% or $4,000 equals $16,000.

2) Add thc place money bet on #4 to the money bet on the horse getting the most action, (i.e. #5): $1,700 + $5,200 equals $6,900.

3) Subtract this amount from the total available to determine the total profit: $16,000 — $6,900 equals $9,100.

4) Divide the available profit into two parts (since both horses will pay to place): $9,100 ÷ by 2 equals $4,550.

5) Divide the profit available by the dollars bet to determine the odds (profit per dollar): $4,550 ÷ $1,700 = $2.46. Round down to the nearest 20¢, and you end up with $2.40 profit. Add this to your original $2.00 bet and you get a minimum place price of $4.40 on horse #4.

Show Price

The same basic approach is employed, except this time we use three horses. Let's determine the minimum show price for horse #7.

1) Deduct 20% from the total show pool: $16,000 — $3,200 equals $12,800.

2) Add the show money on #7 with the remaining top two favorites in the pool (#1 and #5): $2,200 + $3,700 + $4,900 equals $10,800.

3) Subtract this amount from the total pool available: $12,800 — $10,800 equals $2,000.

4) Divide this profit available by three: $2000 ÷ 3 equals $667.

5) Divide this profit available-per-horse by the total bet on #7: $667 ÷ $2,200 equals 40¢ profit per dollar bet. The minimum show price on #7 would then be $2.80.

Estimating these prices will come easily once you understand the technique. Obviously, rounding numbers speeds up the process. Last season there were a number of excellent overlays in these secondary pools. Generally speaking, they existed on favorites who were over-bet to win, yet under-bet to place or show.

A tip ... betting longshots to show is a lousy play because, more often than not, the favorites share in the pool. So if you are betting long-priced horses, bet something to win, then "insure" your bet in the place or show pools.

H. CANTERBURY DOWNS
Par Times - 1985

The following chart shows the Par Times (or average running times on a normal or "fast" track) for races run at Canterbury Downs during its inaugural season. The times are broken out by class of horse. These figures should be viewed directionally, as speed figures can vary significantly from year to year. (Not shown are the "pace figures". A complete chart, including pace figures for each distance is available through Woodside Associates, Millerton, NY.)

	Distance					
Class	**5 1/2f**	**6f**	**6 1/2f**	**1mi.**	**1 70 mi.**	**1 1/16mi.**
Stakes	104.2	110.0	116.3	137.2	142.0	144.1
Top Allowance	104.4	110.2	117.0	137.4	142.2	144.3
NW of 3	105.0	110.3	117.1	138.0	142.3	144.4
NW of 2	105.1	110.4	117.2	138.2	143.0	145.1
NW of 1	105.3	111.1	117.4	138.4	143.2	145.3
Mdn Spl Wt	106.0	111.3	118.1	139.2	144.0	146.1

****

Claiming						
$50,000	104.3	110.1	116.4	137.2	142.0	144.1
$35,000	104.4	110.2	117.0	137.4	142.2	144.3
$25,000	105.0	110.3	117.1	138.1	142.4	145.0
$20,000	105.1	110.4	117.2	138.2	143.0	145.1
$15,000	105.2	111.0	117.3	138.4	143.2	145.3
$13,000	105.3	111.1	117.4	139.0	143.3	145.4
$10,000	105.4	111.2	118.0	139.1	143.4	146.0
$ 8.500	106.0	111.3	118.1	139.2	144.0	146.1
$ 7,500	106.1	111.4	118.2	139.3	144.1	146.2
$ 6,500	106.2	112.0	118.3	139.4	144.2	146.3
$ 5,000	106.3	112.1	118.4	140.0	144.3	146.4
$ 4,000	106.4	112.2	119.0	140.1	145.0	147.1

I. Par Times Comparisons Source Tracks vs. CANTERBURY DOWNS

The following chart provides a rough guide for comparing times run at other tracks versus those run at Canterbury Downs. Dr. William L. Quirin has developed these figures for all the major tracks in North America — and these figures are broken down by class and pace. Individual tracks or a complete set of these charts are available from Woodside Associates, P.O. Box 798, Millerton, NY 12546.

To illustrate the differences between tracks in a general sense, these comparisons are based on only one class — 4YO, males, running in $10,000 claiming races, on a fast track with an "honest" or fast pace.

1985 Par Times

Track	5½f	6f	6½f	7f	1mi.	170	1 1/16	1 1/8
Canterbury	105.4	111.2	118.0	--	139.1	143.4	146.0	--
Ak-Sar-ben	105.0	111.2	--	--	--	143.2	145.4	152.2
Bay Meadows	104.2	110.4	--	--	137.1	--	143.4	150.2
Churchill Downs	--	111.2	118.1	125.0	136.1	--	146.4	153.2
Del Mar (*)	--	110.4	117.1	123.4	137.0	--	143.3	150.1
Fair Grounds	106.1	112.3	--	--	(a) 143.1		147.2	154.0
Golden Gate	104.2	110.4	--	--	138.3		145.1	151.4
Gulfstream	--	111.1	--	124.1	--	--	145.3	152.1
Hawthorne	--	111.1	117.4	--	--	--	145.1	151.4
Hialeah	--	111.0	117.3	124.1	--	--	144.0	150.3
Hollywood (*)	--	111.4	118.1	124.4	138.0	--	145.2	152.0
Keeneland	--	113.1	120.0	126.4	(b) 130.3		148.1	155.1
Longacres	103.3	110.0	--	--	137.1	--	143.4	150.2
Louisiana Downs	--	111.3	118.1	124.4	--	143.4	146.0	152.4
Oaklawn	104.2	110.4	--	--	137.3	141.4	144.1	150.4
Santa Anita (*)	--	111.0	117.2	124.0	138.0	--	144.3	151.1
Sportsman's	--	112.4	118.2	--	140.0	--	146.2	153.1
Tampa Bay	107.1	113.3	--	126.4	--	147.4	150.2	--
Turf Paradise	103.3	110.0	116.2	--	137.1	--	144.0	150.4

(a) 1mi. 40yds.

(b) about 1 mi.

(*) $10,000 is the bottom or lowest claiming level at these tracks. Consequently, par times for "mid-range" claimers are significantly faster.

J. Source Tracks Stats, Records & Specs

The following tracks are the primary "source tracks" for Canterbury Downs. The majority of the horses competing at Canterbury will have generated their most recent Past Performances at these tracks.

****

Ak-sar-ben

Omaha, Nebraska

Abbreviation: **Aks**
Purse Value Index (PVI): 12

Circumference: 1 mile
Length of stretch: 990 feet

Race Day Medications:
Lasix — 6 hours before post
Bute — None

Track Records

5 furlongs	:57
5 1/2 furlongs	1:02
6 furlongs	1:07^{2}
1-70 yds	1:39^{2}
1 1/16 miles	1:40^{3}
1 1/8	1:47^{2}

1985
Trainer Standings:
Wayne D. Lukas
Jack Van Berg
Don Von Hemel
Herb Riecken
Hoss Inman
C.L. Dickey
T.V. Smith
Terry Knight
David Anderson
Orin J. Glass, Jr.

1985
Jockey Standings:
Tim Doocy
John Lively
Dale Cordova
Bobby Walker
Don Pettinger
Tim Masters
Craig McGurn
Tim Brown
Don Frazier
David Pettinger

****

****

Churchill Downs

Lousiville, Kentucky

Abbreviation: **CD**
Purse Value Index (PVI): 12

Circumference: 1 Mile
Length of stretch: 1,234 feet

Race Day Medications:
Lasix & Bute
with no limitations

Track Records

5 furlongs	:57[4]
5 1/2 furlongs	1:04[1]
6 furlongs	1:09
6 1/2 furlongs	1:16
7 furlongs	1:21[1]
1 mile	1:33[4]
1-70 yds	1:41[3]
1 1/16	1:41[3]
1 1/8	1:48[2]

1985 Fall
Trainer Standings:
Bill Mott
C.R. McGaughey, III
Steven Penrod
Don Winfree
Joseph M. Bolero
Jerry Calvin
Lyle Whiting
Carl Dowman
A.J. Foyt, III
G.R. Arnold, II

1985 Fall
Jockey Standings:
Patrick Day
Michael McDowell
Charles R. Woods, Jr.
Keith K. Allen
Larry Melancon
Julio Espinoza
James McKnight
Phil Rubbicco
Mike Smith
Daryl Montoya

****

Fair Grounds

New Orleans, Louisiana

Abbreviation: **FG**
Purse Value Index (PVI): 9

Circumference: 1 mile
Length of stretch: 1,346 feet

Race Day Medications:
Lasix — 4 hours before post
Bute — No restrictions

Track Records

5 1/2 furlongs	1:03[3]
6 furlongs	1:09
1 1/16	1:42[2]
1 1/8	1:48[4]

1986* Trainer Standings:	1986* Jockey Standings:
C.W. Walker	Ronald Ardoin
Frank Brothers	Ricky Frazier
Jack Van Berg	Randy Romero
Bill Mott	Jeff Faul
J.R. Smith	M. Torres
J.P. Dorignac, III	Julio Espinoza
B.S. Flint	Gerard Melancon
W.I. Fox	C.J. Perrodin
Gerald Romero	Bobby Walker
Clifford Scott	Kirk LeBlanc

*thru 4/6/86

****

Hialeah

Miami, Florida

Abbreviation: **Hia**
Purse Value Index (PVI): 12

Circumference: 1 1/8 miles
Length of stretch: 1,075

Race Day Medications:
Lasix — 4 hours before post
Bute — No restrictions

Track Records

5 furlongs	:57[1]
5 1/2 furlongs	1:04[3]
6 furlongs	1:08
6 1/2 furlongs	1:15[4]
7 furlongs	1:20[3]
1 mile	1:36[3]
1 1/16	1:40[3]
1 1/8	1:46[2]

1986 Trainer Standings:	1986 Jockey Standings:
Lester. R.	Tammaro, J.
Belez, J.A.	Pierce, J.H.
Suckie, M.	Olivares, L.
Cruguet, J.	Plesa, E.
Perret, C.	Crupi, J.J.
Gonzalez, M.A.	Sonnier, B.J.
Duarte, J.	Croll, W.A.
Soto, S.	Lepman, B.
Rodriguez, F.	Blengs, B.
McCauley, H.	

****

****

Keeneland

Lexington, Kentucky

Abbreviation: **Kee**
Purse Value Index (PVI): 20

Circumference: 1 1/16 miles
Length of stretch: 1,174

Race Day Medications:
No restrictions

Track Records

5 1/2 furlongs	$1:05^{4}$
6 furlongs	$1:08^{2}$
6 1/2 furlongs	$1:15^{2}$
7 furlongs	$1:21^{1}$
1 1/16 miles	$1:41^{1}$
1 1/8	$1:47^{2}$

1985 Fall Trainer Standings:	**1985 Fall Jockey Standings:**
C.R. McGaughey III	Patrick Day
Bill Mott	Randy Romero
Joseph Bollero	Keith Allen
Del W. Carroll II	Charles Woods, Jr.
J.D. Fredericksen	Don Brumfield
Stanley Rieser	Larry Melancon
James E. Morgan	Mike Smith

****

Louisiana Downs

Bossier, Louisiana

Abbreviation: **LaD**
Purse Value Index (PVI): 12

Circumference: 1 mile
Length of stretch: 1,010

Race Day Medications:

Race Day Medications:
Lasix — 4 hours before post
Bute — No restrictions

Track Records

5 furlongs	$:58^{1}$
5 1/2 furlongs	$1:03^{1}$
6 furlongs	$1:08^{2}$
6 1/2 furlongs	1:15
7 furlongs	$1:21^{3}$
1-70 yds	$1:39^{2}$
1 1/16	$1:42^{2}$
1 1/8	1:49

1985 Trainer Standings:	1985 Jockey Standings:
Frank Brothers	Larry Synder
C.W. Walker	Ronald Ardoin
Gerald Romero	Donald Howard
Gene Norman	David E. Whited
Robert Holthus	Ricky Frazier
R.D. Schultz	Terry Sonnier*
George Hallock	Kenneth Borque
Tim Van Berg	Jeff Faul
Larry Robideaux, Jr.	Dan Delahoussaye
Paul Holthus	Jon Court

****

Oaklawn Park

Hot Springs, Arkansas

Abbreviation: **OP**
Purse Value Index (PVI): 14

Circumference: 1 mile
Length of stretch: 1,155

Race Day Medications:
None

Track Records

5 furlongs	:57[3]
5 1/2 furlongs	1:02[3]
6 furlongs	1:08
1 mile	1:34[2]
1-70 yds	1:38[2]
1 1/16	1:40[1]
1 1/8	1:46[4]

1986* Trainer Standings:	1986* Jockey Standings:
Bill Mott	Pat Day
William Fires	Larry Snyder
Gary Thomas	David Whited
A.J. Foyt III	Mike Smith
Jack Van Berg	Don Howard
David Vance	Dean Kutz
Jean Brennan	Larry Melancon
J.R. Smith	John Lively
Phil Hauswald	Patrick Johnson

* thru 4/4/86

****

****

Santa Anita

Arcadia, California

Abbreviation: **SA**
Purse Value Index (PVI): 29

Circumference: 1 mile
Length of stretch: 990

Race Day Medications:
Lasix — 4 hours before post
Bute — 5 mcg/ml

Track Records

5 furlongs	:58[3]
5 1/2 furlongs	1:02[1]
6 furlongs	1:07[3]
6 1/2 furlongs	1:14
7 furlongs	1:20
1 mile	1:33[3]
1 1/16	1:40[1]
1 1/8	1:45[4]

1986* Trainer Standings:	1986* Jockey Standings:
Charles Whittingham	Chris McCarron
Melvin F. Stute	Gary Stevens
D. Wayne Lukas	Patrick Valenzuela
Bruce Headley	Eddie Delahoussaye
Mike Mitchell	Laffit Pincay, Jr.
John H.M. Gosden	Alex Solis
Jerry Fanning	Corey Black
Robert Frankel	Jack Kaenel
L.S. Barrera	Frank Olivares
Joseph Manzi	William Shoemaker

*thru 4/12/86

****

Sportsman's Park

Cicero, Illinois

Abbreviation: **Spt**
Purse Value Index (PVI): 13

Circumference: 5/8 mile
Length of stretch: 902

Race Day Medications:
Lasix — 4 hours before post
Bute — 2 mcg/ml

Track Records

6 furlongs	1:10
6 1/2 furlongs	1:15[2]
1 mile	1:36
1 1/16	1:42[4]
1 1/8	1:49

1986** Trainer Standings:	1986** Jockey Standings:
Richard Hazelton	Carlos Silva
Frank Kirby	Juvenal Diaz
E.T. Poulos	Ron Hansen
E.W. Reynolds	K.C. Patin
Wm. Catalano	Michael Moran
T. Tomillo	Randall Meier
Steve Specht	Frank Briggs
George Getz	Eusibio Bazo
G.D. McGrath	Brent Bullard
Neil Boyce	Nicholas Meza*

** thru 4/10/86

****

Turf Paradise

Phoenix, Arizona

Abbreviation: **TuP**
Purse Value Index (PVI): 4

Circumference: 1 mile
Length of stretch: 990

Race Day Medications:
None

Track Records

5 furlongs	:55[2]
5 1/2 furlongs	1:01[3]
6 furlongs	1:07[1]
6 1/2 furlongs	1:14[1]
7 furlongs	1:26[1]
1 mile	1:33[4]
1 1/16	1:39[3]
1 1/8	1:48[1]

1986* Trainer Standings:	1986* Jockey Standings:
Creed Botts	Pat Steinberg
R.L. Lockwood	Don Simington
Janeen Haller	Marty Wentz
Kory Owens	Vince Guerra
Kent Jensen	Orlando Garrido
Danny Hunsaker	Jim Powell
Joe W. Weaver	Bill Stallings
Robert Parker	Dan La Grange
Lyman Rollins	George Munsell
Bart Hone	Hugo Ditteach
Kevin Eikleberry	Scott Dahl

*thru 4/7/86

****

K. National Trainer Standings - 1985

Based on Money Won

Trainer	Starts	1st	2nd	3rd	%	$ (000)
Lukas, D. Wayne	1,140	218	183	135	.191	$11,155
Whittingham, Charles	464	68	71	61	.147	5,896
Van Berg, Jack	1,883	235	223	202	.141	4,627
Gambolati, Cam	114	11	11	13	.096	3,704
Frankel, Robert	375	74	69	51	.197	3,572
Mott, William L.	695	154	117	109	.222	3,469
Stephens, Woodford C.	262	53	50	31	.202	3,323
Gosden, John H.	451	77	78	53	.171	3,263
McGaughey, Claude,III	395	94	78	56	.238	3,180
Jones, Gary	435	81	65	52	.186	3,138
Stute, Melvin F.	651	97	77	76	.149	2,979
Drysdale, Neil	248	52	47	36	.210	2,743
Barrera, Lazaro S.	475	63	88	65	.133	2,668
Veitch, John M.	97	17	17	15	.175	2,586
Nerud, Jan H.	286	55	37	32	.192	2,581
Moschera, Gasper S.	593	87	102	97	.147	2,348
McAnally, Ronald	490	70	63	70	.147	2,48
Bothers, Frank L.	604	174	99	58	.288	2,151
Schulhofer, Flint B.	295	52	33	21	.176	2,138
Jerkens, H. Allan	515	62	78	71	.120	2,056

K. National Trainer Standings - 1985

Based on Races Won

Trainer	Starts	1st	2nd	3rd	%	$ (000)
Baird, Dale	1,670	249	201	216	.149	$453
Van Berg, Jack	1,883	235	223	202	.141	4,627
Lukas, D. Wayne	1,140	218	183	135	.191	11,155
Leatherbury, King T.	870	186	136	126	.214	1,505
Benelto, Marlo	817	175	128	112	.214	629
Bothers, Frank L.	604	174	99	58	.288	2,151
Reese, Walter C.	852	170	123	107	.200	1,334
Walker, Charles W.	904	162	108	116	.179	1,359
Mott, William L.	695	154	117	109	.222	3,469
Henry, Billy J.	1.084	133	135	132	.123	1,054
Hilton, Robert R.	596	125	89	72	.210	391
Klesaria, Robert P.	430	123	75	66	.286	854
Alfano, Ronald A.	664	120	119	102	.181	1,006
Hazelton, Richard	602	119	87	74	.198	906
Angella, Dale	654	113	104	99	.173	336
Garcia, Juan	505	105	77	74	.208	395
Borosh, Allen	441	104	81	51	.236	454
Roberta, Tom	551	103	88	85	.187	824
Barrera, Oscar S.	701	103	85	108	.147	1,992
Dandy, Ronald	401	99	70	64	.247	750

Note: Although "Dollars Won" and "Number of Winners" are the standard measures, top trainers with smaller stables may saddle more winners per start. So pay close attention to each trainer's winning percentage.

L. National Jockey Standings

Based on Races Won - 1985

Jockey	Mounts	1st	2nd	3rd	% Wins
Antley, C.W.	2,336	469	371	288	.201
Romero, R.P.	1,829	416	327	229	.227
Day, P.	1,417	323	252	193	.228
McCauley, W.H.	1,509	316	221	197	.209
Baze, R.A.	1,365	306	246	194	.224
Gamberdella, C.	1,290	292	226	200	.226
Pincay, L. Jr.	1,409	289	246	183	.205
McCarron, C.J.	1,367	287	227	192	.210
Miller, D.A. Jr.	1,604	270	262	233	.168
Migliore, R.	1,666	266	200	210	.160
Diaz, J.L.	1,565	284	222	199	.169
Velasquez	1,465	258	259	201	.176
Colton, R.E.	1,304	248	205	172	.190
Snyder, L.	1,025	242	162	100	.236
Santos, J.A.	1,583	242	241	211	.153
Vargas, J.L.	1,139	241	205	179	.212
Fires, E.	1,577	241	205	179	.153
Ardoin, R,	1,520	233	182	214	.157
Borel, B.H.	1,443	234	201	159	.162
Cordero, A. Jr.	1,150	233	182	177	.203

M. 1985 CANTERBURY DOWNS Trainer and Jockey Standings

Final Trainer Standings

Trainer	Starts	1sts	2nds	3rds	Win%
Jack Van Berg	214	36	26	17	16.8
B.S. Flint	104	22	11	15	21.2
Forrest Kaelin	105	21	18	16	20.0
Charles Taliaferro	131	20	18	14	15.3
G.R. Arnold, II	67	18	10	11	26.9
Michael Green	69	17	7	11	24.6
Penny Lewis	79	16	11	4	20.3
William H. Fires	81	15	18	12	18.5
Ray Lawrence, Jr.	76	15	8	13	19.7
Bernell Rhone	167	15	15	27	9.0
Rhoda Warhol	84	15	9	12	17.9

Final Jockey Standings

Jockey	Mounts	1sts	2nds	3rds	Win%	% in the Money
Mike Smith	378	73	57	55	19.3	48.9
Ron Hansen	351	57	56	63	16.2	50.1
Leroy Moyers	319	48	48	36	15.0	41.3
Gerard Melancon	257	48	42	35	18.6	48.6
Steve Bass*	252	47	30	43	18.7	47.6
Charles Woods, Jr.	233	43	40	26	18.5	46.8
Tim Doocy	246	37	49	30	15.0	47.1
Vicki Warhol	279	35	30	34	12.5	35.4
Patrick Johnson	184	32	28	33	17.3	50.5
Dan LaGrange	250	30	26	38	12.0	37.6

* Denotes apprentice rider.

N. Leading Active North American Sires

(Based on Average Earnings Index*)

Rank	Stallion	Index	Rank	Stallion	Index
1.	Seattle Slew	8.35	32.	Raise A Native	2.98
2.	Cox's Ridge	6.91	34.	Affirmed	2.76
3.	Alydar	6.05	34.	Coastal	2.76
4.	Northern Dancer	5.44	34.	Forli	2.76
5.	Nijinsky II	4.80	37.	Ack Ack	2.75
6.	Blushing Groom	4.42	38.	Foolish Pleasure	2.73
7.	Vaguely Noble	4.20	38.	Topsider	2.73
8.	Mr. Prospector	3.96	40.	Sharpen Up	2.72
9.	His Majesty	3.69	41.	Key to the Mint	2.70
10.	Roberto	3.64	42.	Vigors	2.65
11.	In Reality	3.56	43.	Run the Gantlet	2.63
12,	Graustark	3.41	44.	The Minstrel	2.61
13.	Sir Ivor	3.34	44.	Tri Jet	2.61
14.	Alleged	3.24	46.	Big Spruce	2.56
14.	Lyphard	3.24	47.	Exceller	2.55
16.	Damascus	3.20	48.	Nodouble	2.54
17.	Secretariat	3.19	49.	Naskra	2.50
18.	Halo	3.16	49.	Riverman	2.50
19.	Buckfinder	3.13	51.	Our Native	2.47
20.	Majestic Light	3.11	52.	Verbatim	2.45
21.	Stop the Music	3.03	53.	Timeless Moment	2.43
22.	Believe It	3.00	54.	Raja Baba	2.40
23.	Stage Door Johnny	2.97	55.	Youth	2.36
24.	Lord Gaylord	2.92	56.	Drone	2.34
25.	Vice Regent	2.89	57.	Sham	2.33
26.	Valid Appeal	2.88	58.	Mr. Leader	2.31
27.	Tom Rolfe	2.85	59.	Arts and Letters	2.29
28.	Icecapade	2.83	59.	Hatchet Man	2.29
29.	Star de Naskra	2.80	59.	Green Dancer	2.29
30.	Grey Dawn (Fr.)	2.79	62.	It's Freezing	2.28
30.	Ole Bob Bowers	2.79	63.	Explodent	2.26
32.	Caro (Ire.)	2.77	64.	Bailjumper	2.24

* The Lifetime Average-Earnings Index indicates how much purse money the progeny of one sire has earned, on average, in relation to the average earnings of all runners in the same year; average earnings of all runners in any given year is represented by an index of 1.00.

Source: The BLOOD-HORSE. Cumulative statistics through December 31, 1985.

O. Speed and Distance Sires

The following lists contain certain sires whose offspring have shown outstanding speed or an ability to go a route of ground. These lists are by no means exclusive, but will identify the most noteworthy stallions.

Speed Sires

Buckfinder	Christoper R	Cutlass
Distinctive	Duck Dance	Full Pocket
Hard Work	Insubordination	Loom
Mr. Leader	Mr. Prospector	Never Bend
Northern Dancer	Our Michael	Princely Native
Raise A Native	Reviewer	Rollicking
Shecky Greene	Stop the Music	Time Tested
Tumiga	Turn To	What A Pleasure
What Luck		

Distance Sires

Big Spruce	Cougar II	Good Counsel
Graustark	Herbager	Grey Dawn
High Echelon	Le Fabuleux	London Company
Lyphard	One For All	Proud Clarion
Round Table	Run the Gauntlet	Tom Rolfe
Vaguely Noble		

P. Turf and Off-Track Sires

Turf Sires

The following is an abbreviated list of sires whose offspring have proven to be good performers on the grass. Superior turf sires are indicated by a bullet (●).

Advocator ●	Al Hattab	Alydar
Ambernash ●	Bailjumper	Banquet Table ●
Big Spruce ●	Blushing Groom ●	Buffalo Lark
Cannonade	Caro ●	Clever Tell
Coastal	Diplomat Way	Drone
Empery	Exocutioner	Explodent ●
Exclusive Native ●	Forceten	Forli
Graustark	Hagley	Hail the Pirates
Hawaii	Halo	Hoist the Flag ●
Icecapade	Key to the Mint	Khaled
King Pellinore	Le Fabeleux ●	Little Current ●
London Company	Majestic Light	Marshuas Dancer
Mill Reef	Mississippian	Mr. Leader
Native Royalty	Naskra	Never Bend
Nijinsky II ●	Northern Dancer ●	One For All ●
Our Native ●	Prince Valiant	Quack
Raise A Cup	Riverman ●	Roberto ●
Speak John	Stage Door Johnny ●	Star Envoy ●
Text	Told	Tom Fool
Top Command	Tell	TVCommercial
Unconscious	Upper Case	Valdez
Verbatim	Vigors	

In addition to this list, you might favor horses that are foreign-bred in that most racing in Europe and in South America is conducted over the grass. Foreign-bred horses are indicated by a small asterisk preceding their name in both the DRF and in the track program.

Off-Track Sires

There hasn't been much tracking of sires who have consistently produced offspring that excel on an off-track. The following are some who come to mind.

Bagdad	Graustark	Native Charger
Blade	Grey Dawn II	Proudest Roman
Bold Forbes	Herberger	Ridan
Bosum	In Reality	Spanish Riddle
Cinteelo	Key to the Mint	The Pruner
Damascus	King's Bishop	Truxton King

Q. CANTERBURY DOWNS
Track Diagram and Track Records

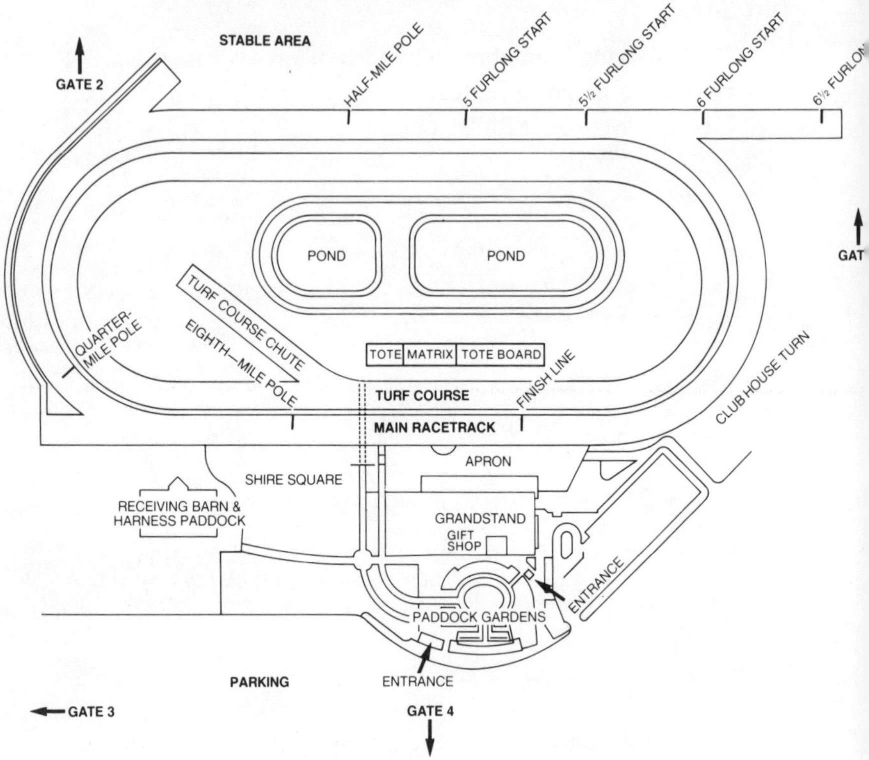

Track Records — Inaugural Meeting

Distance	Time	Set By	Age	Weight	Date
About 3 1/2 Furlongs	:40	Bye For Now	(3)	115	6/30/85
4 1/2 Furlongs	:52[3]	Milkshake	(2)	116	7/6/85
5 Furlongs	:57[4]	Noble Secretary	(3)	116	9/8/85
5 1/2 Furlongs	1:04	Patch of Sun	(4)	114	6/26/85
(Dead Heat)		My Earl	(4)	114	6/26/85
6 Furlongs	1:09[2]	Rapid Gray	(6)	123	9/1/85
6 1/2 Furlongs	1:16[1]	Patch of Sun	(4)	121	8/1/85
1 Mile	1:36[1]	Pitchit	(4)	120	7/10/85
1 Mile 70 Yards	1:40[1]	Come Summer	(3)	112	8/18/85
1 1/16 Miles	1:42[1]	Savannah Slew	(3)	122	9/28/85
1 1/8 Miles	1:48[3]	Come Summer	(3)	114	9/2/85
1 1/2 Miles	2:39[2]	Princess Redoy	(4)	114	10/4/85
1 3/4 Miles	3:00[4]	Luciole	(5)	114	9/27/85

CANTERBURY DOWNS

Mutuel Ticket

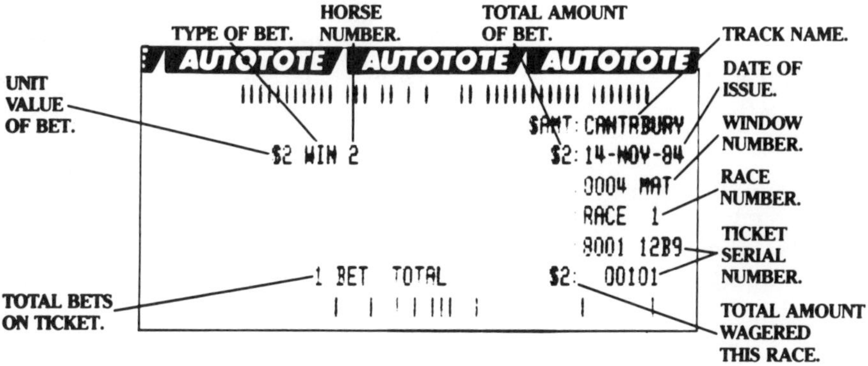

Betting Slips

CANTERBURY DOWNS

Workout Chart

The following should be used as a directional guide. There are a number of factors that can affect workout times — weight of the exercise rider, distance off the rail, degree of effort asked for, track condition, etc. The 1986 Canterbury Downs clocker will be Butch Brown, who considers most workouts to be done "handily" unless the rider has a very firm restraint on the horse. (It should be noted, however, that clockers at other tracks will rate most workouts as "breezing" rather than "handily".) The times below are considered "normal" for each class of horse going "handily" on a "fast" track at Canterbury Downs.

	Distance					
Class of Horse	**3f**	**4f**	**5f**	**6f**	**7f**	**1m**
Maiden $10M Clmg	:39	:52	1:05	1:18	1:32	1:47
Maiden Allowance	:37	:50+	1:03	1:16	1:30	1:45
$5-8M Claiming	:37	:50+	1:03	1:16	1:30	1:45
$10-20M Claiming	:36+	:49	1:02+	1:15+	1:29	1:43
$25-50M Claiming	:36	:48+	1:01+	1:14	1:27	1:41
Non-Winners of 2	:36+	:49	1:02	1:15	1:29	1:43
Top Allowance	:36	:48+	1:01+	1:14+	1:28	1:42
Handicap/Stakes	:35+	:47+	1:00+	1:13+	1:27	1:41

+ equals plus 2 or 3 fifths of a second.

Adjustments:

(b)	Breezing	**-1** second per 3 furlongs
(g)	From the Gate	**-3/5**th's second
(d)	"Dogs Up"	**-1** second per 3 furlongs
(m)	Muddy track	**-1** second per 3 furlongs
(gd)	Good track	**-3/5**th's second per 3 furlongs
(trt)	Training track	**-1** second per 3 furlongs

R. Conformation of a Horse

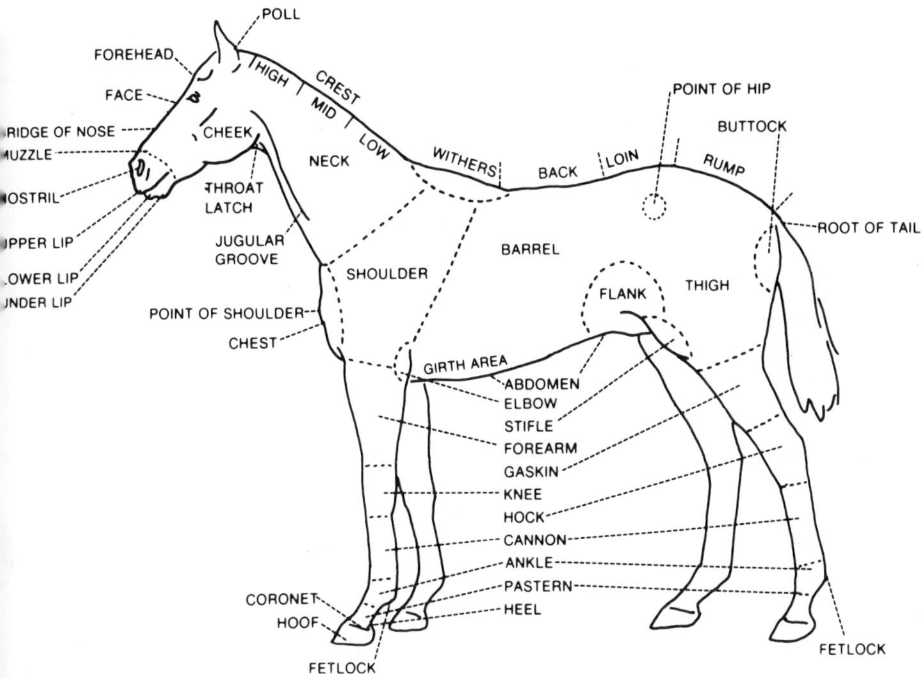
POLL
FOREHEAD
FACE
RIDGE OF NOSE
UZZLE
OSTRIL
PPER LIP
OWER LIP
NDER LIP
HIGH
CREST
MID
LOW
CHEEK
NECK
THROAT
LATCH
JUGULAR
GROOVE
POINT OF SHOULDER
CHEST
SHOULDER
WITHERS
BACK
LOIN
POINT OF HIP
BUTTOCK
RUMP
ROOT OF TAIL
BARREL
FLANK
THIGH
GIRTH AREA
ABDOMEN
ELBOW
STIFLE
FOREARM
GASKIN
KNEE
HOCK
CANNON
ANKLE
PASTERN
HEEL
CORONET
HOOF
FETLOCK
FETLOCK

S. Recommended Reading

The following is but a partial list of the many worthwhile books and reference guides to thoroughbred racing and handicapping.

Books

"Ainslie's Encyclopedia of Thoroughbred Handicapping" by Tom Ainslie. William Morrow and Company, New York.

"Ainslie's Complete Guide to Thoroughbred Racing" by Tom Ainslie (Newly revised 3rd edition due in the summer 1986). Simon & Schuster, New York..

"Thoroughbred Handicapping — State of the Art" by William L. Quirin, Ph.d. William Morrow and Company, New York.

"Body Language of Horses" by Tom Ainslie and Bonnie Ledbetter. William Morrow and Company, New York.

"Betting Thoroughbreds" by Steven Davidowitz. Dutton, New York.

"Picking Winners" by Andrew Beyer. Harcourt Brace Jovanovich, New York.

"Winning at the Races" by William L. Quirin, Ph.d. William Morrow and Company, New York.

"Situation Handicapping" by Henry Kuck. Woodside Associates, New York.

"The American Racing Manual" — This huge reference book and statistical abstract is published by the DRF annually and is a requisite for the serious handicapper. In addition to a totally comprehensive statistical summary of the previous year, it contains other solid reference materials including records and percentages for all horses, trainers, owners and jockeys.

Periodicals

"The Blood-Horse" — *The Blood-Horse* is a weekly magazine devoted to the thoroughbred industry. Aside from the *Daily Racing Form, The Blood-Horse* is the most important reference periodical you can have. It is particularly useful in terms of unravelling the mysteries of breeding and pedigrees. It also contains comprehensive results of stakes races, sales and provides updated schedules of current and future racing dates.

"Minnesota Thoroughbred" — This locally-published, monthly magazine is the official publication of the Minnesota Thoroughbred Association. It is devoted to thoroughbred racing in Minnesota, and will keep you informed on all aspects of the state's newest sport, particularly the breeding industry.

"Thoroughbred Record" — This monthly magazine is similar to the the Blood-Horse magazine, yet offers a broader editorial format.

NOTE: During the off-season, I recommend that you subscribe to the *Daily Racing Form* to keep in touch with the industry and to follow horses. In terms of mail service, second class is more affordable, and you will receive the DRF the same day as you would with first class.

NOTES

NOTES

NOTES